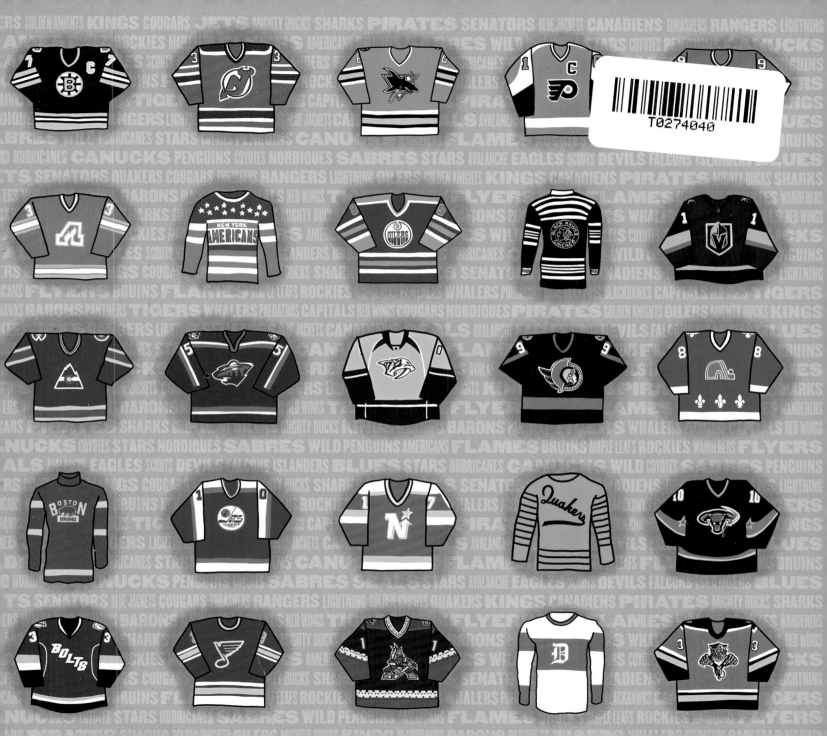

FABRIC
OF THE
GAME

FABRIC
OF THE
GAME

THE STORIES BEHIND THE NHL'S NAMES, LOGOS, AND UNIFORMS

CHRIS CREAMER & TODD RADOM
FOREWORD BY **LANNY McDONALD**

SPORTS
PUBLISHING

Sports Publishing books may be purchased in bulk at special discounts for sales promotion, corporate gifts, fund-raising, or educational purposes. Special editions can also be created to specifications. For details, contact the Special Sales Department, Sports Publishing, 307 West 36th Street, 11th Floor, New York, NY 10018 or sportspubbooks@skyhorsepublishing.com.

Sports Publishing® is a registered trademark of Skyhorse Publishing, Inc.®, a Delaware corporation.

Visit our website at www.sportspubbooks.com.

10 9 8 7

Library of Congress Cataloging-in-Publication Data is available on file.

Cover design and artwork by Todd Radom
Photographs courtesy of the Hockey Hall of Fame: pgs. 18, 55, 136, and 176 (Todd Radom); pg. 167 (Hal Roth); pg. 203 (Dave Sandford); pg. 210 (Matthew Manor); pg. 213 (Imperial Oil – Turofsky)
Photographs courtesy of Rod Palson & Darryl Hartle: pgs. 243, 244
Photographs courtesy of Bill Frederick: pgs. 6, 7
Photographs courtesy of Chris Creamer: pgs. 24, 92, 160, 189, 207, 229, 230
Photograph courtesy of Dean R. Specker: pg. 100
Images from the Public Domain: pgs. 33, 77, 114, 116, 124, 131, 148, 155, 156, 179, 215, 218, 221
Artwork courtesy of Todd Radom: VIII, 20, 22, 38, 48, 71, 78, 80, 81, 94, 112, 116, 117, 121, 122, 124, 133, 138, 139, 141, 150, 157, 167, 169, 174, 177, 179, 180, 185, 193, 203, 212, 217, 219, 251
All photographs, unless otherwise noted above, are courtesy of Getty Images

Print ISBN: 978-1-68358-384-4
Ebook ISBN: 978-1-68358-385-1

Printed in China

For Kristen, Ollie, and Rosie—C.C.

For Susanne—T.R.

CONTENTS

FOREWORD
BY LANNY McDONALD

I may be biased, but I believe that the Hockey Hall of Fame is the greatest sports hall of fame and museum anywhere in the world. Growing up in Alberta and playing the game, becoming a member of the Hall was the furthest thing from my mind. All these years later I have the great, great honour to serve as chairman of the board of the Hockey Hall of Fame, a place that really is like home to me. Like so many of you, I love the game of hockey and I love the history and traditions of the game. Honouring and preserving this history is core to the Hall's mission. All the greatest artifacts and pieces of history are here, and it's such cool stuff—starting with the Stanley Cup. What about the gloves that Gordie Howe wore, or the sticks that Wayne Gretzky scored with—and how could he have scored that many goals with *that* stick? And then there are the jerseys—literally the fabric of our great game.

Hockey fans see a classic jersey—especially any of the Original Six teams—and they're automatically drawn to it. You can take a look at the Red Wings crest and you know it'll be good forever. When I take one look at the Bruins and their crest with the "Big B" in the middle, I'm right back in their tiny rink, knowing I'm about to pay a price one way or another. Then you have teams like the California Golden Seals, who were the brunt of so many jokes. Like, really, why have your players wear white skates? The Vancouver Canucks and how unusual that "V" uniform was with the black, orange, and yellow stripes. Philadelphia also wore black and orange, and it was incredibly menacing for us to see that whenever we played. They were obnoxious, but they were effective.

Growing up, until I was ten years old, we never had a television. My dad and I, as was customary every Saturday night, would sit in the kitchen and listen to Foster Hewitt or Danny Gallivan calling the games on the radio. To be able to sit with my dad and just listen to the games, I'd close my eyes and feel like I was actually there at Maple Leaf Gardens. Dad was an absolutely huge Maple Leafs fan, so much so that when I was picked in the first round by both the Leafs and the World Hockey Association's Cleveland Crusaders in 1973, I knew if I would have signed with Cleveland over Toronto, I may never have been allowed to ever go back home again.

I was lucky enough to be drafted by the Maple Leafs, and I remember walking into the dressing room for the first time at training camp. They had all our jerseys with the names out in the stalls. I had no idea what jersey number I was going to wear—they never asked or said anything to me about it. But I walk up to my stall and there it is, number seven. Right away, I'm thinking, "Oh my God, Tim Horton wore that number, like is this not the coolest thing ever!?" It was such a feeling of pride to be able to put on that jersey, after all those years of listening to Leafs games with my dad. When I'd look down and see that Maple Leafs crest, it was just so powerful. It is such an important symbol of the Maple Leafs and to Canadian hockey fans all around the world.

After six-and-a-half years in Toronto, I got traded to the Colorado Rockies. Even though my time with the Rockies was short, I absolutely loved that jersey and the complete uniform. It was colourful and a little flamboyant compared to what I wore in Toronto, and maybe the team wasn't so great . . . but the look was *really* solid.

Things came full circle for me in November 1981, when I was traded to the Calgary Flames. I grew up two hours east of Calgary, so the opportunity to be able to return, close to home, in front of family and friends, was just so special. When I was growing up there, of course, there was no Calgary Flames. Eventually becoming the captain of the team and winning the Stanley Cup—the first opposing team to ever win the Cup on Forum ice against the great Canadiens—is the kind of stuff that you never think of when you're listening to Foster Hewitt on the radio with your dad when you're five, six, or seven years old.

I've always been so appreciative and so thankful because the fans there treated me as a long-lost son who finally came home. I absolutely loved the Flames' logo. All these years later, I feel immensely proud when I see the team throwing back to the same jerseys we wore when we won the Stanley Cup. Seeing a new generation wearing them and knowing what it means to so many fans—because they were also a part of that '89 team—and that really is what *Fabric of the Game* is all about.

INTRODUCTION

Nothing unites or divides a random assortment of strangers quite like the sports team for which they cheer. The passion they hold for the New York Rangers, Toronto Maple Leafs, Montréal Canadiens, or Boston Bruins allows them to look past any differences which would have otherwise disrupted a perfectly fine Thanksgiving dinner and channels it into a powerful, shared admiration for their team.

We decorate our lives with their logos, stock our wardrobe with their jerseys, and, in some cases, even tattoo our bodies with their iconography and colors. They're so ingrained in our lives that we don't even think to ask ourselves why Los Angeles celebrates royalty; why Buffalo cheers for not one, but two massive cavalry swords; or why the Broadway Blueshirts named themselves for a law enforcement agency in Texas.

Rights to the Cleveland Barons' nickname were secured in exchange for what was described as "a nice dinner." The Detroit Red Wings were once called the Detroit Cougars, but the locals had trouble pronouncing the team's moniker.

James R. Maxwell won a contest to name the Kansas City Scouts and was awarded a new Ford car for his efforts. Nine-year-old Alec Stockard was responsible for having named the Philadelphia Flyers; he won a color television and two season tickets.

The Montréal Maroons, unsurprisingly, were named for the color of their uniforms. The California Seals wore Pacific Blue sweaters, the Mighty Ducks of Anaheim took the ice clad in "eggplant" togs, and the New York Americans' official colors were "stars and stripes."

Fans' passion for the colors of their favorite teams is hardly a new phenomenon.

In Ancient Rome, chariot racing was the sporting obsession of the day. Two thousand years ago, an estimated 150,000 to 250,000 spectators flocked to the Circus Maximus in Rome to watch their favorite professional racing teams, called "factions," participate in often deadly competition. Fans of the factions wore their colors with a fervor that would seem familiar to fans of today's teams. The four factions were the Greens, Reds, Whites, and Blues (fan favorites long before the ones in St. Louis lifted the Stanley Cup in 2019 AD). The emperor Domitian added two expansion teams, the Purples and Golds, both of which folded soon after his assassination in 96 AD.

Pliny the Younger, writing to his friend Calvisius Rufus, described the "childish passion" of the fans and their partisan rooting interests:

If, indeed, they were attracted by the swiftness of the horses or the skill of the men, one could account for this enthusiasm. But in fact it is a bit of cloth they favour, a bit of cloth that captivates them. And if during the running the racers were to exchange colours, their partisans would change sides, and instantly forsake the very drivers and horses whom they were just before recognizing from afar, and clamorously saluting by name.

In the 1979 Canadian children's story *The Hockey Sweater*, author Roch Carrier recalls his youth, gathering with friends on the local pond, all wearing the same rouge, blanc et bleu of the Montréal Canadiens. When he grows too large for his sweater, he's erroneously given the sweater of the rival Toronto Maple Leafs as a replacement. The negative reaction from his peers from wearing the blue and white culminates in the author visiting the local church and asking God "to send, as quickly as possible, moths that would eat up my Toronto Maple Leafs sweater." A story so ingrained in Canadian culture that a passage of it appeared on the back of the five-dollar bill.

The Montréal Wanderers hosted one of the National Hockey League's first two official games, on December 19, 1917. Two weeks later, their home arena burned to the ground, forcing the team out of business. The Wanderers played only six games in the NHL, but their story is here.

The Vegas Golden Knights joined the league as its 31st franchise and began play in 2017–18. They made it all the way to the Stanley Cup Finals in their inaugural season. Their story is here, too.

Cities such as Québec, Cleveland, Hartford, Hamilton, and Kansas City have come and gone since the league's inception, and Seattle has now joined the fray. More than a century after its establishment, the NHL's founding fathers would have a hard time reconciling what has become of their then-modest venture, now a multibillion dollar enterprise that spans the North American continent. They would, however, recognize the red, white, and blue sweaters worn by the Montréal Canadiens.

The game marches forward, and our enduring affection and sense of pride for the looks and names of our teams continues to both bind and separate us. Let the debates rage, but we can probably all agree that Pliny the Younger and Calvisius Rufus would likely have appreciated the Ottawa Senators' Roman centurion logo.

Chris Creamer and Todd Radom
June 2020

ANAHEIM DUCKS
1993-PRESENT

THE TEAM

In the autumn of 1992, a new arena was under construction within sight of Disneyland. After negotiations to attract the National Basketball Association's Los Angeles Clippers had failed, the arena needed a tenant . . . and fast. It was around this time that Walt Disney Co. chairman Michael Eisner was having a good old-fashioned shower-think when it hit him: "...Maybe we would help Anaheim out," he recalled later in a 2018 interview with *The Athletic*. It wasn't because of success of the 1992 Disney hockey film *The Mighty Ducks*, as many would later believe, but quite simply in an effort "to be a good citizen of Anaheim."

While many hockey-hungry markets have waited decades to land a National Hockey League franchise, Eisner and the Disney group only had to endure a few weeks. When the NHL's Board of Governors gathered in Boca Raton, Florida, for their annual meeting on December 10, 1992, the Anaheim expansion franchise (along with an expansion team for Miami) was unanimously approved on the condition they could secure a deal to play at the new Anaheim Arena and sell enough season ticket packages to satisfy the league. Disney paid an expansion fee of $25 million to the league and another $25 million to the nearby Los Angeles Kings in exchange for setting up a new franchise within their territory. The Anaheim and Miami (later the Florida Panthers) franchises were the fourth and fifth expansion teams to be awarded by the NHL in just over two years.

The Mighty Ducks first-ever regular-season game was played less than ten months later, with the opener being held at the freshly coined and appropriately named "Pond" against the Detroit Red Wings on October 8, 1993. A fifteen-minute pre-game show worthy of the Disney name included a light show and a performance of the song "Be Our Guest" from the animated film *Beauty and the Beast*. The show cost more than $500,000 (that's $33,333 per minute!) and was presented before a sellout crowd of 17,174; witnesses to hockey history, armed with the complementary duck-calls handed out before the game. On their first night, despite the pomp, the Ducks weren't so Mighty on the ice, as the Red Wings scored three quick goals and the Ducks ultimately lost, 7–2.

Things turned around for the Mighty Ducks in the following years when future Hall of Famers Paul Kariya and Teemu Selänne helped the team make a "Cinderella story" run worthy of its own Disney film. They made it all the way to the seventh game of the 2003 Stanley Cup Finals before they were stopped by the New Jersey Devils. Just four years later, their first with "Mighty" removed from their name, the Anaheim Ducks won their first and only Cup Championship to date, a five-game victory over the Ottawa Senators in 2007.

THE NAME

The hockey world was first introduced to *The Mighty Ducks* courtesy a feature-length motion picture which hit theatres in October 1992. The film, released by Disney, starred Emilio Estevez as a lawyer who was sentenced to coach a kid's hockey team (to fulfill a community service sentence for drunk driving!) that, by the end of the movie, would be known as the Ducks. The movie was a hit, earning $50.7 million at the box office—a cool $700,000 more than what the NHL charged Disney in expansion fees for the team.

Just two months after the film's release, Eisner appeared at the NHL's Board of Governors meeting wearing the green, purple, and yellow Ducks jersey from the film. Upon the result of the vote, Eisner wasted no time in sharing his pick for the name.

"Ducks are what we are going to call it unless I hear otherwise," Eisner said to the *Los Angeles Times*. "Whenever I suggest the name 'Mighty Ducks,' six people tell me no hockey player will ever play for that team," later admitting, "the trouble is, if we don't win in three or four years we might be called the 'Unmighty Ducks'—or worse!"

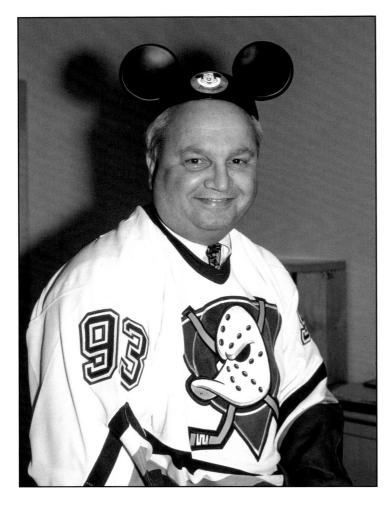

General Manager Jack Ferreira sports Mickey Mouse ears while modeling the original Mighty Ducks of Anaheim home uniform in 1993.

The Mighty Ducks wore their original uniform set for thirteen seasons, including a trip to the 2003 Stanley Cup Finals led by captain and future Hockey Hall of Famer Paul Kariya.

The following day's *LA Times* claimed they received nearly 200 calls in the first twenty-four hours after the new team was announced, with 166 of those calls made to criticize the choice of "Mighty Ducks" as the team name. Callers suggested Thunder, Blades, Matterhorns, Earthquakes, and Tremors as better options.

Despite the negative reaction, Disney went ahead with the then unpopular name, making it official at a news conference on March 1, 1993. Eisner was joined on stage by new NHL commissioner Gary Bettman and Los Angeles Kings owner Bruce McNall for the announcement, with Mickey and Minnie Mouse also on hand. Bettman, Eisner, et al. announced the official name as "The Mighty Ducks of Anaheim," and did so while tooting their wooden duck calls.

"It's a quack—a quack heard 'round the world!" Eisner said, while Bettman noted that he'd "never been to a press

Anaheim briefly wore these unusual jerseys featuring their mascot "Wild Wing" as the NHL introduced a new third-jersey program in 1996.

conference like this one before."

Former NHL player Stu Grimson recalled sitting in his dressing room when he heard the name of the new team. He later told *The Athletic*, "[I] said to teammates, 'can you believe they're going to let them name them that? Imagine playing for that franchise?' That's generally how it works, I'm the lone Blackhawks player that moves to the Mighty Ducks."

In 2005, Disney sold the Mighty Ducks franchise to Broadcom Corporation co-founder and Orange County resident Henry Samueli and his wife, Susan. Following the sale, the Samuelis announced they would consider a new name for the team. After a year of consulting season-ticket holders, during which two-thirds preferred a new name, and flirting with the idea of changing the name to either the Condors or Bears, Samueli announced on January 26, 2006, that the club would simply shorten its name to Anaheim Ducks beginning with the 2006–07 season.

"In selecting the name 'Anaheim Ducks,' we are respecting the heritage of a tremendous organization that has been a very important and visible part of the community," Samueli said to the *LA Times*. Ducks winger Teemu Selänne added, "It's really good the new owners are going to keep the Ducks name. Maybe the 'Mighty' was more about the Disney side of it."

THE LOOK

The original Mighty Ducks of Anaheim logo made its debut to the world courtesy of NHL commissioner Gary Bettman on NBC's *Today* show on the morning of June 7, 1993, ahead of a press conference held by the team later that afternoon. The logo featured an old-fashioned goalie mask in the shape of a duck's head, placed on a black circle and green triangle with two crossed hockey sticks behind it. There were reportedly as many as a thousand logo concepts proposed for the inaugural look, with the bulk of those courtesy of Disney's animation department and still more coming from their television and consumer product staff. The winning design was created by Disney artists Tony Cipriano and Fred Tio.

"We promised our fans we would deliver an exciting logo and we have done just that," Eisner said at the unveiling. "It is one both our players and fans will be proud to wear. We 'Goofy-ized' Jason from *Friday the 13th*. We wanted something between 'Disney-esque' and hockey mean—not too light, not too silly."

Anaheim's burgundy, teal, silver, and white uniforms were shown off at this event, with white for home games and burgundy on the road. Both uniforms featured a diagonal teal slash going up from the bottom-left to the mid-right of the front and back of the uniform. Before even playing a game, the Ducks tinkered with their uniforms, swapping out the burgundy for dark purple. The team would, later on, change the name of their "teal" to "jade" without actually changing the color.

The new look—while unusual to the traditional hockey fan—proved to be a hit when it came to merchandise sales. Disney immediately began selling Mighty Ducks memora-

Corey Perry and Todd Marchant unveil the new black and gold Anaheim Ducks uniforms on June 22, 2006.

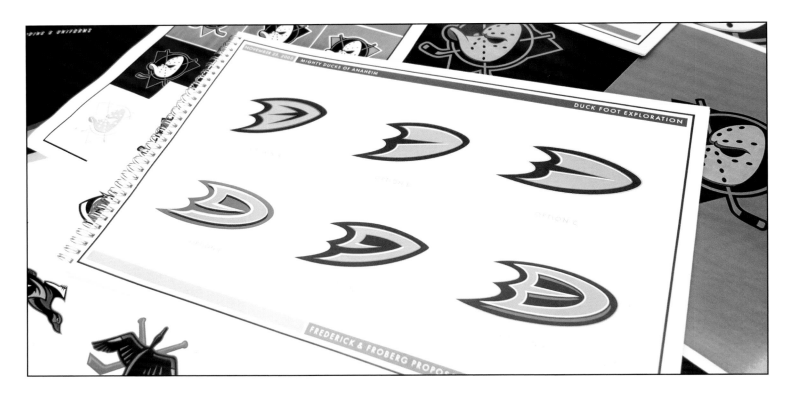

bilia across the country via its 225 Disney stores, as well as the souvenir shops at Disneyland. Within a year of the Ducks playing their first season, the league had reported record league-wide sales with the Mighty Ducks outselling every team—not only in the NHL, but in all of North American professional sports.

"A lot of people have said the name is stupid and the logo is stupid," Disney Sports president Tony Tavares told the *New York Times*. "All l I know is the kids love it."

During the Mighty Ducks' third season, the NHL introduced a new uniform initiative allowing clubs to add an additional "third" uniform option to their usual two-jersey rota-

tion. Anaheim was one of the first five teams to jump on board, adding a green jersey with the team's mascot "Wild Wing" on the front shown leaping out of a sheet of ice. The new look made its debut on January 27, 1996, against the Los Angeles Kings, who were also dressed in their new, equally unconventional third uniforms. The uniforms were met with negative reviews by media and fans, and they naturally didn't last long (both the Mighty Ducks and Kings dropped their new third jerseys immediately following that 1995–96 season).

In 2005, after Broadcom founder Henry Samueli and his wife, Susan, purchased the Mighty Ducks and announced their intention to rechristen the team as simply "Anaheim Ducks," they turned to New Jersey–based Frederick & Froberg Design Office, as well as designer Brian Casscles, to develop the new look.

"We were on an aggressive timeline to develop the new identity, and during one of our presentations in a Newport Beach boardroom, I lined the four walls with dozens of concepts that included angry ducks, animated ducks, aggressive ducks, and ornithologically correct ducks," designer Bill Frederick told the authors. "Around the board table were the owners, Henry and Susan, as well as all of the senior officers including Brian Burke, the new GM. While none of the approaches were resonating with the owners, there was a sudden interest in just one part of a concept that used a duck foot oriented as a capital 'D' as a holding shape behind a duck in flight. I pulled out a pad from my bag and started sketching. Henry and Susan immediately loved it."

The new logo was unveiled—along with the new uniforms and colors—on June 22, 2006, and incorporated Frederick's webbed "D" logo into a horizontal wordmark spelling out the full name of the team with a black, gold, and orange color scheme. The uniforms—black at home and white on the road—featured the wordmark across the chest with a gold diagonal stripe along the bottom as a nod to the original Mighty Ducks jerseys. The Ducks dropped the wordmark in 2014–15, opting for just the "D" logo as their primary look across the board.

In 2015–16, with the designs of the 1990s experiencing a resurgence in popularity, the Ducks brought back their original Mighty Ducks logo as a third uniform, now recolored to match the modern black, gold, and orange look of the team, ensuring the original Mighty Ducks would live on well into the twenty-first century. Quack.

Above: Bill Frederick's original sketch for the Ducks' new visual identity. Below and opposite: Outtakes from Frederick & Froberg's 2005 design exploration.

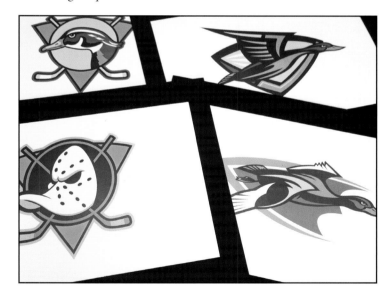

ARIZONA COYOTES
1996-PRESENT

THE TEAM

The Arizona Coyotes—previously the Phoenix Coyotes—sprung to life from the plains of Manitoba as the Winnipeg Jets, charter members of the World Hockey Association (WHA), in 1972. The Jets were a WHA powerhouse, winning the league's Avco Cup championship three times and making the finals five times in the league's seven seasons.

The Jets joined the National Hockey League in 1979, and were playoff participants 11 times over their 17 NHL seasons. By early 1995, Winnipeg was the league's smallest market. Buffered by soaring player salaries, a diminished Canadian dollar, and an old, outdated Winnipeg Arena, the Jets and local officials tried to broker a deal to save the franchise, though those efforts came up short.

In May 1995, a move to Minneapolis was considered to be "imminent," but the arrangement collapsed due to a lack of solid financing. Another potential deal to keep the team in Winnipeg was floated but, again, those efforts failed. Finally, on October 18, 1995, Jets owner Barry Shenkarow officially announced the sale of the franchise to American businessmen Richard Burke and Steven Gluckstern. The Jets would play one final lame duck season in Winnipeg.

On December 19, 1995, the new owners held a press conference to declare that the franchise's future home would be Phoenix, Arizona, and arrangements were made to play home games at the downtown America West Arena. Burke and Gluckstern, along with Phoenix mayor Skip Rimsza and Jerry Colangelo, owner of the MLB Diamondbacks and the NBA Suns, discussed the terms of the lease and held up a Teemu Selänne Winnipeg Jets jersey for the cameras. Observers noted the fact that the "Phoenix Hockey" logo, which accompanied them on the dais, featured purple—the official hue of both of Colangelo's pro teams. The Winnipeg Jets played their final game on April 28, 1996, a home playoff loss to the Detroit Red Wings, 4–1.

The Coyotes' first home game took place on October 10, 1996, in front of a sellout crowd of 16,210. Outdoor temperatures in excess of 100ºF were no match for the boisterous crowd, who witnessed a win over the San Jose Sharks, 4–1. As fans imitated coyote howls, the home team was introduced to Warren Zevon's "Werewolves of London," and a snippet from the

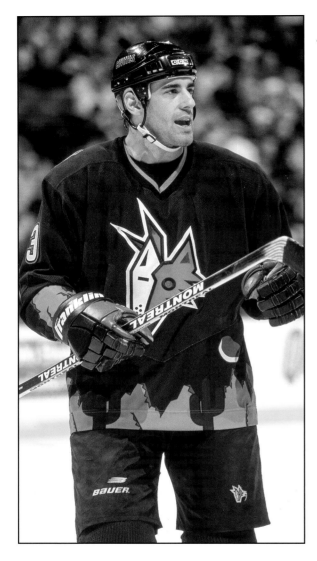

Phoenix wore this desert-themed third jersey featuring cacti and lizards from 1998 to 2003.

movie *Wayne's World*, proclaiming "Game on!" played on the arena's video boards. Robin Wilson, lead singer of the band Gin Blossoms (who were formed in Tempe in 1987), performed the national anthem.

Phoenix's America West Arena was not designed with hockey in mind—it featured more than 3,000 sight-obstructed seats, which proved to be a significant drag on gate receipts. Team losses were pegged at $20 million annually by 2001, and the Coyotes, led by a new ownership group which included Wayne Gretzky, announced a move to a new city-built arena in suburban Glendale. The Glendale Arena made its NHL debut on December 27, 2003. Commissioner Gary Bettman proclaimed it "the best arena in North America."

Despite the shift, the Coyotes continued to struggle both on and off the ice. New owners came in and bled red ink, running up hundreds of millions of dollars in losses, and the team declared bankruptcy in 2009. A shift to Hamilton, Ontario, was rumored to be on the horizon. The franchise was then sold to the NHL. Against a backdrop of continual franchise instability (and more rumors of a potential relocation to Seattle, and even back to Winnipeg), the Coyotes cycled through multiple owners over the years but have continued to hold forth in their desert outpost. Despite all the turbulence, the team's grassroots efforts to grow the sport at the youth level have finally taken root, a hopeful sign for this long-beleaguered franchise.

THE NAME

When the Jets' relocation to Phoenix was made official in December 1995, a Name the Team Contest was announced. "Right now, they're freezing somewhere in Canada," read newspaper advertisements. "But by September of '96 we'll be calling the Winnipeg Jets our very own." The grand prize was two lifetime season tickets.

Eight names were to be considered: the Wranglers, Outlaws, Coyotes, Renegades, Freeze, Mustangs, Jets, and Scorpions. A write-in option was also made available.

The team's identity was revealed at an April 8, 1996, press conference at the America West Arena, attended by some 4,000 fans and the Stanley Cup. Chief operating officer Shawn Hunter did the honors, proclaiming "Coyotes" as the team's moniker. More than 10,000 entries were harvested, with the contest winner announced as seventeen-year-old Brett Thornton. "It's not as drab as a lot of other NHL names. I think it's pretty cool," he said of the name. Scorpions came in a close second, along with off-ballot names such as Dry Ice, Posse, and Phreeze.

In January 2014, the team announced that they were changing the name of the club to the Arizona Coyotes, a nod to the fact that they no longer played in downtown Phoenix. Team president Anthony LeBlanc said, "Becoming the Arizona Coyotes makes sense for us since we play our games in Glendale and the city is such a great partner of ours. We also want to be recognized as not just the hockey team for Glendale or Phoenix, but for the entire state of Arizona and the Southwest. We hope that the name *Arizona* will encourage more fans from all over the state, not just the Valley, to embrace and support our team."

THE LOOK

The Coyotes went all in for their first visual identity.

At the same April 8, 1996, press conference—where they announced the new name, the team unveiled their logo. The unique primary logo, described as "an upright coyote wearing an extra-long hockey mask styled to resemble a menacing Hopi kachina figure from Northern Arizona," generated all kinds of attention. The color palette of dark green, brick red, purple, black, and sand reflected the hues of the team's new desert home.

"We internally refer to it as the 'Coyoteman,'" said team COO Shawn Hunter of the stylized figure, in comments made to the Associated Press. "We think the logo is made with incredible distinction and sophistication. Not only does it capture the Southwest colors that we have, it also weaves in the ice hockey message." The kachina approach made an impression, noted Hunter. "It screamed, 'This is the one.' We pursued a lot of different directions, but when we arrived at this, everybody started to feel comfortable."

Team co-owner Richard Burke said to the AP, "I tested it on two really good fans in my home, ages ten and fifteen. The first day, they were looking at it like, 'what is it?' The second day, they were screaming about wanting to go show their friends." He told the *Arizona Republic* that the conservative leadership at the NHL were not too keen on the look. "It was a stretch, but they like it now."

The logo was the work of Campbell Fisher Ditko, a Phoenix-based design firm that had recently given Major League Baseball's expansion Arizona Diamondbacks their visual identity. The agency's Greg Fisher told the *Republic*, "It's unique. We think it's going to sell big." He added, "The final character is aggressive, witty, and attractive to sports fans of all ages. Its personality will be fully realized through animation."

In 2015, Fisher told foxsports.com, "As we were moving into this the league gave their opinion on the color palette they thought might work for a new NHL team and they were adamant about the logo. There were so many angry animals coming on board at that time that they were like 'do not do an angry animal logo because we'll never say yes.'"

In comments made to nhl.com in 2020, Fisher discussed some of the subtle details that were contained within the character, noting that "[m]ost people don't realize that the Coyote is standing on a puck that's flat down and that the overarching shape of the Coyote is an 'A' for Arizona, even though at the time [the team] was the Phoenix Coyotes." He added, "That crescent moon obviously creates a 'C' for 'Coyotes.'"

Fisher also noted that some of the early variations of the logo depicted a sunglasses-wearing coyote. "Hockey had never been in the Southwest before, so that was the whole reason for the sunglasses at the beginning—it's so hot and sunny in the desert." The Los Angeles Kings cribbed this idea several years later when they included shades on a hockey stick-wielding lion within their primary crest.

Some observers were perplexed and scornful of the decidedly unconventional look. Corky Simpson, writing in the *Tucson Citizen*, opined that the logo "looks like a two-headed dog playing hockey," and "ancient graffiti scrawled on the tomb of an Egyptian pharaoh."

The Coyotes' uniforms were unveiled at an event held at the Hard Rock Cafe in Phoenix on the morning of August 26, 1996. Mike Gartner modeled the black road uniforms while Kris King showed off the home whites. Applauding the new look, King told the *Republic*, "The logo itself on a piece of paper doesn't do it justice. Everybody was thinking about the Coyote, all the abstract designs, the skates and stuff. But I kept telling everybody, 'Wait until it gets on a jersey and you'll really see what it's all about.'"

Rock legend Alice Cooper, a big sports fan and resident of the Phoenix area, received a jersey. "I think it's awful nice you put my name on the shorts," he joked, pointing to the manufacturer's "Cooper" logo on the uniform pants.

The Coyotes' moved to Glendale in 2003; an opportune moment to bring forth a refreshed brand identity, which was executed by Denver-based Adrenalin Design Group. A team press release said, "This evolution of the team's brand mirrors the transition of the Coyotes organization that now combines the ultra-modern experience of the new Glendale Arena with the long-standing traditions of the National Hockey League. The new logos and uniforms reflect the aggressiveness and excitement of Coyotes hockey in the new arena while maintaining ties to the seven years of history that have been created in the Valley."

The new look was the product of "18 months of extensive research and development." It was unveiled at a September 3, 2003, press conference at the food court of the Arizona Mills Mall in Tempe, in front of a crowd of more than a thousand people. The team took out newspaper ads that trumpeted the changes.

Howling at the moon, this new coyote embodies the intensity and passion of our incredible fans while showing respect for our past. The colors brick red, desert sand and black are borrowed from the original logo while several key graphic elements are also carried over—notice the two-tone face with the zig-zag black markings down the middle, the three pieces of mane and the triangular shape of the ear. The new logo continues to showcase the four triangles across the bridge of his snout, representing Four Peaks, a well-known geographical landmark in the Valley.

The Coyotes introduced an entirely new look in 2003. This identity change represented a clean break from their initial identity and it coincided with the team's move to a new arena in suburban Glendale.

"These uniforms have a very traditional look, which is something we think our players, and especially our fans, will really enjoy," Coyotes managing partner Wayne Gretzky told the AP. Gretzky, who was reported to be no fan of the original kachina theme, added, "[W]e wanted to create a classic jersey that our players and fans could be proud of and we are thrilled with the final product.

"We wanted to establish something that had the Valley [of the Sun] taste, had the Coyote intrigue and yet had the stature of the National Hockey League. To me it's the greatest game in the world, and to be part of the NHL, to be a city in the NHL, is something very special," said The Great One.

Forward Shane Doan told the *Arizona Daily Star*, "It's more of a coyote. It's not a fake drawing of one. It's a real coyote. The jersey has a more traditional look to it, sort of a re-turn to the old style. I like the old jerseys—they were different than any other jersey in the league—but change isn't bad."

Coach Bob Francis and winger Ladislav Nagy modeled the new uniforms, which, as Doan observed, represented a sharp departure from the old look. Nostalgia for the kachina never completely ebbed, however, and in 2018 the Coyotes brought back the originals as their designated third jerseys.

Doan, now retired, told azcentral.com, "It's funny because in the beginning they were almost ahead of their time or not quite to the level of uniqueness that they are now. I was hoping that this would be the direction they go, because of the players that have played in those jerseys and the history behind it."

The kachina look, much like the franchise itself, proved to have multiple lives after all.

ATLANTA THRASHERS
1999 - 2011

THE TEAM

Atlanta's first foray into the ranks of the National Hockey League concluded with the Flames' relocation to Calgary in 1980. By the end of the twentieth century, however, the city's sports landscape was quite different. Atlanta served as host to the 1996 Summer Olympic Games, and baseball's Braves were ascendant. Atlanta, the largest American television market without an NHL team, would soon be getting a new state-of-the-art downtown arena. The city's quest for a new NHL entry was further buttressed by the involvement of Turner Broadcasting System and its parent company, media behemoth Time Warner.

On June 25, 1997, the NHL Board of Governors unanimously voted to award expansion franchises to Atlanta, St. Paul, Minnesota; Columbus, Ohio; and Nashville, Tennessee. Nashville took the ice first, in 1998, followed by Atlanta the following season, with Minnesota and Columbus joining the circuit in 2000.

The Thrashers made their NHL debut at home on October 2, 1999, in a 4–1 loss to the New Jersey Devils. A sellout crowd of 18,545 packed the new Philips Arena, and, despite the loss, the team was awarded with a standing ovation once the game ended. The Thrashers' inaugural season went about as expected, with only 14 wins and a last-place finish in the Southeast Division. Even so, Atlanta was back on the NHL map and an enthusiastic fan base was beginning to develop.

Attendance remained strong over the course of the next few seasons, even if the on-ice product was of less than championship caliber.

In September 2003, Turner and Time Warner—now AOL-Time Warner after a $165-billion media mega merger in 2000—sold their interests in the Thrashers and the NBA's Atlanta Hawks to an eight-man group of investors who called themselves "Atlanta Spirit LLC."

The 2006–07 season represented the high-water mark for the Thrashers. The team averaged more than 16,000 attendees per game, and made the playoffs for the first (and only) time in their history, bowing to the New York Rangers in a first-round sweep. The team was consistently mediocre from there on out, winning 34, 35, 35, and 34 games over its next four seasons.

Atlanta Spirit's stewardship of the franchise was never solid. The Thrashers, much like the Flames before them, hemorrhaged money, and members of the group feuded with one another. Rumors of a potential relocation began to fly.

Mark Bradley, writing in the *Atlanta Constitution* in April 1997, assessed the franchise's future chances of success as a mortal lock. Touting Turner's prospective ownership, he noted that the Flames left town because they were perpetually strapped for cash. "The new team," he wrote, "will be the property of an empire on which the sun never sets. Ted Turner and Time Warner think globally but pay locally: No team of theirs will be allowed to go under, or, worse still, leave town."

The Atlanta Spirit group, however, never had the deep pockets or the local civic commitment of Turner and Time Warner. On May 31, 2011, a deal was announced to sell the team to Manitoba's True North Sports & Entertainment, who moved the Thrashers to Winnipeg, where they would be reborn as the Jets.

THE NAME

The Atlanta Thrashers were named in honor of *Toxostoma rufum*, also known as the Brown Thrasher—the official state bird of Georgia. "Thrashers" was a runner-up to "Flames" when the NHL expanded to the Deep South back in 1972.

The nickname was bestowed upon the team by its founder, media mogul and America's Cup–winning skipper Ted Turner, who also founded CNN. Turner was all in on "Thrashers" right from the outset of Atlanta's efforts to land a new NHL team.

"Ted got his way," quipped team president Harvey Schiller.

"We were walking somewhere and he turned to me and said, 'You know it's Thrashers.' I immediately called the lawyers and had them register the name." Schiller said that he sent an e-mail to his staff that said, "Forget any name research. It's the Thrashers."

Turner's wife, actress Jane Fonda, said that her husband first discussed the name while riding horses with her at their Montana ranch.

Not everyone was thrilled with the team's tribute to the diminutive songbird. Local hockey fan Liz Shaw told the *Constitution*, "My two nephews and I think it shows they're going to be a bunch of sissies." On the other hand, E. J. Williams, a Georgia biologist and bird specialist, told the newspaper, "They're a real strong bird, real aggressive...they'll fuss over you."

An additional dollop of local relevance was accorded by the fact that Atlanta was once informally called "Thrasherville" in honor of "Cousin" John Thrasher, who built a settlement in 1839 in what is now downtown Atlanta.

One final bit of business needed to be attended to before the name was secured. In February 1998, the franchise reached an out-of-court settlement with *Thrasher* magazine, a skateboarding publication, before officially launching the look of the new team.

THE LOOK

The Thrashers unveiled their logo at a press conference, held in the atrium of Atlanta's CNN Center, on April 23, 1998. A crowd of 2,000 witnessed the event, which featured interviews with former members of the Flames and a video of NHL highlights.

The emblem featured a stylized representation of a scowling thrasher, depicted in profile, formed into a tight, tornado-like vortex, rendered in five colors: Capital copper, Georgia bronze, Peachtree gold, Atlanta midnight blue, and Thrasher ice blue.

New York's Sean Michael Edwards (SME) was credited with having created the identity. SME's body of work was formidable. They were responsible for the New York Islanders "fish sticks" look, as well as the identities for the Florida Panthers, Minnesota Wild, and a host of other teams across all four major North American pro leagues.

Derek Schiller, the team's vice president of sales and marketing, said that the team reviewed more than a thousand potential logos before landing on the final version.

"We look at this as the real beginning of our franchise," Dave Maggard, vice president of administration for Turner Sports, told the AP. "Now," he said, "People have something they can identify with."

Maggard added, "We didn't want to have a silly comic book character or a weak-looking logo...the idea was to have a bird, yet at the same time a bird of prey. That's a bird that will go after more than worms."

On April 24, 1997, when Turner was closing in on the new franchise, the *Constitution* quoted Turner as saying, "They'll wear brown and white, and they'll thrash people." SME nixed the brown, which was deemed to be "too bland" for the dynamic sports logo landscape of the coming millennium. "The people at SME tell us that the hot new colors are bronze and gold," said Maggard.

The Thrashers' livery was decidedly modern and more than a bit unconventional, with the team's primary logo worn on the home sweaters and an alternate logo on the road. In 2003, the Thrashers broke out asymmetrical light blue alternate sweaters that featured the city name "Atlanta" cascading vertically down the left sleeves. This look proved popular with the Thrashers fan base during their final seasons. The club embraced the love for the new colors by making the light blue jerseys their full-time home set while adopting the team motto "Welcome to Blueland"—a move that included a recoloring the stanchions between the panes of glass light blue instead of the usual silver. This would end up being the uniform that they wore for their final game, on April 10, 2011, a 5–1 home loss to the Pittsburgh Penguins.

Atlanta's original road uniform employed their secondary "T" logo on the front; a third jersey introduced in 2008 went with numbers.

BOSTON BRUINS
1924 - PRESENT

THE TEAM

America's first NHL team, the Boston Bruins, were officially born on November 1, 1924; a new expansion franchise which was awarded to New England grocery store mogul Charles Francis Adams for a reported $15,000.

The Bruins' first game took place a month later to the day, at home against their expansion-mates, the Montréal team later designated the Maroons. A "comparatively small crowd" witnessed the game at the Boston Arena, a 2–1 Bruins win, and with that the franchise was on its way. The *Boston Globe* deemed it "an auspicious start."

The team was, as many new teams are, a disappointment during that first season. Things improved in year two, and, in 1927, the Bruins ascended all the way to the Stanley Cup Finals, where they were defeated by the Ottawa Senators. Enthusiasm for the team began to swell, and, in 1928–29, the team moved into a new arena, the Boston Garden. They also won their first Stanley Cup that season with a Finals victory over the New York Rangers.

Cup triumphs in 1939 and 1941 were followed by a few bright rays of sunshine, with several Finals appearances along the way, though only four winning campaigns between 1947 and 1967. The franchise was faced with fiscal ills during this era, too, and their long-neglected farm system suffered.

A savior would soon appear in the form of defenseman Bobby Orr. A native of Parry Sound, Ontario, Orr made his Boston debut in 1966 at the tender age of eighteen, changing the face of the team, the league, and the sport itself. The Bruins won the Cup in 1970, with a soaring Orr tallying the winning goal against St. Louis in overtime of Game Four. The team delivered another Cup in 1972, defeating the New York Rangers in six games.

The final decades of the twentieth century saw the Bruins participate in the playoffs in 29-consecutive seasons, from 1967–68 through 1995–96. They moved out of the outdated and deteriorating Boston Garden and into a new facility, the Fleet Center, a mere nine inches to the north of the old arena, in 1995.

As the new millennium dawned, the Bruins delivered solid teams and, in 2011, added a sixth Stanley Cup to their franchise trophy case.

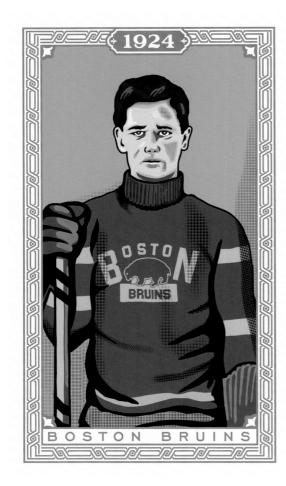

1924

BOSTON BRUINS

THE NAME

The team has been the Boston Bruins right from the outset.

An article in the November 14, 1924, edition of the *Boston Globe* stated, "the name Browns was considered, but the manager feared that the Brownie construction that might be applied to the team would savor too much of kid stuff."

A catchy and alliterative nickname, "Boston Bruins" also connoted positive attributes such as speed, power, ferocity, and agility.

A 1948 item in the *Windsor Star* cites Betty Moss, secretary to coach and general manager Art Ross, as having been responsible for the name.

"Miss Moss was aware of the correspondence between Ross and Adams regarding the team's name and colors. It was decided to have the Boston colors brown and gold, the same colors as were used on the store fronts of the chain of grocery stores of which Adams was president.... The fact that the colors were to be part Brown prompted Ms. Moss to suggest the name Bruins."

THE LOOK

The same *Boston Globe* item that trumpeted the new team name described the Bruins' colors and uniform design: "The Boston uniforms will be brown with gold stripes around the chest, sleeves and stockings. The figure of a bear will be worn below the name Boston on the chest."

The team's original color palette had special significance for team owner Charles F. Adams, according to the article.

> *An interesting item is connected with Pres. Adams' partiality toward brown as the team color. The pro magnate's four thoroughbreds are brown; his 50 stores are brown; his Guernsey cows are of the same color; brown Is the predominating color among his Durco pigs on his Framingham estate, and the Rhode*

Bobby Bauer, Woody Dumart, and Milt Schmidt of the Bruins' famed 'Kraut Line' in 1942. Boston wore player numbers on the front of their sweaters instead of a logo from 1936 to 1948.

Island hens are brown, although Pres. Adams wouldn't say whether or not the eggs they lay are of a brown color.

In 1932, the team began to feature a solitary serifed letter "B" as their crest. Brown and gold gave way to the team's present colors, black and gold, in 1935–36. Boston's *Christian Science Monitor* noted the change, stating, "the Brown in the old uniform has been changed to black, and the new color combination is black, gold and white…. The players used the new uniforms for the first time in practice yesterday, and they presented a colorful appearance. They will be a distinct change from the brown, gold and white color scheme which the Bruins had worn for 11 years."

The following season, Boston relegated the "B" to the arms of the sweaters and began to feature large player numbers on both fronts and backs, making the Bruins look more than a little like a football team.

Boston's familiar "spoked-B" insignia dates back to 1948–49. It was created to commemorate the team's 25th anniversary, and the original iteration featured the numbers "24" and "49" flanking the "B," denoting the years of celebration. This first version contained an oddly shaped, rounded letter "B," rendered in gold with a black outline. The aforementioned numbers were gold and the spokes— six of them—as well as the circle that contained the whole thing—were black.

While many ascribe the design of this logo to Boston's inveterate standing as the "Hub of the Universe," research into the origins of the symbol reveals no contemporaneous evidence to support such a claim.

The following season, 1949–50, saw the logo take on a more familiar configuration, with eight spokes anchoring a block "B." The coming decades would bring small changes, including outlines and the addition of serifs to the core "B," but the silver anniversary logo provided a clear start to the franchise's long-standing visual identity.

In 1995, the team embarked on a new era and a new facility. A gold third jersey was introduced into the mix, the crest of which featured a rather docile-looking bear

1948   1949   1995   2007

head, modeled after a print by artist Guy Coheleach. Team president Harry Sinden told the Associated Press that he "had a brush with a bear during a Canadian camping trip with former President Bush," and that he "wasn't interested in a growling grizzly." The bear emblem, he added, telegraphed a dual message. "Don't fool with me. I can be friendly...but I can also bite your head off." The sweaters were soon dubbed the "Winnie the Pooh" uniforms by snarky observers.

Modifications were made to the spoked-B logo and uniforms, and Sinden needed to provide solace to traditionalists who were fretting about the possibility of potential changes.

In comments to the *Globe*, Sinden said, "We are not getting very far with finding anything that makes sense." Of the spoked-B, he went on to say, "it's a pretty identifiable logo and you better be careful before you mess it up."

We found, if you start messing around with the design of the uniform too much, it doesn't blend in with the logo. If you start tilting a lot of stuff (the spokes or the B itself,) it looks off-balance. So we found, if we are going to keep that logo—which we want to do—we're limited as to what we can do with the uniform. We would have changed it, and changed it in good taste, and never ever given up the spoked-B—it would've been there somehow, somewhere. Maybe it would have been a different configuration, perhaps a different look, 3-D or something. But we know our fans were concerned about it, and, in the end, we didn't see anything we liked.

In the end, the changes were evolutionary in nature. Traditionalists breathed a sigh of relief and the Bruins powered forward into the new century, looking like the Boston Bruins.

Dubbed the "Winnie the Pooh" logo by some, the Bruins wore this grizzly bear on the front of their third jerseys for eleven seasons.

BUFFALO SABRES
1970-PRESENT

THE TEAM

A natural fit for the National Hockey League, the city of Buffalo, New York, had to wait until 1970 before a big-league puck was dropped in the Queen City. Located directly on the border with Canada, Buffalo had been home to professional hockey for several decades prior to the arrival of the NHL. From 1940 right up until 1970, the Buffalo Bisons were members of the American Hockey League, winning five Calder Cups—including a championship in their final season.

Interest in bringing an NHL team to Buffalo began in 1965, when Bisons general manager Fred Hunt approached Seymour Knox III and his brother Northrup about applying for an expansion team. The Knox brothers, heirs to the Woolworths fortune, loved the idea and, upon hearing the league had plans for a large wave of expansion, made it clear that Buffalo should be included among those cities. The pair made a pitch to the league in 1966, which one team owner called "the best of all," but with concerns about a team invading the television territory of the Toronto Maple Leafs—as well as much larger markets also making bids—the league passed.

Undeterred, the Knox brothers looked to bring major league hockey home by other means. On January 9, 1969, they announced they'd entered an agreement to purchase the struggling Oakland Seals, who were only in their second season, and move them to Buffalo. The league stopped this plan just a month later, citing the following reasons: they didn't want to give up on a new market so soon, leave the Los Angeles Kings all alone on the West Coast, and lose the Bay Area TV market. Still interested in being a part of the NHL scene, the Knoxes instead purchased just a 20 percent stake of the Seals that summer, a move that Seymour III later said was crucial to getting Buffalo into the NHL.

In the fall of 1969, when the league announced their plans to add two teams for the 1970–71 season, interest was immediate from the Knoxes, as well as potential ownership groups in Baltimore, Cleveland, and Vancouver. Baltimore and Cleveland would eventually balk at the high expansion fee, set by the league at $6 million, leaving Buffalo and Vancouver to apply virtually unopposed. On December 2, 1969, following presentations made by both groups to the Board of Governors in New York, the league approved expansion to both cities. The Buffalo bid was conditional on renovating the War Memorial Auditorium to increase seating capacity, and the Knoxes withdrawing their stake in the Seals.

"We are extremely enthusiastic with the prospect for major league hockey in Vancouver and Buffalo," NHL president Clarence Campbell said at the time. "We are confident they will bring new and important strength to the league."

The Sabres hired legendary Maple Leafs boss Punch Imlach to be their first coach and general manager, and chose future Hall of Famer Gilbert Perreault with their first-ever amateur draft choice. Buffalo's tenure on the ice also got off to a great start when, on October 10, 1970, they defeated the Pittsburgh Penguins on the road in their inaugural game, with Perreault netting the game-winner in a 2–1 victory. Five days later, the Sabres made their home debut against the Montréal Canadiens at "the Aud," which was still undergoing renovations to (literally) raise the roof. With construction reducing access to seating, only 10,331 were in attendance, and opening ceremonies included a speech from league president Clarence Campbell, a ceremonial faceoff with Seymour Knox III dropping the puck, and figure skater Sundae Bafo performing, appropriately enough, to Khachaturian's classical piece "Sabre Dance." The fun would stop there for fans of the new team, as the Habs shut out the Sabres, 3–0.

Buffalo found early success in the NHL and, in 1974–75, just their fifth season, qualified for the Stanley Cup Finals against the Philadelphia Flyers. Game Three of the Series was infamously interrupted a dozen times due to foggy conditions at the Sabres' home barn. Buffalo couldn't pull off the victory over the Flyers, nor would they be able to top the Dallas Stars in the 1999 Final, a series ending in controversy which many Sabres fans will be quick to tell you ended with a "no goal."

THE NAME

"The Buffalo Buffs...how does that sound?" St. Louis Blues owner Sid Salomon Jr. whispered into the ear of Seymour Knox III, a suggestion for a team name just moments before Knox found out the league had approved his expansion bid. Despite Salomon's suggestion, Knox and his Niagara Frontier Hockey Corporation decided to move forward with a Name the Team Contest in the early part of 1970 to find a suitable tag for their new club.

After receiving more than 13,000 entries suggesting 1,047 different names, Knox III announced the team would be known as the Buffalo Sabres, as Khachaturian's Gayane Ballet, featuring the "Sabre Dance," played to a press luncheon on February 17, 1970. The team was named for the saber, a sword with a curved blade used commonly by the United States Cavalry into the early part of the twentieth century.

"Our name denotes an aggressive, sharp, and penetrating weapon on offense, and a parrying weapon on defense," Knox said. "The committee wanted a name which wouldn't be confused with the [hockey and baseball] Bisons, and we felt that name had already been overworked. Our new name will be readily identified with Buffalo."

Sabres VP Northrup Knox explained that the name was spelled the Canadian way, as "SAB-RES" rather than the American "SAB-ERS" to help any potential fans from nearby Southern Ontario feel some identification with the club.

Knox III shared some of the other names they considered, including Flashes, Pumas, Bandits, Hesters, Sky Hawks, Buzzing Bees, and Cavaliers. "And there were also some like Baboons, Beasties, Hard Knox, Queens, Mugwumps, and even Veni Vidi Vici...of course these never made it to the finals but they are unusual."

With entries coming in from as far away as Munich and Vancouver, it was Williamsville, New York, college student Robert Sonnelitter Jr. who was drawn as the winner from the four who suggested "Sabres" by Buffalo mayor Frank Sedita. Robert won a pair of inaugural season tickets as the top prize for submitting the name.

Nearly twenty years later, Robert's brother Mark came clean, revealing that he had submitted the name "Sabres" on behalf of his brother to get around contest rules limiting one entry per person. Mark explained his choice of "Sabres" to the *Buffalo News* in 1989, saying, "I thought about skates being sharp, cutting edges, and came up with Sabres and Blades," adding that the alliterative Buffalo Blades was his original choice.

THE LOOK

No logo more perfectly expresses its team's full name without having to say a word than the Buffalo Sabres and their original logo from 1970. With a white buffalo leaping in between two crossed sabers placed within a blue circle trimmed in gold, it's quite literally a buffalo and sabers. At the event announcing the Sabres name in 1970, Knox gave a preview of what the team would wear in their expansion season, describing it as a bison between crossed sabers on a home sweater that is blue trimmed with red, white, and yellow.

"My great grandfather trained racehorse trotters and they had jockey silks which were blue and gold," Knox's son Seymour IV told the authors, "My grandfather, dad and uncle all got into playing polo and they used the same colors on their pinnies. As time marched on they were very accom-

plished, and wore what we'd call the 'Aurora colors' [in reference to their estate in East Aurora, New York]. So it was pretty easy when they started the Sabres as to what the colors were going to be."

Originally designed to show a gold buffalo in motion in between the two white sabers, the animal in the Sabres' first logo was quickly changed to white—as it was a symbol of good fortune in local Native American lore—during the creation process. The only inclusion of red within the entire set was in the eye of the buffalo.

"When they were doing the logo they wanted to have the buffalo moving, they wanted him to be mad so they gave him a red eye," said Seymour Knox IV. "He was going to be on the warpath, so to speak."

As the team approached their 25th anniversary season in the early 1990s and the move into a brand-new arena neared, the Sabres looked to make a big change. Knox IV got to work with Vermont-based design firm Jager Di Paola Kemp Design—who were known more for their work in snowboarding—to develop an all-new look for the Sabres.

"I went to JDK to take a look at the first rough cuts of the jersey and the colors were teal, and khaki, and cranberry," Knox IV recalled. "We didn't really know what to say we just sort of looked at each other and they asked, 'Well, what are you gonna tell your dad?' I said, 'We're just going to tell him you're still looking into it.'"

The NHL's player lockout in 1994–95 pushed back the implementation of the new look, which had included silver originally in honor of the team's 25th anniversary season, but it wasn't until an open midday practice held on April 11, 1996, that the team announced the changes. With 16,000 fans crammed into the soon-to-be-closed War Memorial Auditorium, Sabres players took to the ice to rock music, dry ice, and laser lights while wearing the brand-new, aggressively redesigned, black, red, and silver uniforms.

The Sabres had dropped the blue and gold, scrapped their original logo, and debuted a modern design, which featured the head of a white buffalo trimmed in black, red, and silver on the chest of the sweater. No saber was present in the team's new primary logo, but was still represented courtesy a shoulder patch with a "B" wrapped around a sword. Several large stripes drove diagonally from each hip up toward the player's armpit to form the horns of a buffalo.

"What we're trying to do is revive interest in Sabres hockey," Sabres president Doug Moss said at the time. "To be honest, I think this town could use something to be excited about. I said we were in the entertainment business."

Moss added that there were problems with their previous colors in that they were incredibly inconsistent.

"The shades of blue and gold depended on what piece of dry goods you looked at. There wasn't any consistency in the colors. Some of the stuff was light blue, some of it royal blue, some of it navy. Some of the gold actually was yellow, some of it was brown. We looked at this design in every imaginable color and the black absolutely was the best."

It was a major departure from the look most associated with the Sabres, the *Tampa Bay Times* mentioning that one reporter claimed the new logo "looks like 'Elsie the Cow' in drag."

"Dad was sick at the time and he loved the Sabres original logo," Knox IV recalled when asked how his father felt about the change. "He didn't think that there was a necessary need to [change] it. He was pointing to the Maple Leafs, the Canadiens, the Blackhawks and how they've made minimal changes to their uniform over the years." Seymour III died just a few weeks after the new look was unveiled.

"The big thing was, do we focus on the buffalo or do we focus on the saber? In talking with the people there, they wanted the buffalo," Steven Farrar, senior design director at JDK told the *Bennington Banner*. "I wanted to convey the idea of a stampede, the aggressive nature of it as well as the skating movement. We wanted to stay with the deep colors and get away from the light blue to build mass and power in the uniform. We just want to make them look bigger and more powerful than their opponents."

It wasn't long before Sabres fans began to miss the old colors and logo and, despite a near Stanley Cup Championship while wearing the black and red in 1999, they made it quite clear they wanted to go back.

In the summer of 2006, the Sabres teased the return of the classic look. Fans got their hopes up for a return to the logo and colors they missed so dearly.

But then there was a leak...

"Donald Trump comb-over!"; "Bobby Hull's toupee!"; "a slug."

These were just some of the mountains of negative reactions the new look received upon first viewing, accidentally leaked by a licensing firm in July 2006. The logo featured the head and body of a leaping gold buffalo—shown with no legs and trimmed in blue and silver with a red eye.

"What I saw, I couldn't believe," chimed in former Sabres goalie Dominik Hasek. "I was shocked. It reminded me of [the] Atlanta [Thrashers] or something." Several websites

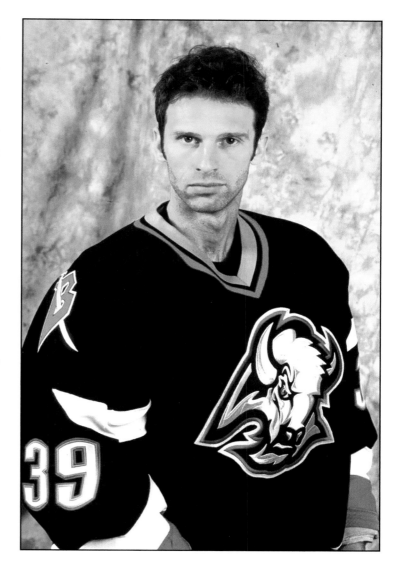

Dominik Hasek poses in Buffalo's "aggressive" uniforms, 2000.

Jochen Hecht, Martin Biron and Daniel Briere getting set to reveal the Sabres' infamous "Buffaslug" uniforms on September 16, 2006.

popped up such as fixthelogo.com and Sabres Not Slugs, which collected signatures petitioning the team to abandon the new mark and allowed a platform to express their displeasure with it.

The reaction to the leak was so overwhelmingly negative that the team took the unprecedented step of holding a press conference to address the leaked logo in the hopes of calming the fan base.

"Given the outpouring of fan concern the last few weeks, we decided to make this announcement now," said Sabres managing partner Larry Quinn. "We are still committed and enthusiastic about our new uniform and believe that fans will embrace it once they have a chance to actually see it."

Designed by Kristopher Bazen and Reebok, the logo and uniforms were "officially" released two months after the leak at an open practice in front of just 8,000 fans on September 16, 2006. After the unveiling, Quinn commented that he appreciated the passion shown with the petitions and was happy with the way it all worked out, adding that he felt fans like the jersey.

"We wanted to create something that would be iconic and a little more forward thinking," Bazen told Greg Wyshynski of Yahoo! in 2012. "Reebok wanted to push the envelope somehow. I give them credit, because they tried to be innovative but the Sabres also wanted to go in a new direction, based on what they decided on." Bazen added that the Sabres logo itself was partially inspired by the lightning bolt logo of the National Football League's then San Diego Chargers. "We

tried to convey this image of strength. For inspiration, we looked at the front end of the buffalo. I tried to take the boldness from that."

For such a simple design, there was plenty of confusion over which part of the logo was which. Bazen, to his credit, has tried to clarify his logo.

"The front part is not legs, it's the gruff of his face, and I never understood why the logo came to that abrupt stop [in the back]," Bazen told Chris Creamer's Sports Logos Community in 2012. "That one was out of my hands. If it were up to me, the back would've come to a point, for consistency purposes."

Unsurprisingly, with all the vitriol directed toward it, the Sabres moved away from the new logo as fast as they could. During that first season on the ice with their new look, the team tried to smooth things over by adding the original 1970 road blue sweater as a temporary alternate uniform. Two years later, in 2008, a more permanent alternate uniform was added featuring the original team logo—now modernized to match the new darker color scheme and silver streaks with piping added throughout. But all that wasn't enough to save the slug. After just four seasons, the "Buffaslug" was dead, replaced full-time by that newer retro-inspired alternate sweater from 2008, retaining the darker colors and silver additions. In 2017, much of the silver was removed from the uniform and for the 2020–21 season the team announced that they would finally, after nearly twenty-five years, return to the original shade of royal blue.

CALGARY FLAMES

1980-PRESENT
ATLANTA FLAMES, 1972-1980

THE TEAM

The Flames' National Hockey League history extends across two nations and some 2,000 miles. The team initially were the ones to introduce NHL hockey to the Deep South, but were a major box office flop. Conversely, their 1980 relocation to Alberta was an immediate success and the Flames won the Stanley Cup in 1989.

Atlanta, along with Long Island, New York, was awarded a new NHL franchise on November 9, 1971. The league fast-tracked its third expansion in five years, a preemptive strike against their new and aggressive rivals, the World Hockey Association. The Flames' NHL debut came on October 7, 1972, in a 3–2 road victory against their expansion brethren, the New York Islanders.

The team's on-ice performance was solid—the Flames qualified for the NHL playoffs in six of their first eight seasons, but won only two postseason games along the way. A multitude of business ills plagued the Flames during their tenure in Atlanta. The team was battered by a combination of receding attendance and expanding debt, which was eventually fuelled by a toxic one-two punch of a deep economic recession and spiraling inflation. Local television and radio revenues were paltry, and attendance at their home arena, The Omni, plummeted. Rumours of a potential move swirled and, on May 23, 1980, Flames ownership announced that they were selling the club to Canadian millionaire Nelson Skalbania for $16 million, the highest price ever paid for an NHL franchise up to that point. The team was to be shifted to Calgary for the 1980–81 season.

The new Calgary Flames were instantly embraced by the local community, and ticket sales boomed at the team's diminutive first home, the Stampede Corral. The team moved over to the 16,683-seat Olympic Saddledome in 1983. There was a lot to cheer for, as the team went all the way to the Stanley Cup Finals in 1986. They lost to the Montréal Canadiens, but exacted sweet revenge on the Habs three years later, winning their first Cup Championship.

The Flames, along with a couple of their Canadian counterparts, faced economic headwinds as the new millennium approached, but a surprise run to the 2004 Finals recaptured the imagination of the community and solidified their place in the hearts and minds of Calgarians.

THE NAME

Atlanta's new NHL franchise held a Name the Team Contest. A total of 9,415 people submitted entries, which included such nicknames as the B-72s, Yucca-Pucks, Y'alls, and Rednecks. While "Thrashers" was described as a popular choice, the team announced on June 2, 1972, that they would be called the Atlanta "Flames."

Team president Bill Putnam said that the name resonated with judges and that they "agreed on 49 of 50 points that Flames was the ideal name."

The winning entry was credited to Mickey Goodman, a nineteen-year-old sophomore at DeKalb College (now Perimeter College), who was awarded four season tickets for his efforts. Goodman was one of 198 entrants to suggest "Flames."

*   *   *

In announcing the 1980 shift to Calgary, new owner Nelson Skalbania decided to give fans seven days to decide on a new nickname for the relocated franchise. "Originally," he told the *Calgary Herald*, "I thought we might be able to keep the same name, the same logo, the same red and white uniforms and embellish the flaming 'A' with a 'C.' It seemed like a natural. The 'A' would stand for 'Alberta' and the 'C' for 'Calgary.'"

Calgarians, it seemed, were weary of western-themed names such as Stampeders or Wranglers. A four-member committee vetted some 400 different suggestions, among them Americans, Executives, Critters, Yahoos, and Bush-

wackers. Other entries included Sodbusters, Hillbillies, Pumpers, Prairie Dogs, and Homesteaders. "We got all sorts of weird suggestions," said part-owner Normie Kwong. "One person even mailed us their utility bill."

At the end of the day, retaining the "Flames" moniker made sense. The existing designation received a total of 152 votes, with "Chinooks" coming in second with 95, followed by Spurs, Cowboys, and Mustangs. The Calgary Flames were officially christened as such at a June 3, 1980, press conference, held at the Calgary Convention Centre. Many noted that the name evoked an image of flaring natural gas wells, a natural fit for the team's new region.

The Atlanta Flames wore "Coca-Cola red" with a flaming "A" logo.

THE LOOK

The Atlanta Flames' logo represented the very model of modernity. Introduced on July 6, 1972, the mark was streamlined and bold; a spare, yet highly effective trademark.

The task of creating a visual identity for the new team was assigned to Atlanta ad agency McDonald & Little. Bob Wages, a twenty-four-year-old designer at the firm, came up with the new look. Wages simultaneously created both the Flames' mark and a new logo for the Atlanta Hawks, now referred to as the "Pac-Man" logo.

Wages later said that he rendered the two marks in "Coca Cola red," a hue with great local relevance and recognition.

Agency head Tom Little told the *Atlanta Constitution*:

> *We feel the Flames' logo is graphically more sophis-*
> *ticated than the usual athletic symbols. The mark*
> *blends sports tradition with modern design. The*
> *block letter is used throughout sports, but we added*
> *a couple of elements to give it a new dimension. The*
> *letter is slanted and the addition of the tendrils of*
> *flame in the centre give a feel of graceful flow and*
> *speed, which is hockey. The design is very simple,*
> *very bold and will be highly visible at a distance*
> *and instantly recognizable even on a fast-moving*
> *wing man.*

The team's uniforms—white at home and red on the road—were handsome and unembellished, featuring the team crest front and centre, accompanied by minimal striping of red and gold.

* * *

The Flames' move to Calgary, of course, required a rethinking of the franchise's visual identity. Their hasty relocation resulted in an equally hasty call for entries to determine a new logo, open to "professional firms," announced on June 18, 1980, with a deadline of June 27. There were 58 submissions considered by the team's board of directors, and the results were released at a July 21, 1980, press conference.

The winners of the competition were Keller/Lussier Designers, Ltd., and Brad Bennett, who split a first prize of $1,000. The team, however, discarded their winning efforts.

"We knew we couldn't go through with one of the designs; it was so close to the Philadelphia Flyers' logo, it would not have been accepted by the NHL," explained Flames public relations director Al Coates, in comments made to the *Calgary Herald*. "The other design was quite creative, but not functional. It would've cost too much money to reproduce on novelties like T-shirts and buttons."

A logo created by Calgary Intergroup was thus unveiled as the team's new symbol. The mark closely tracked the old Atlanta branding, an italicized letter "C" aflame. Critically, it was met with the approval from Nelson Sklabania's twenty-year-old daughter, Rozanda.

An early Flames official publication stated, "The logo is symbolic of the Flames' aspirations in the National Hockey League. The Flames ... qualified for the playoffs six of eight seasons, but have one major hurdle to overcome—getting by the preliminary round of the Stanley Cup playoffs. The Flames' logo ... represents the hopes of Flames fans, ecstatic Calgarians and saddened Atlantans."

Atlanta's red and gold colour scheme made the trip north with the Flames to Calgary. A modified logo featuring a flaming "C" instead of an "A" was the only change to the uniform.

A fire-breathing horse graced Calgary's jersey from 1998 to 2006.

The Calgary Flames' uniforms looked much like the togs of their Atlanta predecessors, with the obvious substitution of a new crest design; the red and yellow gold colour palette moved across the northern border with the team.

The Flames, like so many sports teams in the 1990s, added black into the mix. On September 29, 1994, new uniforms introduced an unorthodox diagonal striping pattern with an italicized player name and red, black, and gold uniform numbers. The new look was created by Bill Brownridge, who had previously designed the logo for the Western Hockey League's Calgary Centennials. Brownridge was an illustrator for the Francis, Williams & Johnson advertising agency and given the task of adding black to the Flames' red and gold colour palette.

"I really am a great believer in the diagonal in uniforms," Brownridge told Paul Lukas at *Uni Watch* in 2020. "You don't see too many diagonals—and my thought was to put the flaming 'C' on a podium, sort of a soaring-up podium. And then of course I used the diagonal slashes on the pants and the sleeves."

In 1998, the Flames unleashed a black alternate uniform, the focal point of which was a new crest that featured an angry, front-facing, fire-breathing horse. This became their full-time road outfit for a spell before disappearing into history in 2006–07.

Fittingly, the Atlanta Flames' classic and identifiable "A" logo was restored in the form of the "A" uniform patch that identifies alternate captains, a reverent and classy nod to the team's distant, Southern origins.

CALIFORNIA GOLDEN SEALS
1967-1976

THE TEAM

Before the Sharks came ashore in San Jose, it was the Seals who first represented the Bay Area in the National Hockey League. Added as part of the league's great expansion in the late 1960s, the franchise was awarded to the "well-organized" San Francisco Seals, Inc. group on February 8, 1966. Despite the name of the group, NHL president Clarence Campbell immediately revealed the team would actually play their home games across the bay in Oakland as the California Seals. The Seals went through a colorful cast of owners during their brief existence, from twenty-seven-year-old millionaire Barry Van Gerbig to crooner Bing Crosby to the infamously eccentric owner of baseball's Oakland Athletics, Charles O. Finley.

The franchise went through an identity crisis that would make even baseball's Angels shake their head, using five different names between their 1967–68 inaugural season and 1970, before finally settling on the name California Golden Seals in the fall of 1970. All the while the Seals struggled mightily to attract fans to the brand-new Oakland-Alameda County Coliseum, averaging just 5,600 fans per game over nine seasons.

Never finishing with a record above .500, the team lost money during each season they played. By 1976, team co-owner Mel Swig sought to move the franchise across the bay to San Francisco but ran into difficulties building a new arena there. Throughout the course of the summer, Swig had considered moving to or fielded offers from Denver, Edmonton, Miami, San Diego, and San Jose—all looking to be the new home of the Golden Seals before Swig settled on Cleveland, the home of co-owner George Gund III. On July 15, 1976, the NHL approved the relocation of the Seals to Ohio in time for the 1976–77 season, where they would continue on as the Cleveland Barons; it was the first relocation in the NHL since the Ottawa Senators moved to St. Louis to become the Eagles forty-one years earlier, in 1935.

THE NAME

The Seals assumed the name used by the San Francisco Seals, a pro hockey team from the old Western Hockey League (WHL), from 1961 to 1967. Those original hockey Seals were named following a Name the Team Contest, in which more

than 3,000 entries were submitted. Front-runners included Golden Gaters, Blades, Penguins, and Vigilantes, but it was Seals which took the top spot. Donald Naify, a state social worker, was officially recognized as the one to submit the winning name, earning a trip to see the new WHL team on the road in Los Angeles—much to the dismay of Mrs. Naify, who insisted he choose the alternate prize of a new watch. The new name immediately ruffled some feathers in the city's sporting scene, as a roller derby team announced they'd also be known as the San Francisco Seals, even threatening to take the issue to court, while others pointing out both of these teams had just taken the name from baseball's long-running Seals of the Pacific Coast League.

In an effort to match the new NHL club, the WHL Seals moved across the bay and changed their name from San Francisco to California in 1966. The team was disbanded after just a single season, just in time for the NHL Seals to take the ice for their inaugural campaign.

Just a month into their inaugural season, Seals owner

Barry Van Gerbig told the league they were changing their name to the Oakland Seals, stating that the original "California" name was "not of our doing when the franchise was awarded … it was the desire of the league that we try to identify with San Francisco; the only way we could identify with both cities would be to play in the middle of the bridge." The new name was made official on November 4, 1967, after playing just 10 games as the California Seals.

In the summer of 1970, Charles O. Finley purchased the franchise for $4.5 million. Finley, who at his introductory press conference, announced "I know absolutely nothing about hockey," immediately made his mark on the team by changing the name once again, now from the Oakland Seals to the Bay Area Seals. Finley defended the decision, saying, "we are the only hockey team in the area, why not call it an area team," adding that taxpayer money from several different counties—not just Alameda County—was used to build the arena. While merchandise, including a few pennants and posters, were produced and sold featuring the new name, it didn't last long. After just two games as the Bay Area Seals, the team was rechristened yet again. An article in the *Chicago Examiner* published quotes from Finley saying the team would play out the season as the San Francisco Golden Seals despite remaining in Oakland. Hearing the response to the article, Finley immediately changed his mind once again, opting to use California as the location name instead. The Golden Seals bit stayed, and the official announcement of the California Golden Seals name was made on October 14, 1970.

Why *Golden* Seals? "That's for the Golden West," Finley explained. "The Golden Gate Bridge as well … on my first visit to San Francisco I went out to Seal Rocks and I was very impressed by the seals romping around out there after passing by the Golden Gate Bridge." From that point on, the California/Oakland/Bay Area/San Francisco/California Seals-Golden Seals never changed their name again during the remainder of their final five seasons in Oakland.

THE LOOK

While the Seals are remembered now for their more "out-there" looks, the club started out with a very conservative, traditional design. The first team logo showed a green-and-black seal holding a hockey stick upon a blue "C" trimmed in black. Simple green and blue uniforms were shown off at the news conference announcing Van Gerbig's purchase of the team on April 20, 1967. Charlie Burns and Gerry Odrowski—both of the WHL's Seals—modeled the new look, which included a road uniform incorporating a SEALS wordmark arched over the club's new logo. This SEALS wordmark was dropped before the team took the ice that fall.

When the Seals changed their name from California to Oakland in November 1967, a new logo came with it, the "C" surrounding the seal was simply changed to an "O," although the club would continue to wear the "C" logo on their jerseys for the remainder of the 1967–68 season. During this time, the new Oakland "O" logo was used only on team publications and merchandise, not making its debut on their uniform until the following season.

In 1970, Finley took over the club and, as was his style, everything about the look of the team changed. In addition to the numerous revisions to the name of the club under his watch, the Seals revamped their colors to match those of his Oakland A's: Fort Knox gold and Kelly green. "Regardless of what you're selling—baseball, insurance, hockey, you've got to put color into it," Finley said. "If people think a colorful uniform is flamboyant, then it's too bad, I like color and my players like their uniforms." The logo featuring the seal on an "O" was scrapped, replaced with a simple *Seals* italicized wordmark. Each player's last name was added on the back of the uniforms, a first in the NHL. Much to the chagrin of other team owners who felt it would hurt their program sales, the practice caught on quickly with the league mandating its use across the league by 1978.

But Finley didn't stop there. He also wanted the Seals and A's to match on another piece of the uniform, white footwear. After some pushback from the league's Board of Governors, Finley eventually won out, the league allowing the Seals and three other clubs to try out colored skates "as long as every member of the team wears the same color." Finley backed off using white at the time due to reluctance from his players, instead having the players wear green and gold skates

Golden Seals players memorably wore white skates from 1972 to '74.

matching their uniforms for a handful of games to start the season. The idea of white skates stayed with Finley, and it wasn't long until he eventually got his way. One season later, on January 14, 1972, the Golden Seals debuted their white skates with a victory at home over the Vancouver Canucks. They'd continue to wear them through the end of the 1973–74 season.

With Finley's departure in the summer of 1974, the white skates were gone, and so too were his preferred color scheme. The Golden Seals dropped the green and shifted to teal—which the team called "Pacific Blue"; white uniforms returned for home games and a unique series of stripes now looped around the top of each arm down around to the armpit. The Seals wordmark remained, recolored to accommodate the new Pacific blue. After the team relocated to Cleveland in 1976, the Golden Seals uniforms almost made the trip with them across the country, as the newly formed Barons didn't have their new duds ready in time for their first preseason game. Fortunately, the club managed to find their new black and red threads in time to drop the puck on their even briefer tenure in the NHL.

CAROLINA HURRICANES

1997-PRESENT

THE TEAM

The National Hockey League arrived in North Carolina by way of Hartford, Connecticut, when the struggling Whalers moved south in 1997. A press conference was held on March 26, 1997, to announce the Whalers' departure. Unable to secure an agreement for a new arena in Hartford, franchise owner Peter Karmanos Jr. and Connecticut governor John G. Rowland announced that the team would leave the state's capital city after the conclusion of the NHL season. The Whalers agreed to pay the state a $22.7 million exit fee to escape its lease obligation a year before the commitment was set to expire.

Unlike most team relocations, no new home was announced for the soon-to-be ex-Whalers. A host of potential landing spots were rumored to be in the mix, including Las Vegas, which was reputed to be Karmanos's first choice. NHL commissioner Gary Bettman, however, reportedly didn't want his league to be the first major professional circuit with a franchise in the gambling epicenter of America.*

Within weeks of the announced move, Karmanos said that Columbus, Ohio, was his first choice, followed by Raleigh, North Carolina. "I know it will be one of those cities," he stated.

Finally, on May 6, 1997, Karmanos, general manager Jim Rutherford, and North Carolina governor James B. Hunt held a press conference and officially announced that the Whalers would be shifting to Raleigh.

> We have spent a harrowing four to six weeks crisscrossing the country looking for a place to relocate. We were on the East Coast. I have been on the West Coast, I've been into gambling meccas, I've been into the north, into some very cold areas, and was down south. Very, very easily in our minds this area finished on top.

* Two decades later, the NHL did exactly that when they voted to award an expansion outfit to Vegas, later named the Golden Knights.

This is a market where the people have a good feeling about themselves, have a good feeling about the future. I think they want a sports team here as a quality-of-life issue, something they can identify with.

The team, however, would have to play in Greensboro for two seasons while a new arena was constructed in Raleigh. Greensboro, 80 miles northwest of the team's planned permanent home, proved to be a less-than-auspicious choice. Crowds were sparse—the team's season ticket base was a paltry 3,000, the lowest in the NHL.

The Hurricanes' Greensboro debut took place on October 3, 1997—a 4–3 loss to the Pittsburgh Penguins, with NASCAR driver Jeff Burton dropping the ceremonial first puck.

The crowd, which was announced as 18,661, included a large contingent of Whalers fans who made the 12-hour drive south from Hartford. Some of them hung a banner from the upper deck that read, "We Still Bleed Green." One fan, Jennifer St. Laurent of Bristol, Connecticut, was asked about the Hurricanes' new logo by the *Greensboro News & Record*. Her sense of bitterness was probably representative of many of the Whalers' fans in attendance: "To be honest," she said, "I think it looks like a flushed toilet."

Gerry Callahan, writing in *Sports Illustrated*, noted that the Hurricanes were "like some down-on-its-luck country band playing in front of small crowds, in a small city, with no home and no hope. Their nickname, the Hurricanes, is the only thing about them that makes sense, because thus far the NHL's incursion into tobacco country has been a natural disaster."

The Canes made their debut at the new Raleigh Entertainment & Sports Arena on October 29, 1999, where they dropped a 4–2 decision to the New Jersey Devils. A sellout crowd of 18,730 welcomed the team to their new home.

Carolina secured playoff spots in 1998–99 and 2000–01, and made it all the way to the Stanley Cup Finals in 2002, dropping a five-game series to the Detroit Red Wings. In 2006, the team climbed to the top of the hockey world when they defeated the Edmonton Oilers in seven games to win their first (and only, to date) Cup.

THE NAME

When the team formally announced their intentions to move to North Carolina on May 6, 1997, the name of the new team was also officially conveyed: the Carolina Hurricanes.

Team owner Peter Karmanos told the assembled media that the name IceHogs was also considered, but that Hurricanes was the selected sobriquet. In comments made to the *Charlotte Observer*, he conceded that naming his team after a destructive natural force was sure to be seen by some as a polarizing issue. "That was our first concern when we started talking about the name. We wanted something that people would remember and be germane to the area. When you think about the Avalanche in Colorado, that is a big disaster there. It's unfortunate these things happen. At the same time, when people talk about hurricanes, they talk about them with awe and sometimes with a warm feeling in the sense that they went through tough times and survived them. We are sensitive to all that. But, at the same time, I think it's a great name for a hockey team."

Governor Hunt acknowledged the fact that hurricanes Bertha and Fran had recently wreaked havoc upon his state. "After last year, I didn't think I'd ever want to see a hurricane

come to this state again. Today, I am delighted."

Karmanos said that the new team would sport a "traditional" look. "I guarantee you it won't be teal," he said, seemingly referring to the popular signature color of the NBA's Charlotte Hornets.

THE LOOK

The Hurricanes' logo was revealed on June 16, 1997, at an event held at the Sheraton Imperial Hotel in Research Triangle, North Carolina. A crowd of more than a thousand attendees witnessed the ceremony, which included a light show and a parade of youth hockey players from Greensboro and Raleigh, sporting various NHL team jerseys. The logo was unveiled to "Rock You Like a Hurricane," the 1984 anthem by the German metal band Scorpions.

The new team opted for a traditional visual approach, which represented a sharp departure for the era. "We wanted a good, straightforward, high-powered traditional hockey logo," said Karmanos. "We tried to come up with the kind of logo that would give us an identity and would be separate from other teams and have powerful colors—you know, all that advertising talk. Nobody will ever mistake us for anyone else.

"You want a sense of identification, but we thought that a good, strong, traditional hockey crest would be nice for a change. We were willing to give up a few early retail sales for something that will last and be traditional in the long run. We didn't want any gimmicks."

NHL director of creative services David Haney said, "The inspiration for the logo comes from the power, the strength, the speed and the tenacity of a hurricane. It happens to be the same kind of qualities of a great hockey club and the great game of hockey."

Keen-eyed observers noted the fact that the new team's secondary logo—intended to represent a hurricane warning flag—was actually the symbol for a gale warning, centered around a single flag, as opposed to a pair of vertical flags for a hurricane. The flag, lashed to a hockey stick, was backed up with a black triangle in honor of the Raleigh-Durham-Chapel Hill Research Triangle area.

"That's just a stiff breeze," Haney said of the single flag. "Two flags up is a hurricane, so we will give you two flags." A double flag logo was finally introduced in 2018.

The Hurricanes' colors, red and black, were chosen with a nod to North Carolina State University, whose men's basketball team would be sharing their future arena in Raleigh. Rick Bonnell, writing for the *Observer,* said, "Consider the hockey color scheme a subtle concession to Wolfpack fans. Karmanos wants to be a good neighbor, and NC State has been around a lot longer than the Whalers."

In an interview with the authors, Haney said that the Hurricanes' red color was directly connected to Detroit, via Karmanos, a Motor City native, and GM Jim Rutherford, who played ten seasons with the Red Wings. Of the NC State homage, Haney recalled Rutherford's suggestion, "If there's a strong second color, let it be black."

Haney gives great credit to Rutherford for his leadership role in what was necessarily a hasty branding process. "I really admired the way Rutherford navigated all of this," he says. "He exhibited great support for what we were doing."

The long arc of history eventually connected the 'Canes back to their New England roots.

In January 2018, Karmanos sold a majority interest in the

franchise to Texas billionaire Tom Dundon. Later that year, the Hurricanes announced they would wear green Whalers throwback uniforms for two games against Boston, thus reviving one of professional sports' all-time most popular logos. "I think we should have a store that sells that Whalers merchandise online and we should explore playing games in that jersey and selling that gear. It's part of the legacy," Dundon told EPSN.

"We're proud of the history and traditions that we've built in 21 years in North Carolina. But we've never thrown away the records established during this franchise's 18 NHL seasons in Connecticut," said team president and GM Don Waddell on the Hurricanes website. "This is a chance to celebrate our team's heritage and the players and coaches who laid the groundwork for this franchise."

Revisiting the Whalers' look opened up raw wounds for many in New England. Matt Vautour, writing for masslive.com, said, "It's like your ex decided to have a day to 'honor' you, by wearing that outfit you saved up to buy them, on a date with their new spouse. It's opening an old wound and dumping vinegar-based BBQ sauce into it. It not only hurts, but would taste better if they'd used sauce from Memphis or Kansas City."

In North Carolina, however, the sentiments were quite different. Luke DeCock of the *News & Observer* wrote of Karmanos, "While a great number of people in the Nutmeg State have their Cooperalls in a bunch over what they see as the Hurricanes' cultural appropriation of their beloved Whalers, their primary antagonist—the man they blame for the loss of the team, with all the bile that comes with that—isn't quite as bothered. Having sold the team to Tom Dundon a little less than a year ago, he's as operationally detached from the day-to-day operations as he is emotionally

detached from everything that seemed so important two decades ago."

"I'm going to watch the game with morbid curiosity," Karmanos told him. "I'll let you know how I feel afterward."

Neutral observers relished in the spectacle, a full circle turning back of the clock to the roots of the franchise and its broadly beloved symbol.

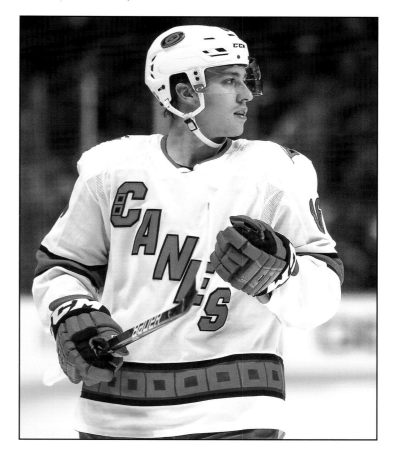

Road uniforms in 2019-20 featured CANES down the front.

CHICAGO BLACKHAWKS
1926-PRESENT

THE TEAM

Chicago's 1926 arrival into the National Hockey League was a tumultuous one. Applications for new franchises for Chicago and Detroit were hotly debated by NHL owners and leadership, and, at one point, the discussions were so heated that they threatened to break the league apart. An agreement was eventually reached, however, and on May 15, 1926, the two cities officially gained admittance to the NHL.

The Chicago club was awarded to Huntington R. "Tack" Hardwick, a former Harvard football star and future inductee into the College Football Hall of Fame. The cost was a cool $50,000. Hardwick's ownership tenure was short-lived, however, as he soon sold his majority of the franchise to a group headed up by Major Frederic McLaughlin, a Chicago coffee magnate.

The new Windy City entry was stocked with players from the Western Hockey League's Portland Rosebuds, purchased for a reported $100,000.

The Chicago Black Hawks' first NHL game took place at home on November 17, 1926, a 4–1 victory over the Toronto St. Pats in front of 7,000 fans at the Chicago Coliseum. The team played in their first Stanley Cup Finals in 1931 and won the Cup in both 1934 and 1938. The franchise fell on hard times in the 1940s and 1950s, frequently finishing in last place and making only two playoff appearances between 1945 and 1958.

Starting in the late 1950s, the team began to develop a talented and deep farm system. The Hawks broke through for a Cup Championship in 1961, and made Finals appearances in 1962 and 1965.

Another pair of Finals losses took place in 1971 and 1973. The Blackhawks were perennial playoff participants through the end of the twentieth century, and made it back to the Finals in 1992, when they were swept by the Pittsburgh Penguins. They moved into the new United Center in January 1995, a replacement for their longtime home of Chicago Stadium.

Finally, in 2010, the Blackhawks again hoisted Lord Stanley's silver chalice as champions of the National Hockey League. They followed this up with Cup victories in 2013 and 2015, a truly golden era for an NHL Original Six franchise.

Chicago's inaugural NHL team. Major Frederic McLaughlin is seen at center, wearing a fedora.

THE NAME

The Blackhawks' name is attributed to Major McLaughlin's World War I Army division, the 86th "Blackhawk Division," which was itself named for Chief Black Hawk (1767–1838), leader of the Sauk tribe, located in America's Midwest, home to present-day Chicago.

On August 27, 1926, the *Chicago Tribune* reported, "The name of the team was picked yesterday. McLaughlin and his associates decided that the team should be called the Black Hawks. Uniforms will be symbolic of the name."

In January 1937, McLaughlin revealed a scheme to "Americanize" his team, with plans to stock the Black Hawks solely with US-born players. The club was to develop their own "hockey factory" of American natives, starting in 1938–39. "I think an all-American team would be a tremendous drawing card all over the league," he said.

Irene Castle McLaughlin's 1935 Chicago Black Hawks uniform design, inspired by the garb of the Sauk people.

Notably, he announced that his club would be called "Yankees," starting in 1937–38.

In March 1937, with his team out of contention, McLaughlin's plan moved forward in earnest. Five American natives—all rookies—took the ice for the team's March 11 game against Boston. The Black Hawks lost the game, 6–2, but Bruins boss Art Ross was none too pleased. Chicago's use of the five Americans made the game a "laughing stock," he said, and demanded that the league cancel Chicago's franchise. "Never in hockey's history has such a farce been perpetrated on a National League crowd," he added in disgust.

The rookies put up a good battle three nights later in Toronto, though losing a tight game to the Maple Leafs, 3–2. The sound system at Maple Leaf Gardens blared "Yankee Doodle" as the Hawks took the ice, and the crowd expected a mismatch. But after an impressive showing, Leafs fans wound up giving the Chicago skaters a hearty round of applause for their efforts.

The team soon abandoned the plan—as well as the intended name change—but shocked the league by winning the Stanley Cup the following season—with eight Americans on the eighteen-man roster.

Finally, in 1986, the team officially clarified the name of the franchise when they proclaimed themselves to be "Blackhawks"—one word—as opposed to "Black Hawks." "'Hawks' makes it sounds like they're birds, which they aren't," declared owner Bill Wirtz.

On March 23, 1952 Chicago's Bill Mosienko scored three goals in 21 seconds against the New York Rangers at Madison Square Garden, the fastest hat trick in National Hockey League history.

THE LOOK

The Blackhawks' first logo and uniforms are credited to Irene Castle McLaughlin—famed ballroom dancer, Broadway actress, movie starlet, and fashion icon. She was purportedly the first film actress to have her own line of clothing. She was also the wife of team owner Frederic McLaughlin.

The logo, a profile of a Native American, enclosed within a circle, surrounded by the name of the team, was closely inspired by (if not directly lifted from) the insignia of the Onwentsia Club in Lake Forest, Illinois, where Major McLaughlin, one of America's top polo players, held sway.

Irene Castle McLaughlin's original uniforms were black and white and chock full of horizontal stripes. More than a few pundits compared them to the outfits worn by convicts of the era.

She spiffed up the monochromatic uniforms in 1934–35, eliminating the signature stripes, but her sartorial creations for the 1935–36 season broke new ground. They were designed to echo the garb of the Sauk people, accompanied by a few timely and trendy Art Deco flourishes in the form of geometric patterns on the pants and socks.

Edward Burns, writing in the *Chicago Tribune*, described them as such: "The shoulders are black, but with no white stripes. The torso and arms are circled with three wide stripes, the outside ones red and the middle one buckskin. This color scheme, with Indian embellishments, has been used in the design of the panties and the socks. The socks have diagonal stripes rather than the Joliet solitary confinement motif.

"The gloves are uniform for the first time. The three color idea is carried out on these flashing gloves and fringe on the gauntlets gives that Indian touch." The colorful new look captured the attention of fans and media alike. One headline in the *Christian Science Monitor* noted, "Hawks Adopt Uniform to Dazzle Opponents."

The Native American head on the sweaters was now composed of green, brown, red, and yellow—a direct connection to the crest worn today.

While the look that she created endures, her marriage to Major McLaughlin did not. News of their contentious divorce proceedings filled the newspapers in 1937 and, coincidentally or otherwise, the Black Hawks adopted yet another new set of uniforms for the 1937–38 season.

These were the creations of the team's new coach, Bill Stewart. Stewart, a Major League Baseball umpire and NHL referee, dressed his team in flashy togs that featured a multistriped red, white, and black "barber pole" pattern, with black silk pants. Arch Ward, writing in the *Chicago Tribune*, noted that Stewart "designed the club's new uniforms before he knew they were displacing the ones designed by Irene Castle McLaughlin."

This look persisted through the World War II era straight into the mid-'50s. What came next bears a very close resemblance to the uniforms that the team employs today, one which was voted "best in league history" in a 2018 NHL fan poll.

The design of these uniforms is attributed to Dorothy Ivan, wife of then Chicago general manager Tommy Ivan. They were first worn at the Black Hawks' training camp in Welland, Ontario, in September 1955, and garnered positive reviews upon first reveal.

Steve Larmer, Al Secord, and Denis Savard wearing the iconic Chicago Black Hawks red jersey during the 1982-83 season.

The signature Native American head was redrawn and liberated from its circular retaining shape, and the striping pattern was eliminated in favor of a more subdued look. A "C," backed up by a pair of crossed tomahawks, was added to each sleeve, thus completing the look.

While there have been stylistic modifications to the logo and the uniforms over the decades, they are directly connected to the ones unveiled in 1955, when the NHL was a six-team circuit and Chicago was its westernmost outpost.

CLEVELAND BARONS
1976-1978

THE TEAM

The Cleveland Barons' two-season membership in the National Hockey League was hardly the stuff of legend. The on-ice product was lousy, home games were sparsely attended, and the team struggled mightily to make ends meet before giving up and merging with the Minnesota North Stars following the conclusion of the 1977–78 season.

Despite its short life span, the franchise does, however, hold a unique distinction. They are, as of this writing, the most recent major North American sports team to simply disappear and fold, ceasing operations and vanishing into memory after their brief flirtation with big-league status.

The Barons arrived in northeast Ohio in July 1976, from Oakland, California, where they began life as the Oakland Seals, one of the six teams that were added in the 1967 expansion which doubled the size of the league.

THE NAME

The Barons took their name from Cleveland's American Hockey League (AHL) franchise, a highly successful and well-attended entry that won nine Calder Cups during their three-and-a-half-decade run. These Barons, facing competition from the World Hockey Association's Cleveland Crusaders, had moved to Jacksonville, Florida in the middle of the 1972–73 season.

The AHL Barons gained their moniker via the result of a "Name the Team" contest that attracted some 23,000 entries. The new name, it seems, did not sit well with some observers. A September 29, 1937, article in the *Akron Beacon Journal* said, "hockey officials want a name that is simple enough for Cleveland headline writers to spell but which will not permit abbreviation. But they don't like Barons." The item went on to note the fact that one of the contest judges admitted to have never having attended a hockey game.

Other suggestions included Nordics, Comets, and Foresters, in honor of Cleveland's nickname "Forest City." Team owner Al Sutphin, citing the city's previous hockey club's nickname of "Falcons," said that he decided to change the name because newspaper headline writers had shortened Falcons to "Falcs." That, he quipped, "sounded pretty close to 'Talcs,' and we don't have any talcum powder guys on our team."

Whatever the case, the city's new NHL entry decided to glom onto a time-honored appellation that still conveyed fresh equity and relevance. Names that were "seriously considered" included Americans, Buccaneers, Cougars, and Seals—but Barons it was, and there's a story behind the transfer of the name.

Mel Swig was the owner of the relocated Seals franchise. Swig, a Bay Area real estate developer, had tried and failed to build a new arena for his team in San Francisco. When he shifted the team to Ohio, he sought out Cleveland sports magnate Nick Mileti, the man who moved the AHL Barons to Florida three years earlier. (Mileti was also the founder of the NBA's Cleveland Cavaliers.) He still controlled the rights to the Barons name, and a deal was soon struck: Swig acquired the name in exchange for a meal. Mileti, he said, "sold me the name in exchange for my wife and I taking Nick and his wife out for a nice dinner."

On July 22, 1976, Swig held a press conference at the Richfield Coliseum, his club's future home. He announced that his team would be called "Barons," and held up a rendering of the team's road jerseys and new logo.

THE LOOK

The Cleveland Barons' logo was designed by Walter Lanci of Maple Heights, Ohio. Lanci, owner of Offset Color and Printing Company in Bedford Heights, said that he wanted the team's identity to be "attractive, distinctive, and have a strong traditional feeling."

A 1976 game program quotes him at length. "It was generally felt all along that we would work with a large 'C' that would be original and different," said Lanci. "We also wanted to work in the configuration of the state of Ohio, because the Barons are sole representatives of the state in the NHL. This was to be a whole new thing, something with dignity that you would remember."

"We feel that the words Cleveland Barons within the "C" have an

Cleveland Barons uniforms included numbers inside state maps of Ohio during their first season.

elegant look, like an official seal. Also, the "B" to represent Barons is not really gothic, but a modification of the old English. The Ohio map is, we think, a truer representation than most Ohio state configurations in use now."

The man was clearly going for a traditional look. "You won't get tired of it as people tend to do with it so-called 'modern' graphics," he said, a tacit dismissal of the abstract visual identities then in vogue.

Black and scarlet red were the colors.

Close inspection of the team logo reveals some oddities, the reasoning behind which is lost to the ages. The letters that form "Cleveland" and "Barons" are joined in some-times-awkward combinations. The "O," "N," and "S" in "Barons" appear to contain pieces that should be snapped off into separate forms. And the "V" in "Cleveland" consists of two opposing-angled pieces that are begging to be united.

The Barons' 1976–77 uniforms were white at home and red on the road; white being the designated host color for NHL teams of the era. Sleeve numbers were rendered in white were contained within the shape of the state of Ohio, a unique and interesting touch. The logo crests were screened, a decidedly cheap look that might well have been borne out of expediency.

An AP story about the Barons' September 22, 1976, pre-season debut stated, "the Barons … may not be in their new white, red and black uniforms, but in their old green and gold Seals outfits. Team officials were still waiting and hoping that the new uniforms would arrive Wednesday, but there was no word from the manufacturer."

The uniforms made it, but the Ohio sleeve numbers were missing. Indeed, the Barons did not wear their Ohio-numbered jerseys until October 13, at home against the Atlanta Flames. This distinctive element was eliminated from the uniforms the next season in favor of a more conventional approach.

The Barons' financial situation was precarious from day one. The team struggled both on and off the ice, and owner-ship, unable to make payroll, considered folding the team in January 1977. Players threatened to strike (they also consid-ered a uniform-centric protest for their February 8 game against Colorado in the form of black armbands), but the team was saved by a $1.3 million loan from the National Hockey League Players Association. This only represented temporary relief, as the Barons' short tenure in Cleveland would soon draw to a close.

While the Barons did not live to see the 1978–79 season, there is a tantalizing piece of evidence that exists which pro-vides a look at what they *might* have looked like.

The Hockey Hall of Fame has, in its collection, a jersey. It is red, and features large black letters, trimmed in white, that read "BARONS," displayed on a diagonal. This jersey was created by Barons general manager Harry Howell in antici-pation of a season that never came.

Howell, a Hockey Hall of Famer who would soon be-come the head coach of the newly merged Barons/North Stars franchise, spent seventeen-consecutive seasons with the New York Rangers, famed then, as now, for their signa-ture sweaters with bold diagonal letterforms. There is no mistaking the similarity or the connection.

The Cleveland Barons evaporated into the ether of hockey history after only 160 contests, a seldom-remembered red and black ghost team that literally wore their state on their sleeves.

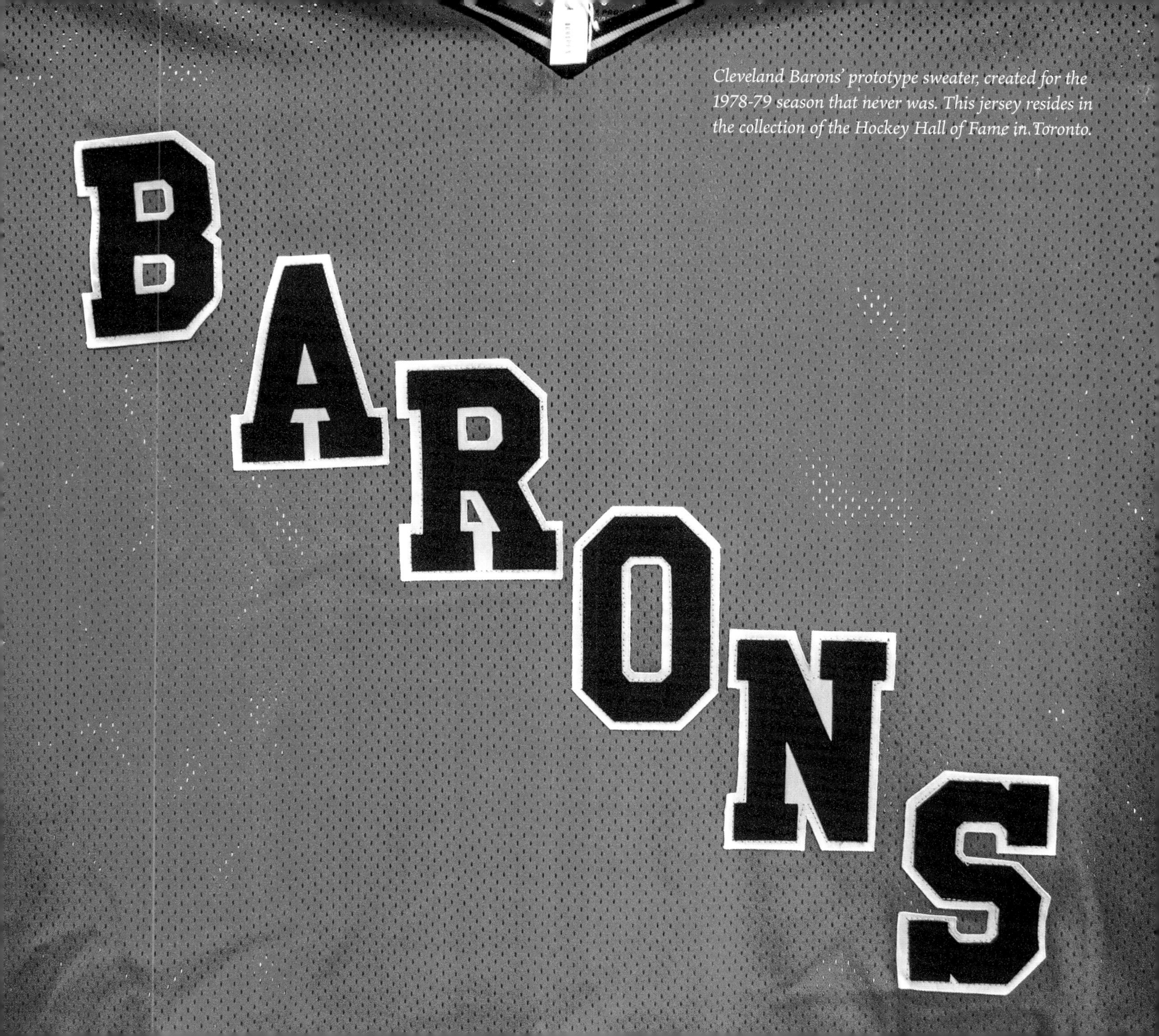

Cleveland Barons' prototype sweater, created for the 1978-79 season that never was. This jersey resides in the collection of the Hockey Hall of Fame in Toronto.

COLORADO AVALANCHE
1995-PRESENT

THE TEAM

In May 1995, the Québec Nordiques, charter members of the World Hockey Association and a National Hockey League franchise since 1979, were running on fumes. Québec, by far the league's smallest market, was being buffeted by a weak Canadian dollar, escalating player salaries, and an inability to secure funding for a new arena. A little more than a year later, the team—relocated and reborn as the Colorado Avalanche—won the Stanley Cup.

The Nordiques were a team on the rise at the time of the shift, an attractive property with a strong roster. As discussions for a new playing facility in Québec broke down in the spring of 1995, the club was rumored to be headed to Denver, Phoenix, or Atlanta. Finally, on May 25, 1995, Québec team president Marcel Aubut announced that a deal had been reached to sell the club to Comsat Entertainment Group, which would move the franchise to Colorado.

"We're bringing winners into Denver," said Comsat executive Charlie Lyons. "Let's face it—this is a great young team. They lost in the first round of the playoffs to the defending Stanley Cup champions [the New York Rangers], but they're young and they have a lot of heart. We think the NHL is going to be great in Denver. The Rocky Mountain region is really becoming sort of the center of the universe, and we think our fan base will be considerable." The move was formally approved by the NHL Board of Governors on June 21.

This would be Denver's second shot at an NHL franchise. The Colorado Rockies played six seasons in the Mile High City before fleeing to New Jersey in 1982, where they were transformed into the Devils. Enthusiasm for NHL hockey was strong this go-around. By the time the deal closed, on July 1, 1995, the team had banked more than 10,000 deposits for season tickets.

The Avalanche made their regular-season debut at Denver's McNichols Sports Arena on October 6, 1995, with a 3–2 win over the Detroit Red Wings. More than 16,000 fans witnessed the NHL's return to Denver, which was preceded by a modest fireworks display and the words "DANGER: AVALANCHE WARNING" illuminated on the scoreboard high above the ice. A banner commemorating the event was raised to the rafters, and the Avs magical inaugural season was officially underway.

The team won the Pacific Division with a record of 47–25–10, good for 104 points. They defeated Vancouver, Chicago, and Detroit in the playoffs before sweeping the Florida Panthers in the Stanley Cup Finals. The decisive game started in Miami on June 10, 1996, and ended at 1:15 the following morning when Colorado defenseman Uwe Krupp's slap shot won the Cup in triple overtime . . . 4 hours and 58 minutes after the start of play.

The Avalanche were perennial contenders during their early years, taking home eight-consecutive division titles over the course of their first eight seasons in Denver. The team moved into the new $160 million Pepsi Center in 1999. On June 10, 2001, the Avalanche hoisted Lord Stanley's Cup for the second time in team history after a 3–1 Game Seven victory over the New Jersey Devils.

THE NAME

The Avalanche revealed their name at a press conference at the Westin Tabor Center on August 10, 1995—less than two months before the team's first game. Shawn Hunter, the team's vice president of marketing, said that he fielded hundreds of potential names in the months after the Nordiques move was made official. "The nicest thing is we can stop answering the phone, 'Colorado NHL.'"

The road to being named "Avalanche," however, was a meandering one.

When the deal to bring the Nordiques westward was announced on May 25, 1995, team officials indicated that the organization's new name would reflect a regional, rather than a Denver-centric approach.

In June 1995, the *Denver Post* reported that team ownership had settled on a name: the Rocky Mountain Extreme. The designation was supposedly favored by Comsat execu-

tive Charlie Lyons, a skiing enthusiast who doubtlessly wanted the new team to appeal to a younger demographic with an affinity for "extreme" sports. Public reaction to the proposed name was fiercely negative. A day after the initial report was published, Hunter issued a denial, saying, "the name 'Extreme' was discussed, as many names were discussed. But we are still quite a ways from making a decision."

On June 23, 1995, team officials publicly asked Colorado residents to help them select a name from a list of eight potential monikers: Avalanche, Black Bears, Cougars, Outlaws, Rapids, Renegades, Storm, and Wranglers. Fans were asked to either fax or phone in their votes. Nearly 15,000 opinions were registered, and later the following month "Avalanche" was widely reported as the final name. The *Post* quoted an anonymous source as saying, "this is the NHL, a rough and tough sport, and Avalanche is something that matches the 'on the edge' feel they want to create."

Reactions were varied, and some could even be described as … extreme. *Post* columnist Mark Kiszla slammed the name as "dumb, insensitive and slightly offensive to any thinking person who has called Colorado home for longer than a spring ski vacation.

"Naming your team the Avalanche is akin to scribbling a smiley face on a deadly natural disaster," he added. The *Post*'s anonymous source had a rebuttal at the ready. "Hey, Cougars and Bears kill people too."

When the name was officially announced, the *Post* said, "The decision to call the team the Avalanche was reached about two weeks ago. … Comsat management at first entertained ideas of having 'Rocky Mountain' as a first name, but they felt Colorado was 'more appropriate.'"

Winning a Stanley Cup in your first season buys you a lot of positive equity. As the team gets ready to celebrate its golden anniversary in the Mile High City, the Avalanche name is now firmly established.

THE LOOK

The Avalanche have employed a consistent look throughout their history, dating back to the unveiling of the team's name and logo on August 10, 1995.

The club's press release said that their primary logo "features a dominating letter 'A,' which stands like a mountain, representing Colorado's Rocky Mountains and the strength required to succeed in the NHL. In contrast, an avalanche on a puck whips around the solid 'A,' representing the power and speed of the skating, passing and shooting in the game."

The *Post* quoted team marketing executive Hunter as saying that, "the team's colors were decided well before Comsat decided on Avalanche. Everybody involved with the group seemed particularly pleased with the burgundy-red color, which Hunter said is only being used by the Washington Redskins."

"Everybody we've talked to thinks burgundy is going to be the hot color of the '90s," said Hunter. "There was a lot of research done on it. We think we're the first team in pro sports to have it as our primary color." The *Colorado Springs Gazette-Telegraph* further quoted him in stating that burgundy "will be the next great color in sports."

"Now I get to sleep," he added. "It was probably a little longer than we wanted, but it's a hot logo that Colorado is going to be happy with."

Dan Price, creative director of the NBA's Denver Nuggets and Colorado Avalanche (also owned by Comsat), worked with David Haney and the NHL's creative services group—which included designer Joe Bosack—in developing the look of the new team. Others involved in the process were Colorado Avalanche art director Michael Beindorff, who collaborated with Price in Denver, and Frederick & Froberg Design Office in Montclair, New Jersey.

When the logo was released, Price told the *Post*, "The hardest thing was the snow. It took a while to get a design that made it look realistic, but I think it does now. We brought a puck in at the end as a place for it to stop. We were always working around a design that would have an 'A' as the centerpiece, though."

In an interview with the authors, Price said that there was no single reason why the identity has endured for as long as it has. "People connect their logos to more than just the visuals," he said, noting the fact that the Avalanche won the Stanley Cup in their very first season in Denver. "The logo is still popular, and if the fans wanted a change it would have been changed," he added. Team owners have remained committed to the look, he said, which is always an important factor when determining if a logo will go through a redesign.

He also discussed the Avalanche's color scheme, which has similarly remained consistent as the decades have rolled along. "When the [NBA's] Nuggets streamlined their colors [in 1993], we went with something that was aged and rugged, not bright and shiny. We decided on red, blue, and gold, which were based on the Colorado state flag. Thinking ahead to the Pepsi Center, we wanted to pick a common color theme between the two teams, with seats, signage, and infrastructure in mind. Even if the reds and blues were different, there was commonality to be found."

Veteran sports designer Joe Bosack was just starting out, working in-house at the NHL when the identity was created. Echoing Price's 1995 comments, Bosack, in an interview with the authors, said, "the one big challenge that kept coming up involved the detailing in the snow and the puck that wrapped around the 'A.' We all kept hammering away, trying to figure it out."

Astonishingly, Bosack notes that the team's blue color was the result of a happy technical accident. "Burgundy was always going to be the core color, but we [on the NHL end] were working with hunter green as the secondary. We had a Tektronix Phaser color printer in the office, an expensive, primitive thing that took an eternity to print and wasn't always accurate. The output kept emerging as a dusky blue color, not the green that we were looking for. We showed it around and everyone embraced the blue, even if it wasn't what it was supposed to be. I remember taking out a Pantone fan deck and matching the blue—Pantone 647 C." This is the color that's still used by the team all these years later.

Bosack remembers finalizing the project. "We were into to the final logo, it was into the evening, and David [Haney] wanted to share the design with the commissioner before sending it out into the world. He took one of those Phaser prints of the logo and walked it down to Gary Bettman's office. A few minutes later they both returned, and Gary asked me to change a small detail around the swirling puck. A couple clicks of the mouse and his eyes lit up, he said, "How much did we pay for this machine!?'"

Colorado Rockies remembered on Avs' third uniform introduced in 2015.

An extreme Rocky Mountain design for the outdoor 2020 Stadium Series.

The team's first sweaters were white at home and burgundy on the road, with bold blocks of zig-zag striping and spiky player numbers. A "Bigfoot" logo was featured on the shoulders, designed by the Frederick & Froberg team.

Bill Frederick recalls working on the Bigfoot logo. He told the authors, "the foot translated so well into a signature idea. We created a footprint and started dragging it wider and wider until it looked like a Bigfoot print. We made the big toe super wide and knew that we'd nailed it."

David Haney recalls being asked by an NHL marketing executive to supply a narrative in order to help sell the Bigfoot mark. "Well," he said, "Bigfoot's the guy who started the Avalanche."

In 2001, the Avs introduced a third jersey—it was burgundy with "COLORADO" spelled out on a diagonal path, much like the New York Rangers' sweaters. Burgundy was swapped out for blue in 2009. Navy blue was added to the team's color palette in 2015 with a new alternate look, one that featured a crest that was inspired by that of the old Colorado Rockies.

Brought to life by multiple designers, working at great speed, Colorado's on-ice look has proven to be an enduring one.

COLORADO ROCKIES
1976-1982

THE TEAM

The Colorado Rockies were a National Hockey League team long before they were a Major League Baseball team. The NHL Rockies represent the meat in the New Jersey Devils' franchise sandwich. The franchise started out as the Kansas City Scouts, a 1974 expansion entry, and now reside in downtown Newark, New Jersey, as the Devils.

The Scouts were less than good during their brief run in Missouri, going 27–110–23 over the course of their two seasons there. The team was undercapitalized, and their ownership structure was an unwieldy one, with thirty-seven partners on board. The Scouts averaged but 8,200 fans per game at KC's Kemper Arena over their short history. Faced with multiple headwinds, the team embarked upon a season ticket drive during their second season that was met with tempered enthusiasm. Something had to give.

The Scouts threw in the towel on July 26, 1976, announcing their intent to sell the franchise to a group of Denver investors, fronted by Jack Vickers. The deal, however, became bogged down in legal entanglements, and league approval was stalled for many precious weeks. Training camp was scheduled to open on September 10, so decisions needed to be made quickly on what the club would be called and what they would look like when they next took the ice.

Like their Kansas City ancestors, the Rockies struggled mightily on the ice. Multiple ownership and coaching staff changes helped destabilize the franchise. Despite it all, the Rockies featured several notable players, including future Hockey Hall of Famer Lanny McDonald. They made the playoffs during their second season, and even employed colorful coach Don Cherry for one year (when billboards throughout the Denver area noted, "Come to the fights and watch a Rockies game break out.").

Vickers, Palmer, and crew sold the team to New Jersey trucking magnate Arthur Imperatore in 1978. This, along with the planned development of a sparkling new arena in the New Jersey Meadowlands, spurred rumors of yet another franchise shift. Imperatore planned to play two seasons at New York's Madison Square Garden while the new arena was being built, but the league wanted Denver to remain an NHL city, so they stayed put.

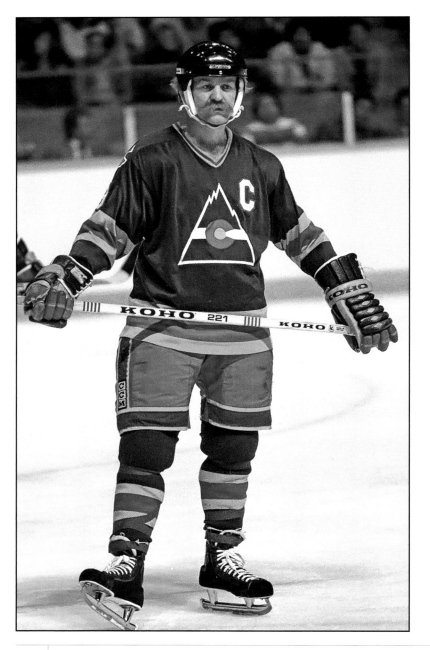

Imperatore jettisoned the Rockies in February 1981, to cable television operator Peter Gilbert who, in turn, flipped them to Houston Astros owner (and New Jersey native and resident) John McMullen a little more than a year later. The Rockies were Garden State bound after six losing seasons.

THE NAME

Denver's professional hockey history included minor league hockey teams called the Falcons, Invaders, Mavericks, and Spurs. The Spurs name was also utilized by a short-lived World Hockey Association (WHA) team, which made its debut on October 10, 1975, before moving to Ottawa several months later, reborn as the Ottawa Civics. (That move was so hastily planned that the Civics played their inaugural game on the road in Cincinnati on January 2, 1976, clad in Denver Spurs uniforms.)

The WHA Spurs and NHL Scouts both failed within months of each other, opening the door to a new professional hockey team for Denver's McNichols Sports Arena.

When it came time to name the city's new NHL entry, ownership considered a name-the-team contest, but went ahead and announced their new moniker on August 21, 1976: the Colorado Rockies.

"Rockies is a natural," said co-owner John "Bud" Palmer. "It sounds mean and aggressive—the same attributes we expect our club to have on the ice." Designating the team as "Colorado," as opposed to "Denver," was a deliberate decision, according to

Palmer. "We want to be a team for the entire state, not just Denver," he said.

Palmer, who passed away at the age of ninety-one in 2013, lived a full, rich, and fascinating life. Born in Hollywood, the son of a silent film actor and a wealthy aspiring soprano, Palmer was a pioneering sports broadcaster and producer, an actor and a model, a World War II US Navy bomber pilot and, according to many, the inventor of basketball's jump shot. Whatever the case, he was certainly one of the first to shoot one.

He was a charter member of the New York Knicks and their first team captain. He later originated *Glamour* magazine's "Ask Jake" advice column, served as New York City's commissioner of public events and official greeter, and became involved with the development of the Vail ski resort before helping bring NHL hockey to Colorado.

THE LOOK

The team carried over their royal blue, red, and gold color palette from their previous home in Kansas City. A happy coincidence, these colors synched up with those of Colorado's distinctive state flag, and the team rebranded them as "mountain blue, Colorado gold, and sunset red."

The logo, described as "a mountain base with the red 'C' symbol from [the] state flag and a gold sun in the 'C,'" was simple and recognizable. Rockies president Munson Campbell said it "represents what Colorado is all about. The greatest sources of pride are the mountains and the blue sky. We hope that this pride will serve as an extra bit of motivation to our players and organization."

The team opened their exhibition season at the Broadmoor World Arena in Colorado Springs on September 19, 1976, against the Pittsburgh Penguins. The uniforms they wore that evening were recycled Scouts garb featuring the same complex striping patterns that the team wore in Kansas City, but with the Rockies' new crest displayed front and center. They continued to use these uniforms throughout the preseason, but the team's regular-season debut in Denver on October 5 saw them hit the ice in white sweaters with simple, bold stripes of red and gold, bookended by thin blue stripes around the sleeves and hem. The central "C" element was plunked from the primary logo and placed on each shoulder, a subtle touch. Blue pants rounded out the uniform.

The Rockies wore blue sweaters and red pants on the road. While the traveling sweaters did not contain player names, they were added in 1977–78. The uniforms drew high marks, with the Toronto *Globe and Mail* calling the blue road sweaters "splendid."

They would wear this look throughout their entire tenure in Colorado.

Denver eventually found a new NHL team in the Colorado Avalanche, who won the Stanley Cup in their first season in the Mile High City. Twenty years later, the Avs unleashed a new alternate jersey that borrowed elements from the Rockies' look of yore, a reminder of Colorado's first NHL franchise who sported a team name that's now firmly associated with baseball.

COLUMBUS BLUE JACKETS

2000-PRESENT

THE TEAM

The city of Columbus, Ohio, officially joined the National Hockey League on June 25, 1997, when the league's Board of Governors unanimously voted to admit four new entries. Columbus, along with St. Paul, Minnesota, would join the circuit in 2000, with Nashville (1998) and Atlanta (1999) getting a head start.

Efforts to land an NHL team for Columbus began in earnest in November 1996, when a group of investors seeking to attract a franchise for Ohio's capital city submitted a formal application to the league. They followed this up with a presentation to NHL officials a few months later. Columbus-based Nationwide Insurance soon agreed to privately finance a new downtown arena, to be constructed on the site of the historic Ohio State Penitentiary, which dated back to 1834.

Local steel magnate John H. McConnell led the team's ownership group. McConnell, a self-made, civic-minded community leader, considered the team to be his gift to the city. "Columbus has been good for me; I think this is good for Columbus," said McConnell when Nationwide Arena opened.

The Columbus Blue Jackets made their NHL debut at home against the Chicago Blackhawks on October 7, 2000, where they lost, 5–3, before a sellout crowd of 18,136. As would be expected from an expansion outfit, a few rocky seasons followed, but the team sold out their first 58 home games, thus firmly establishing themselves and NHL hockey in the hearts and minds of Columbus' sports fans.

The Blue Jackets broke through with their first winning season in 2008–09, when they also made the playoffs for the first time. On April 21, 2009, a then-record crowd of 19,219 packed Nationwide Arena for the state of Ohio's first Stanley Cup playoff game. Columbus lost to the Detroit Red Wings by a score of 4–1, and were swept two nights later. Detroit made it all the way to the Cup Finals, but Columbus would have to wait until 2013–14 for their next postseason appearance.

The Blue Jackets hosted NHL All-Star Weekend in January 2015. In 2016–17, the club finished the regular season with a team-record 108 points, but lost to Pittsburgh in the first round of the playoffs. Columbus made postseason appearances in the next two seasons as well, winning their first playoff series in 2018–19, when they swept the Presidents' Trophy winners, the Tampa Bay Lightning, in the first round.

THE NAME

A Name the Team Contest, sponsored by the Central Ohio–based restaurant chain Wendy's, launched in July 1997, with more than ninety Columbus-area restaurants distributing entry blanks. Dave Thomas, the chain's ubiquitous founder and pitchman, wanted "Frostys" according to a Wendy's spokesperson, a joking tribute to their signature frozen dessert.

Some Columbusites wanted to embrace the city's "Cowtown" nickname. The effort was spurred by a local alternative weekly's tongue-in-cheek campaign to name the new franchise the Columbus "Mad Cows."*

When the name of the new team was officially announced, on November 11, 1997, it was the Columbus Blue Jackets.

Majority owner John McConnell said that ten potential names were submitted to the NHL, and that two came back: Blue Jackets and Justice.

The Name the Team Contest produced some 13,000 entries, with seven contestants submitting Blue Jackets. Jared Berry, a nineteen-year-old sophomore at Wright State University, won a raffle to determine the ultimate winner, and was awarded a pair of season tickets for their inaugural campaign for his victorious efforts.

Critics complained that the new designation bore no meaningful ties to Columbus nor Ohio.

The *Columbus Dispatch* sought out local opinions, and reported a range of negative reviews. Westgate Avenue resident Michael Scherl said, "A hockey team shouldn't sound like a sports coat. Hockey is brutal. It should have a brutal name." Mollie O'Donnell of Bryden Road thought that the name was too long. "It's got too many syllables," she said.

"The colors are ugly, the name is stupid," said a caller to a local sports radio station. "I'm ashamed to be in Columbus, Ohio, right now."

Others expressed relief that the name wasn't based on the eighteenth-century Shawnee war chief Blue Jacket.

John Christie, president of JMAC (a venture capital firm owned by Blue Jackets principal owner McConnell), noted, "We wanted to have something with a patriotic feel that represented the heartland." He said that fans would better understand the team name once they saw the team's logo, which he described as "an insect with attitude."

"I think any name thrown out would have been met with a negative reaction," he added. "There were so many other names thrown around—it's not Explorers, or Armada or one of the obvious names—this came to them out of the clear blue sky. It surprised a lot of them."

Carolina Hurricanes owner Peter Karmanos, fresh off from moving the Hartford Whalers, had been criticized for naming his club after a destructive force of nature. He offered up some advice for Columbus, via the *Dispatch*. "If someone wins the presidential race 60 to 40 [percent], they call it a landslide. But that also means four out of 10 people didn't like the winner, maybe hated his guts. You must remember, you generally hear from the most vocal people first." He approved of the new name, noting, "I didn't shrink back and say, 'Oh my God,' and that's pretty good—I usually hate everything."

---

* Columbus' minor league hockey club, the Chill, went so far as to transform themselves into the Mad Cows for one game, opening night of the 1997 season. The team wore customized Holstein jerseys and featured a 40-foot inflatable cow, as well as a contest where fans bobbed for cow tongues.

The team, however, had the final say. They described the moniker as one that "pays homage to Ohio's contributions to American history and the great pride and patriotism exhibited by its citizens, especially during the Civil War as both the state of Ohio and the city of Columbus were significantly influential on the Union Army. Ohio contributed more of its population to the Union Army than any other state, while many of the uniforms worn by the Union soldiers were manufactured in Columbus."

THE LOOK

The Blue Jackets revealed their new visual identity at the same November 11, 1997, event at which they announced their name. The team's primary logo depicted "Stinger," a lime green–colored bug with gritted teeth and bulging red eyes, wearing a federal blue coat with stars on the collar and a Civil War cap. A secondary logo was also shown; an angular, star-spangled red ribbon, unfurled in the shape of the team's initials, CBJ, with a lime-green hockey stick cutting through the center to represent the "J." This was all topped off by a beveled star, symbolizing Columbus' status as the state's capital.

News reports indicated that the color blue was a fait accompli, a tribute to owner John McConnell's Worthington Industries, as well as to arena developer Nationwide Insurance, both of whose logos contained blue.

Executive John Christie described the team's primary colors as federal (also capital) blue and patriotic red, and noted that the lime green color was "unique to pro sports."

The design work was the result of a collaboration between NHL Enterprises, Columbus-based Rickabaugh

Columbus' original look included neon green, mascot "Stinger."

Graphics, and The Mednick Group.

The Blue Jackets' first uniforms were unveiled in front of 4,000 fans on October 14, 1999—nearly two years after the team name was announced. Mike Emrick, television voice of the New Jersey Devils and FOX Sports, emceed the event, held at the Easton Town Center shopping mall. Both uniforms featured the team's alternate CBJ logo front and center.

Former Columbus Chill minor league players Rob Shriner and Mike Ross modeled the uniforms, with Shriner sporting the white home jersey and Ross clad in the dark road togs. "We felt, 'how can you go wrong with red, white, and blue'" said team president and general manager Doug MacLean. "With the stars it's a little unique," he added.

The Blue Jackets, however, recalibrated their look before they even took the ice.

By April 2000, team merchandise sales had slowed considerably. An Associated Press story reported Blue Jackets' VP Michael Humes as saying that sales began slowing after the team decided that their uniforms wouldn't feature their bug mascot, Stinger. "There's one primary reason and one reason only" for the slowdown, he said. "We changed our colors and relayed to the NHL that we are not a Stinger-led team."

"He's not the logo, he's the mascot," added Humes. "Sales suggest that fans want CBJ, not Stinger, and all that old merchandise had a rather unattractive blue and not our deep red." Navy blue and a deep red thus replaced the original lighter blue and brighter red hues.

On October 13, 2003, the Blue Jackets unveiled a new third jersey, one that featured a new logo based on a stylized version of Ohio's pennant-shaped state flag, the "Ohio burgee," in the shape of a "C," overlapping the Blue Jackets' italicized star. This became the team's primary logo in 2007.

Columbus simplified their color palette in 2007, eliminating the lime green hue that accompanied them into the league. The new colors were now simply navy blue, red, and silver. According to the Blue Jackets, the streamlined colors "help define the team and tell its story. The colors consist of Union Blue, Goal Red, and Capital Silver. Union Blue represents the color worn by the Union Army, Goal Red references the most exciting moment in hockey, and Capital Silver is reflected in the star on the logo, which signifies Columbus as the capital of Ohio."

In November 2010, the club introduced their next-generation third jersey, which represented a departure from their previously established look. The uniform, according to the club, sported a "felt crest depicting the hockey club's signature 1857 Napoleon cannon that fires each time the Blue Jackets score at Nationwide Arena. The team name 'Columbus Blue Jackets' encircles the cannon in a ribbon inspired by Civil War medals while a single star centered at the bottom of the crest signifies Columbus as Ohio's capital."

The cannon logo was designated as the team's official secondary mark in 2015.

Two decades after their NHL debut, the Columbus Blue Jackets continue to hold forth in Ohio's capital city, proudly sporting the unique star-spangled burgee of the Buckeye State.

DALLAS STARS
1993-PRESENT
MINNESOTA NORTH STARS, 1967-1993

THE TEAM

The Dallas Stars' story begins in Minnesota, where they entered the National Hockey League as one of the "Second Six," the largest expansion in professional sports history.

In March 1965, the NHL struck upon a plan to double the number of member franchises to twelve, a far-reaching expansion that would broaden the league's reach westward to the Pacific Ocean. A total of thirteen applicants were considered for the new slots, but on February 9, 1966, Minneapolis-St. Paul—along with Pittsburgh, Philadelphia, the San Francisco Bay area, Los Angeles, and St. Louis—were announced as new NHL entries. Each group paid in $2 million for the privileges of membership.* This expansion represented the first disruption of the league's Original Six configuration since 1942, when the Brooklyn Americans passed from the NHL scene.

The Twin Cities group was headed up by an eight-man syndicate who promised the league that they would deliver a new arena in time for the 1967–68 season. The Metropolitan Sports Center (later called the Met Center), located in Bloomington, was built in just a year at a cost of $6.5 million. The arena and its green, yellow, white, and black seats would serve as home to the North Stars for their entire tenure in Minnesota.

The North Stars' first home game took place on October 21, 1967. Construction workers were still installing seats a half hour before faceoff, but the 12,951 fans in attendance were treated to festive pregame ceremonies featuring a red-coated jazz band, as well as the franchise's first-ever victory, a 3–1 win over the California Seals.

Success, however, proved elusive during the franchise's first decade. By the mid '70s, the team was plagued by a host of economic problems, including sharply declining attendance and competition for the local market from the World Hockey Association's (WHA) Minnesota Fighting Saints. Losses—both on and off the ice—piled up, and things were getting desper-

---

* It should be noted that the average salary of an NHL player at the time of this expansion was $16,630.

ate. A stunning and historic solution was reached on June 14, 1978, when the North Stars merged with the similarly cash-strapped Cleveland Barons. The Cleveland franchise, which began play in Oakland as the California Seals, was killed off, while Barons owners George and Gordon Gund took control of the newly combined entity.

Renewed and invigorated, the North Stars made it all the way to their first Stanley Cup Finals in 1981, where they fell to the mighty New York Islanders. A few moderately successful seasons followed, but the franchise bottomed out in 1987–88, winning just 19 games.

Faced with sustained attendance problems and frustrated by chronic financial losses, the brothers Gund threatened to move the North Stars to the San Francisco Bay area in 1990. The league pushed back, but an arrangement was eventually reached in which the brothers were granted a new expansion franchise—the San Jose Sharks—enabling them to sell the North Stars to a group led by Hartford Whalers founder Howard Baldwin. The complicated transaction, which was made public on May 2, 1990, also involved the transfer of 30 players from the Minnesota organization to help stock the new San Jose team.

Baldwin's tenure at the top of the North Stars' organization lasted but a month. On June 6, 1990, it was announced that Norman Green, former co-owner of the Calgary Flames, had purchased a controlling interest in the Stars. Faced with low expectations, the team drew only 5,730 fans to the 15,000 seat Met Center for the 1990–91 home opener. The North Stars squeaked into the playoffs with a record of 27–39–14. Springtime magic ensued, however, as the Stars knocked off Chicago, St. Louis, and the defending champion Edmonton to reach the Cup Finals for the second time in franchise history. They lost to Pittsburgh in six games, but the North Stars' Cinderella run is considered to be one of the greatest in NHL history.

A year later, the Stars were once again rumored to be on the move. A deal was in the works to shift the team to Anaheim, but, as Green told *D* magazine in 2010:

> *We made a deal to move the North Stars to Anaheim, California, to become the LA Stars. Anaheim had a new building for hockey that was immediately available. My plans were canceled when Disney offered to put a team in Anaheim and use Disney talent to help market the NHL. In December 1992, the league asked me to allow Disney to come into the league. In return, I would have NHL approval to move the Stars wherever I could make the best deal. In January 1993, I selected Dallas, after encouragement from the only Texan I knew: Roger Staubach.*

Staubach, the former Cowboys quarterback, extolled the virtues of Dallas' Reunion Arena.

The Minnesota North Stars' final home game took place on April 13, 1993, a loss to the Chicago Blackhawks, 3–2. Speculating on what the team would be called once the journey to Texas was completed, fans displayed a huge banner that read "North Stars or Lone Stars. They'll Always be Our Stars."

The Stars' first game in Dallas took place on October 5, 1993—a 6–4 win over the Detroit Red Wings. The newly

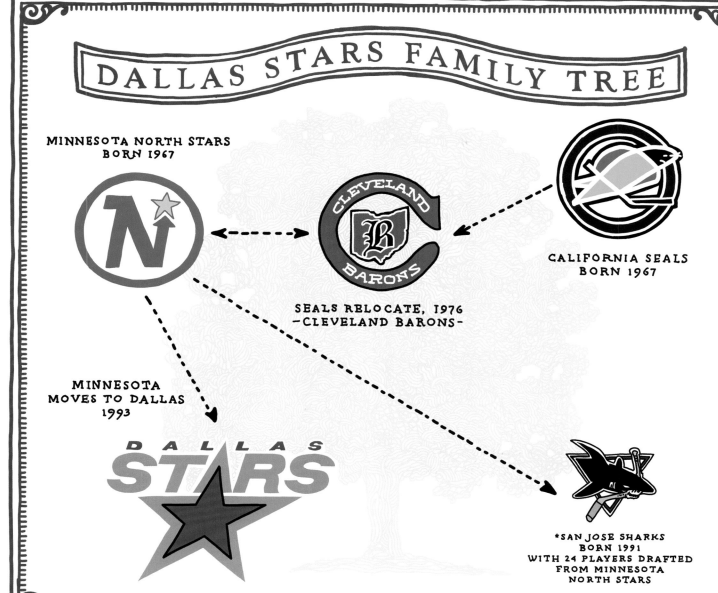

DALLAS STARS FAMILY TREE

MINNESOTA NORTH STARS
BORN 1967

CALIFORNIA SEALS
BORN 1967

SEALS RELOCATE, 1976
-CLEVELAND BARONS-

MINNESOTA
MOVES TO DALLAS
1993

*SAN JOSE SHARKS
BORN 1991
WITH 24 PLAYERS DRAFTED
FROM MINNESOTA
NORTH STARS

relocated franchise flourished, winning games and winning over fans in their new home. On June 19, 1999, Brett Hull's controversial Game Six triple-overtime goal gave the Stars a 2–1 victory over Buffalo, thus securing the first Stanley Cup Championship in franchise history.

THE NAME

As the new franchise readied itself for its looming debut, it began the process of marketing itself and selling tickets and sponsorship. A name and image would be needed to assist in these efforts.

On May 25, 1966, the name "North Stars" was announced as the winner of a "Name the Team" contest. Six hundred and eight different entries were submitted by 1,536 individuals. Fifty-two people wrote in "North Stars," but Mr. and Mrs. William Swanson of Shoreview, Minnesota, took home the grand prize. The Swansons, both physical education teachers, took home a $100 US savings bond for their efforts. The state of Minnesota's official motto, L'Étoile du Nord—or "The Star of the North"—provided the inspiration for the team name. Additionally, team president Walter L. Bush Jr. said that North Stars was selected because the team "wanted a name which is synonymous primarily with the state of Minnesota, but which also would be acceptable to surrounding areas from which we will draw our fans."

In February 1991, team owner Green announced that a rebranding was in the works, and that "Stars" would be newly emphasized. When the franchise moved to Dallas in 1993, they flirted with a new name, "Lone Stars," but went into their maiden season in Texas as simply "Stars," indicating that it would be a one-year moniker, after which fans would be given the opportunity to vote on a new name. That never happened, and the team remains Stars, a connection that binds the franchise's roots in the north to its current location in the south.

THE LOOK

The Stars' visual identity has remained remarkably consistent throughout their history, with three distinct crests gracing the team's sweaters across that span.

With the North Stars name officially in hand, the franchise announced their color scheme on November 9, 1966. The North Stars would be clad in green and white, a palette which hadn't been employed in the NHL since the Toronto St. Pats became the Maple Leafs in February 1927.

"Several color combinations were considered," team president Bush said, "but several were rejected because of being too similar to present and future NHL teams' colors and colors used by local teams. We especially did not want to conflict with the Gophers, Twins and Vikings."

"Ideally, blue and white would have more connotation with the idea of the North Star, but the Toronto Maple Leafs use blue and white. Green connotes forests and trees and grass, and Minnesota also is known for these assets, so we feel green is an ideal choice."

The task of creating the team's logo and uniforms fell to George Karn, a St. Paul–based artist. Karn was the right man for the job. A graduate of Hamline University in Minneapolis, Karn played two years of professional hockey, was a coach, and served as a referee in the International Hockey League. Working out of his Minneapolis-based Studio One, Inc., Karn designed, illustrated, wrote, and created televi-

Goaltender Gump Worsley celebrates a Minnesota North Stars playoff victory with teammates in 1972.

sion ads. His body of work eventually included the original characters for Trix, Count Chocula, and the Lucky Charms leprechaun for local cereal powerhouse General Mills. He also would go on to create the logos for the WHA's Minnesota Fighting Saints and the North American Soccer League's Minnesota Kicks.

Karn's North Stars identity, unveiled in mid-January 1967, featured an italicized "N," topped by a star, enclosed in an elliptical shape. This original logo would eventually be embellished with additional detail, but it was clean, strong, and plainly influenced by corporate design trends of the era. Modern marketing—including the need to create an identity that would show well on television—was a clear consideration for the North Stars and their expansion brethren, a criterion that the Original Six never had to deal with.

Karn passed away in September 2000, "at his art table with a pen in his hand," according to his obituary as published in the *Minneapolis Star Tribune*.

His logo was applied to the new team's sweaters, which were green at home and white on the road. An oddball version of the mark was worn during the North Stars' first preseason games, but the logo that adorned the uniforms for their first-ever game in St. Louis on October 11, 1967, would be the one that would carry them through the coming decades—albeit with small changes along the way.

In 1981, the North Stars added black into the mix as an accent color, a foreshadowing of what would come a decade later.

The franchise underwent a complete rebrand in 1991, after their Cinderella run to the Stanley Cup Finals. Black was now the primary color, and the word *Stars* was the focal point, with the top of a huge green five-pointed star forming the letter "A."

Of the change, owner Green said, "Green isn't a powerful color. It's a nice color. Black is powerful. The uniforms will be all black with green and gold piping. It's very creative. The gold will be reflective. Nobody's done that before." Of the drastic change, he told the *Star Tribune*, "The only person who questioned it was my mother. She thought the reason I bought the team was because the logo was an 'N' and the team color was green."

"Black is a modern, intimidating color for sports teams," he added. "We like that image."

These uniforms accompanied the franchise to Texas, where the city name "Dallas" was added to the fronts of the sweaters a couple of years later. Striping and trim changes evolved over the next two decades, and alternate uniforms were added and subtracted to and from the mix. (The 2003 to 2006 "Mooterus" sweater warrants mention. The crest featured the head of a bull and the constellation Taurus, but many observers saw something quite different.)

On June 4, 2013, the Stars unveiled a totally new look, centered around a bold crest with a dimensional italicized letter "D" set atop a similarly beveled star. Victory Green, described as a mix between Kelly green and forest green, was now the dominant hue, accompanied by silver and black. Stars owner Tom Gaglardi said that the club looked at 236 variations of colors and uniforms before they landed on the final product.

Gaglardi told the Associated Press, "I think green was important because it was in our history and in our DNA. We were worried we would just blend in with so many other teams. We realized we had the ability to own our own color across the league."

In comments made to NHL.com, team VP Jason Walsh noted, "I hope that they look at it and say it's the Dallas Stars. This is who we are. It's a D and a Star. We're the Dallas Stars, in Big D. We looked at a variation of things that just seemed too cute. We just wanted it to be simple and classic with a modern look to it. I think that is exactly what we ended up with."

The new look, developed with apparel supplier Reebok, was well received by fans and media alike. The vibrant green color seamlessly harkens back to the earliest days of the franchise, a reverent acknowledgment of the team's rich visual heritage.

DETROIT RED WINGS
1926-PRESENT

THE TEAM

The Motor City's National Hockey League history dates back to May 1926, when the league conditionally awarded franchises to Detroit and Chicago. These two cities would join the New York Rangers in expanding the circuit's roster to ten teams. The nucleus of Detroit's new outfit was to be composed of players from the Victoria (British Columbia) Cougars, who had been the champions of Canada's recently disbanded Western Hockey League.

After months of acrimonious debate, a deal was finally reached. A Detroit syndicate purchased the Victoria club for $100,000, and the Detroit Cougars were officially admitted to the NHL on September 25, 1926.

The club's NHL debut took place on November 18, 1926—not in what was later dubbed "Hockeytown," but across the Detroit River, at the Border Cities Arena in Windsor, Ontario (as the franchise's new permanent home in Detroit was undergoing construction that first season). That evening, a crowd of 6,000 fans saw the Boston Bruins shut out the Cougars by a score of 2–0. Motown's new entry finished their inaugural season with a dismal record of 12–28–4, good for a mere 28 points and a last-place finish.

Season two witnessed the arrival of Jack Adams as general manager and coach, as well as a move to Detroit's new state-of-the-art Olympia Stadium, which would serve as the franchise's home until 1979.

The Cougars scuffled along during these early years, both on and off the ice. The club was renamed the Falcons in 1930, but the change in identity brought them no real change of luck. The Great Depression pressed down upon Detroit in particularly brutal fashion, driving tens of thousands out of work and, in many cases, out of their homes. The Falcons, the Detroit Olympics (their minor-league affiliate), and Olympia Stadium were forced into receivership in 1931.

In August 1932, the Union Guardian Trust Company, acting as creditor, sold the two hockey teams and the arena to Chicago-based grain magnate James Norris. Toronto Maple Leafs owner Conn Smythe later said, "Jim Norris simply was fortunate to have a load of money at the right time and he was smarter than the rest of us. When major arenas in US cities were going broke, Norris bought them up at 50 cents on the dollar."

Norris soon changed the name of the team yet again, this time to Red Wings. Detroit advanced to the semifinals of the Stanley Cup Playoffs in Norris's first season at the helm, and made it to the final round the following season.

The Wings won their first Stanley Cup in 1936, and repeated the next year, becoming the NHL's first American franchise to win back-to-back Cups. The club played in three consecutive Finals during the World War II years, winning it all again in 1943, when they swept the Bruins.

The postwar era saw the arrival of Gordie Howe, who teamed up with Sid Abel and Ted Lindsay to form Detroit's vaunted "Production Line." From 1947–48 to 1955–56, they appeared in seven Finals, winning four and losing three.

While the team made it to the Finals four times in the 1960s (dropping all four), they fell upon hard times as the league doubled in size, making the playoffs just four times between 1966–67 and 1985–86. They also shifted arenas, playing their final game at Olympia Stadium on December 15, 1979, before moving over to the new Joe Louis Arena a couple of weeks later.

In 1983, Detroit selected center Steve Yzerman as the fourth overall pick in the NHL Draft, a move which kicked off a new era of prosperity, culminating in back-to-back Conference Final appearances in 1987 and 1988.

The Red Wings rolled into the 1990s with a global cast of new stars, breaking a 42-year Stanley Cup drought in 1997, and winning it all again the following season. Two more Cups followed in 2002 and 2008, before the team shifted over to the new Little Caesars Arena in 2017.

Detroit's rich "Hockeytown" tradition includes a slew of Cup victories, powered by some of the greatest players the game has ever seen. It all started with a roster full of Cougars, imported from British Columbia.

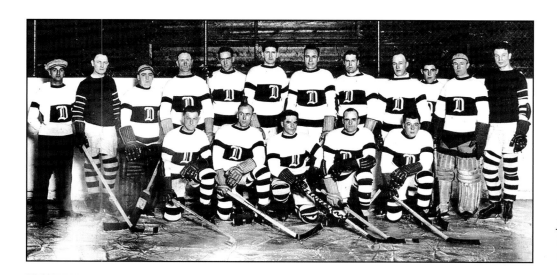

The 1926-27 Detroit Cougars. The club's first set of sweaters featured an Old English "D," similar to that worn by baseball's Detroit Tigers.

DETROIT HOCKEY FANS HAD
TROUBLE PRONOUNCING THE
NAME OF THEIR NEW TEAM.

THE NAME

Detroit's new NHL entry opted to retain the Cougars nickname that was attached to many of the players on their inaugural roster. The Cougars moniker was first applied to the team—previously known as the Victoria Aristocrats—in November 1922. In announcing the new name, the *Victoria Daily Times* noted, "'Cougar' is the local name by which the panther, a wild animal belonging to the cat family, is recognized. It is found on Vancouver Island." Other names that were under consideration were Oaks, Sunbeams, and Roses.

The Cougars name was cast aside after four seasons in Motown. Little equity remained in the nickname, especially after several down seasons and the departure of the key players picked off of the Victoria roster.

The *News-Palladium* of Benton Harbor, Michigan, quipped, "The reason for renaming the team was the fact that fans couldn't pronounce 'Cougars.' Most of 'em called the team the 'Cowgders' or the 'Cowgars.' And the squad's dignity suffered tremendously." While the sentiment was clearly delivered with a generous dollop of snark baked in, other newspaper accounts of the day confirm the part about local fans not being able to properly pronounce the team name.

Additionally, the *Ottawa Citizen* noted, "The name 'Cougars' was never applicable to a club in Detroit. It originated in Victoria, which is located on Vancouver Island, the home of the marauding Cats."

In early October 1930, the club announced plans for a new team nickname. A committee of three local newspapermen—Lloyd Northard, Frank MacDonell, and Jack Carveth—were tasked with vetting fan suggestions. They met on October 17 and 18 to review the nearly 2,000 entries submitted. Dynamics, Wol-

verines, and Ambassadors (a nod to Detroit's new $23 million Ambassador Bridge) were among the many suggestions that were offered up. The journalists opted to narrow things down to four finalists: Falcons, Trojans, Wanderers, and Magnetos. Falcons won the day.

On October 5, 1932, the team announced that the team's name would be changing once again, this time to the Red Wings. The move coincided with the arrival of new owner James Norris. The *Detroit Free Press* later reported, "He [Norris] wanted to christen the team the 'Winged Wheelers'—there was a team in Montréal once called that, he remembered. He accepted the world of friends, however, that the name was too clumsy." Red Wings it was, and has been ever since.

During World War II the Red Wings' sweaters featured the Morse Code message of three dots and a dash for "victory." A sleeve patch urged citizens to invest at least 10 percent of their pay in War Bonds.

THE LOOK

The Detroit Cougars first took the ice in white sweaters that featured a broad-red stripe across the center, with a white Old English "D" (not unlike that worn by baseball's Detroit Tigers) centered within. The Cougars sported several different uniforms over the course of their four seasons, though each one was red and white. The team's second set of uniforms were particularly flashy, highlighted by a series of horizontal red stripes across the front of the sweater with the city name *Detroit* spelled out in condensed sans serif letterforms.

The club's 1930 nickname change to Falcons, of course, required new togs. The red and white theme carried over, as did the red striping, although the bands were now draped across the shoulders of the team's sweaters. The entire team name, "DETROIT FALCONS," was boldly displayed on two lines. Three games into the new season the *Ottawa Citizen* said, "The Falcons paraded in new uniforms. They are a pleasing red and white combination and make a very natty appearance on the ice."

The franchise's October 1932 shift to Red Wings designation gave birth to one of the most iconic logos in all of professional sports, and the team's winged wheel has been a Detroit staple ever since.

THE DETROIT RED WINGS' LOGO,
INSPIRED BY THAT OF THE MONTREAL AMATEUR
ATHLETIC ASSOCIATION'S "WINGED WHEELERS"

Detroit's white sweater has remained largely the same since 1961.

Team owner James Norris gets the credit for the insignia. He was inspired by the emblem of the first ever Stanley Cup Champions, the Montréal Amateur Athletic Association's "Winged Wheelers." Norris, a Montréal native, was a defenseman in his youth for Montréal's Victoria Hockey Club, which regularly competed against the Winged Wheelers.

In January 1933—a few short months after the Falcons became the Red Wings—a profile of Norris in the *Free Press* said, "He himself drew the insignia of the auto wheel with wings sprouting from it on the Red Wing jerseys." Detroit's status as the automobile manufacturing capital of the world no doubt provided additional relevance for the wheel element of the mark.

All logos evolve over time, but Norris's creation currently looks nearly identical to the one first worn by the Red Wings nearly ninety years ago. The same sentiment applies to Detroit's familiar uniforms. "[Jack] Adams' team will blossom out this season in cardinal uniforms, decorated with a white winged wheel," reported the *Free Press* on October 9, 1932. When the Red Wings made their debut the following month, they were outfitted in sweaters that look remarkably similar to those worn by the club today.

A handful of tiny, incremental changes have been rolled out over the years. Detroit added a white uniform option into the mix in 1934, for games against the similarly clad Canadiens. Contrasting sleeves were added to the white sweaters in 1961, and player names came along the following decade. This time-honored look connects Larry Aurie, the Wings' captain in 1932–33, to Ted Lindsay, Gordie Howe, Steve Yzerman, Nicklas Lidström, and the Detroit players of today.

EDMONTON OILERS
1979-PRESENT

THE TEAM

The Edmonton Oilers—originally the Alberta Oilers—started out as one of the ten charter members of the upstart World Hockey Association (WHA), which were announced on November 1, 1971—along with Calgary, Winnipeg, Chicago, St. Paul, Los Angeles, San Francisco, Miami, Dayton (Ohio), and New York.

The notion that Edmonton, a city of some 440,000 souls in 1972, would someday host one of the sport's most celebrated dynasties probably seemed like a far-fetched notion when the team was created.

The driving force behind the Oilers was William Dickenson "Wild Bill" Hunter, a colourful, hyperbolic, natural pitchman. Hunter was the owner, general manager, and coach of the Edmonton Oil Kings of the Western Hockey League (WHL), a circuit he helped form in 1966.

A proud son of Western Canada, Hunter was the perfect man for the task. At the WHA's introductory press conference, he proclaimed, "Ladies and gentlemen, this is the greatest day in the history of the world." Wayne Gretzky later called Hunter "the father of hockey in Edmonton." In 2016, the Oilers named their lynx mascot, "Hunter," in his honour.

The new franchise's main stumbling block was its decrepit arena, the 5,200-seat Edmonton Gardens, a facility originally built in 1913 to host livestock shows as well as two local hockey clubs, the Eskimos and the Dominions.

The Oilers launched the WHA by playing one of the first two games in league history on October 11, 1972—a 7–4 victory over the Ottawa Nationals, in Ottawa.* The Oilers featured a roster that included eleven Alberta-born players.

The team finished the regular season deadlocked with Minnesota for the last playoff spot in the league's Western Division, and a special one-game tiebreaker was hastily arranged. The Fighting Saints defeated Alberta, 4–2, thus ending the Oilers' inaugural campaign.

The 1973–74 season was one of transition for the team, newly designated as the Edmonton Oilers. The following season

---

* The Cleveland Crusaders and Québec Nordiques dropped the WHA's navy blue puck simultaneously in Cleveland in a synchronized faceoff.

marked a milestone with the team's move into the new Northlands Coliseum on November 10, 1974.

In 1976, Hunter sold his interests in the franchise to Vancouver real estate mogul Nelson Skalbania, who soon brought local entrepreneur Peter Pocklington aboard as co-owner. The unusual arrangement was worth some $700,000, including a diamond ring, rare artwork, and a Rolls Royce that was used in the filming of the 1974 film *The Great Gatsby*. Skalbania later sold Pocklington the balance of the club for $500,000 in real estate.

The WHA, always a struggling enterprise, was running on fumes by the end of the decade. Franchises moved and folded with regularity, yet the Oilers endured. The fate of the franchise was secured in 1978, when the club acquired seventeen-year-old phenom Wayne Gretzky from the soon-to-be defunct (Skalbania-owned) Indianapolis Racers.

The Oilers, along with the Québec Nordiques, Winnipeg Jets, and New England Whalers, agreed to join the NHL for the 1979–80 season. The WHA's swan song took place on May 20, 1979, when the Oilers played the final game in league history, a 7–3 loss to the Winnipeg Jets in the Avco Cup championship series. Edmonton thus became the only WHA entry to have played in the league's first and last seasons to not win the Avco Cup.

The Oilers had more losses than wins during their maiden NHL season, but still made the Stanley Cup Playoffs, though were swept by Philadelphia in the first round. As expected, Gretzky led the way, finishing the year with 137 points—tied for the league lead. The seeds of the great Oilers dynasty were soon sown, with young stars Mark Messier, Glenn Anderson, Jari Kurri, Paul Coffey, and Grant Fuhr

forming the foundation of a team that would go on to win five Cups over seven seasons.

The 1988 trade of Gretzky to the Los Angeles Kings, however, altered the trajectory of the franchise. The Oilers' 1990 Cup victory—led by Messier—gave way to a bleak era. The club struggled to stay afloat—with relocation a real possibility—and small-market Edmonton faced an uncertain future. In 1998, Pocklington nearly sold the team to Les Alexander, owner of the NBA's Houston Rockets, but a consortium of Alberta-based investors saved the day at the last minute, purchasing the franchise and saving them from being moved to Texas.

The team had to wait until 2006 for its next appearance in the Finals, which they lost to the Carolina Hurricanes. In September 2016, the Oilers moved into the new state-of-the art 18,641-seat Rogers Place. The arena's footprint was designed in the shape of an oil drop, a fitting homage to the franchise's now-classic logo.

THE NAME

Edmonton's WHA team was originally slated to be called the Oil Kings, a moniker which duplicated that of Bill Hunter's established WHL entry. He soon had second thoughts. In December 1971, Hunter told Terry Jones of the *Edmonton Journal*, "There may be too much conflict with having the same name for two teams. We may hold a name-the-team contest, but we haven't made a decision in that area."

On June 8, 1972, the team announced that it would be named the Alberta Oilers. Hunter pointed out that the Calgary Broncos, unable to come up with the $100,000 bond to join the new league, had dropped out, leaving the entire

Wayne Gretzky, seen here before the Oilers' October 24, 1979 game against the New York Rangers at Madison Square Garden, just two weeks into the club's first NHL season.

province of Alberta up for grabs. He referenced the B. C. Lions, Minnesota Vikings, California Angels, and Texas Rangers as examples of team names with regional appeal. The Oilers planned to play some home games in Calgary, but that never happened.

Citing Edmonton's ties to the oil industry, Hunter later said, "Edmonton was a blue-collar, hard-working town, and I wanted to give the team a name fans could identify with."

On June 22, 1973, the team officially announced that it would henceforth be called the *Edmonton* Oilers, eschewing the Provincial designation. Hunter told the *Journal,* "The change of our name from Alberta to Edmonton Oilers should eliminate once and for all any talk that we are contemplating moving the club to any other centre or playing some league games at Calgary."

THE LOOK

The Oilers' distinctive oil drop logo and blue and orange colour scheme dates back to the very beginnings of the franchise; back to the WHA and inaugural 1972–73 Alberta Oilers. The logo has been credited to "a local artist," whose creation remains largely unchanged after nearly a half century in use.

An image appears in the July 7, 1972, edition of the *Journal,* depicting newly signed players Derek Harker, Rusty Patenaude, Bob McAneeley, and Ken Baird thoughtfully admiring the new logo. The mark is wholly a creation of its time—contemporary, bold, and mod, devoid of needless embellishment.

The Oilers' blue and orange colours were the result of a sponsorship pitch that was intended to win over Gulf Oil executives. Hunter sold Gulf on a $10 million deal which would include the team wearing the company's signature hues, but the arrangement was scuttled by the oil company's board of directors.

Hunter relayed the story behind the Oilers' colours in his 2000 autobiography *Wild Bill: Bill Hunter's Legendary 65 Years in Canadian Sport.* He describes a meeting with Charles Hay, head of Hockey Canada, who had recently retired as president of Gulf Oil in Canada. Hay was still a member of that company's board. With strategy in mind, Hunter shared the fledgling team's orange and blue logo with Hay.

"I pointed out how it complemented the logo Gulf used at the time. I also told him we would be more than happy to use Gulf's colours: blue and orange." Hunter noted that the Gulf name wouldn't appear on the sweaters, but fans would doubtlessly make the connection. "Charlie loved the idea, and we shook hands then and there. The deal was worth $10 million, enough to set up the Oilers for years."

The agreement never came to fruition, however, as the oil company's board opted out, citing rival Imperial Oil's long-standing sponsorship of *Hockey Night in Canada,* which garnered them strong public association with pro hockey. "Down the drain went $10 million," wrote Hunter. "But the name, colours and crest all stuck."

The Oilers' first set of sweaters showcased the logo front and centre. They wore white at home and orange on the road, with the province name "Alberta" initially replacing player names on the backs of the jerseys. The team soon shifted to blue on the road; a look which would come to define the club as it joined the NHL and dominated the league.

The first big changes to the Oilers' familiar visuals were announced on May 31, 1996, when the team unveiled their new uniforms. The Oilers adjusted their colour palette, deepening the royal blue to midnight navy and ditching the orange in favour of a metallic copper hue. Red was added to the mix as an accent colour, used minimally as trim detail and as a thin outline around the crest. A new secondary mark was also introduced, featuring a helmeted roughneck working a rig, his wrench replaced by a hockey stick. This was created by New Jersey–based Frederick & Froberg Design Office.

Team marketing executive Stew MacDonald described the royal blue as "soft and dated." The changes were made at a time when the NHL's visual landscape was shifting away from tradition, with bold, aggressive elements supplanting long established looks. Oilers players seemed relieved to find that the team's optics remained largely unchanged. Team captain Kelly Buchberger told the *Journal*, "I'm glad they kept the traditional logo—they've just changed the colours a little bit. Remember, this organization isn't really old. It's seventeen years old. To keep this logo after winning five Stanley Cups with it, obviously it's something we wanted to keep. I'm glad they did."

In 2001, the Oilers debuted a new third jersey, featuring a logo created by *Spawn Comics* founder and Oilers minority owner Todd McFarlane, with an assist by artist Brent Ashe. The uniforms were deep navy blue with silver trim, a chromatic departure for the team. The look was intended to be fashion-forward, with McFarlane saying, "We wanted it to be a hockey jersey but also a good wear if you were just walking down the street."

The Oilers described the sleek, futuristic logo with abundant detail:

Edmonton's third jerseys, introduced in 2001, represented a sharp departure from the steady look that was associated with five Stanley Cup winners.

Sharp, blade-like shapes signify both the blades of a hockey skate and the fast-paced, exciting tradition of Edmonton Oilers Hockey. The Five Rivets that form around the oil drop represent the five Stanley Cups won by the Edmonton Oilers Hockey Club since its entry into the NHL in 1979. There are also ten gear teeth on the primary mark; five on the large outer gear, and five on the inner gear. Each gear tooth represents each of the previous team captains in the Edmonton Oilers NHL History. Inner and outer gear shapes signify strong and formidable force while reinforcing the concept of teamwork and industriousness.… The Oil Drop is derived from the original Edmonton Primary mark. It has been turned on its side to accommodate and reinforce the speed of the new primary mark. It has also been given a highlight to help define and distinguish it from the rest of the logo.

This now-polarizing uniform was last worn in 2006–07.

In October 2008, the Oilers replaced the McFarlane third jerseys with a retro-inspired set that harkened back to the team's glory years. Orange was restored, and the bold striping of the Gretzky era was revived as well. Team captain Ethan Moreau said, "The cool thing about playing here is the history of the team and when you can put that retro jersey on, it makes you feel more like an Oiler. You relate to the Oilers in these colours."

This formed the basis of the team's new primary uniform set in 2011, a full-circle reversion to what the Oilers looked like when they dominated the hockey world.

FLORIDA PANTHERS
1993-PRESENT

THE TEAM

Just two months into the state of Florida's first season of National Hockey League action—by way of the cross-state Tampa Bay Lightning—the league "pulled a major surprise," according to the Canadian Press, when they announced an expansion franchise for Miami, as well as Anaheim, California, on December 10, 1992. Miami's expansion franchise was awarded to Wayne Huizenga, president of Blockbuster Video and owner of baseball's Florida Marlins, in exchange for $50 million in expansion fees. "The fact that the NHL has been able to attract ownership with the stature and prestige of Disney [Anaheim] and Blockbuster speaks volumes to the momentum and growth the league is experiencing," announced NHL president Gil Stein. "The league footprint needed to be a little broader, this will help."

The Florida Panthers played their first game on October 6, 1993, a 4–4 tie against the Blackhawks in Chicago. The Panthers' first home game didn't come for another week, a 2–1 loss to the Pittsburgh Penguins at the Miami Arena, where they spent their first five seasons. The young Panthers shared their first home with the NBA's Miami Heat as they awaited the completion of their own arena in Sunrise, Florida, a small city on the very edge of the Florida Everglades located just west of Fort Lauderdale.

Success came quickly to the Panthers at the Arena. In just their third season, the club made it all the way to the Stanley Cup Finals before being swept at the hands of the Colorado Avalanche. During their unexpected run, Panthers fans would rain plastic rats onto the ice following each Panthers goal, this in reference to an incident in which a rat was killed with a hockey stick by Panthers forward Scott Mellanby in their locker room before a game earlier that season. Mellanby went on to score two goals later that night—using the very same rat-killing stick—leading goaltender John Vanbiesbrouck to quip that Mellanby had scored the league's first (and probably last) "rat-trick." When more than 3,000 rats were flying onto the ice at its peak, the league was forced to step in, and a new rule was introduced following the season that would penalize the home team if fans delayed games by throwing objects onto the ice.

In 1998, the Panthers finally moved into their new Sunrise home, where they have struggled both at the box office and on the ice. In their first twenty years at the new building, the Panthers qualified for the playoffs just three times and never won a single playoff series.

THE NAME

Chosen to focus attention on the endangered species of the same name, "Florida Panthers" was announced as the name of the team by president Bill Torrey at Burt and Jack's restaurant in Fort Lauderdale on April 19, 1993; while well-intended, the new name was nevertheless immediately met the next morning with a literal "yawn" on the front page of the South Florida *Sun-Sentinel*'s sports section.

Overall, more than 6,000 entries were submitted into the Name the Team Contest launched in March 1993, the only real guideline heading into it was that the team would use either Florida or South Florida—not Miami or any other city name. With names such as South Florida Freeze as well as the eventual winning choice floating around in the minds of local journalists of the era, dozens of fans ended up sending in the winning suggestion of Florida Panthers.

"It was the clear-cut, most popular choice," Torrey said. "We hope to draw attention to the panther in the rest of the United States and Canada," also adding "the panther is the quickest striking of all cats and hopefully that's the way we'll play on the ice." Via a draw, the winner of the Name the Team Contest was Tony Scornavacca of Coconut Grove, Florida, who received four inaugural season tickets as the top prize.

"We vacillated between 'Florida' and 'South Florida,'" Huizenga revealed. "But when the name 'Panthers' came out we went with Florida because it's the Florida state animal."

Huizenga had previously obtained the rights to the name Florida Panthers as an option for his expansion baseball team, purchasing the rights from Tampa businessman Frank Morsani for $5,000 in 1991. Morsani had hoped to use the name for an expansion National League baseball team in Tampa Bay, but he and his group lost that bid for the franchise to Huizenga and his eventual Florida Marlins.

At the time the team was named, biologists believed there were only thirty to fifty Florida panthers remaining in their habitat; in 2017, less than a quarter-century after the hockey team revealed its name meant to increase awareness, that number had risen considerably with the US Fish and Wildlife Service estimating there were now as many as 230.

THE LOOK

With 1,500 fans on hand at Miami Arena, Huizenga unveiled the first logo and uniforms of the Florida Panthers on June 14, 1993, declared "Florida Panthers Day" by the city of Miami. With free champagne, T-shirts, and pucks for all those in attendance, the crowd cheered loudly when Scott Collette and Luc Rivek, two local hockey players, took to the stage wearing the brand-new Panthers uniforms.

Designed by the Sean Michael Edwards (SME) design firm out of New York, the original Panthers logo was described by the *Palm Beach Post* as looking like "*Jurassic Park* in the Ice Age"; it featured a full-bodied gold panther, teeth bared and claws out, leaping out of the center of the jersey toward the opponent. Secondary logos included a hockey stick crossed with a palm tree in front of Florida's shining sun, and a version with the panther snapping a hockey stick in two like a twig in its mouth.

The uniforms were white at home with red shoulders

coming to a point with red, gold, and blue stripes around the waist and each sleeve, with the palm tree logo included on each shoulder. For road games, the main color was red with a similar design, shoulders blue. "I'm very prejudiced," said Torrey, "but I don't think any uniform in the league looks better than the one we showed today. We think this uniform is sleek and aggressive—something we hope to be on the ice."

"This is a hot color," Huizenga said referring to the Panthers, new red, blue, and gold. "The Dolphins and Marlins colors are very similar, we wanted something different, something to stand out."

Huizenga's Panthers indeed stood out; the team kept the logo for more than twenty years before a couple of changes in ownership led to a new-look logo while still maintaining some ties to the spirit of the original design including the entire color scheme.

The Panthers, now owned by New York businessman Vincent Viola, introduced their new look on June 2, 2016. The new design was inspired by Viola's ties to the US Army and his years at West Point Academy. The logo was a shield, loosely based upon the badge worn by the Army's 101st Airborne Division, which included the head of a panther appearing within the shield. Two versions of the logo were revealed, both with text scrawled above the panther head, one reading PANTHERS, the other FLORIDA.

"The idea was to create a uniform that represents the core values of a winning organization, a winning team," Viola told SportsLogos.Net. "From my perspective there's no organization in our society that has more victories to its credit than the United States Army. That's what a winning hockey team looks and feels like."

John Vanbiesbrouck in Florida's original road uniform, 1996-97.

"I thought here are five or six different directions we could take this," said John Viola, son of Vincent, "but pretty quickly we said, 'the Army, South Florida, and the pride in this very distinct animal that lives outside our arena.' That was what we decided to brand with."

The two uniforms remained red and white, while gold was emphasized on the jerseys and blue was reserved mostly for the helmets and pants. A single horizontal stripe similar to the famous Montréal Canadiens red sweater was added—not as a nod to the Habs but instead as an evolved element from the design process that began as a large "X" for the Florida state flag. Army-style badges adorn either sleeve with an extra badge added for a team captain or alternate. A nod to the original look was also included via a simplified and modernized version of the first leaping Panthers logo on each side of the player's helmet.

Aaron Ekblad and Vincent Trocheck model the Florida Panthers' new home and road uniforms for fans on June 2, 2016.

HAMILTON TIGERS
1920-1925

THE TEAM

Canada's Steel City played host to a National Hockey League franchise from 1920 to 1925. The franchise played a single season in Québec in 1919–20 before being sold to Hamilton's Abso-Pure Ice Company for $5,000, and shifted westward. The NHL formally admitted the team on November 27, 1920, and the Hamilton Tigers opened up the season at home with a 5–0 victory over the Montréal Canadiens on December 22.

Hamilton was Canada's fifth-largest city at the time, and Abso-Pure housed their club in a new state-of-the-art arena, located on Barton Street, which was loaded with amenities such as an artificial ice plant, a press box, and multiple locker rooms.

The Tigers' first four seasons bore witness to four last-place finishes. Their fifth campaign, however, saw them go from worst to first, a remarkable turnaround. Hamilton went on a tear at the outset of the 1924–25 season, starting out with a record of 10–4–1. They finished first overall, and looked to be solid contenders for the Stanley Cup. Alas, things went downhill from there.

That season, the NHL expanded the schedule from 24 to 30 games. Tigers players were none too happy about the fact that their salaries remained unchanged, regardless of the additional workload. Sensing leverage, they went on strike. The league pushed back, noting the fact that player agreements ran from December 1 through the end of March, and were not based on the number of games played.

The standoff culminated in NHL president Frank Calder suspending the striking players and declaring the Canadiens league champions. Montréal then went out west to play the Victoria Cougars of the Western Canada Hockey League for the Stanley Cup, losing in four games. This marked the final time the Cup was won by a non-NHL franchise.

That offseason was characterized by a flurry of tumultuous change. In April 1925, the league announced plans to expand to New York, to play at the new 18,000-seat Madison Square Garden, starting in the fall. The troubled Hamilton franchise saw the writing on the wall. While ownership made noises about a newer and more modern arena to replace their 3,800-seat facility, the franchise remained in limbo throughout the spring and summer of 1925.

A deal was eventually secured to sell the Tigers' roster—but not the franchise itself—to the new New York club for $75,000. That

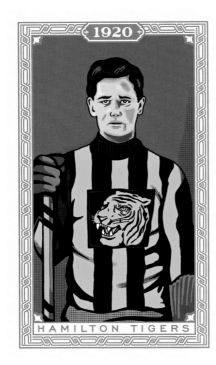

team was officially named the "Americans" in November 1925, and the Hamilton Tigers franchise quietly slipped away.

THE NAME

By the time the NHL got to Hamilton in 1920, "Tigers" was a well-established name for sports teams in "The Ambitious City," with the Canadian Football League team—now known as the Hamilton Tiger-Cats—having begun play as a rugby outfit there in 1869. That club was commonly referred to as "Tigers" within a few years, and they adopted a colour scheme of black and yellow—a look that was embraced by the NHL Tigers decades later.

THE LOOK

The Tigers' visual presence was striking. Their first uniforms apparently caused some confusion with the outfits that were worn by the Ottawa Senators. After only four games, the *Ottawa Citizen* reported, "in view of the fact that their Tiger striped uniforms were confusing with those of the Ottawas, the Hamilton players will get new outfits."

These togs made an impression. The same paper chimed in with the following description, in their January 18, 1921, edition: "Hamilton's new uniform seems to have created a real furore at Montréal. Joe Malone and his men wear yellow and black striped jerseys and heavy gaping Tiger head on the front. They top off the regalia with odd stockings, one black and the other yellow. This was adopted because their first outfit was somewhat similar to that of Ottawa, causing much confusion during the play."

The team wore black and yellow for the rest of their time in Hamilton, but adopted a new look for their second and third seasons. These sweaters featured a series of black and yellow horizontal stripes across the body and sleeves, with a full-body, left-facing bengal as their crest.

Their final two seasons saw the Tigers clad in sweaters with a series of narrow stripes emblazoned across the sleeves and a crest that featured a large black "H" with the word *Tigers* nestled within the crossbar, rendered in yellow. These were the uniforms that were worn by Hamilton's striking players, the last to represent the city in the National Hockey League.

HARTFORD WHALERS
1979-1997

THE TEAM

The New England Whalers were charter members of the World Hockey Association (WHA), winning the league's inaugural Avco Cup championship in 1973. The team made the playoffs in each of the WHA's seven seasons. They were then invited to join the National Hockey League in March 1979, along with the Edmonton Oilers, Winnipeg Jets, and Québec Nordiques, after which the WHA officially folded on June 22, 1979.

The Whalers were a nomadic crew in their early years, playing home games at the Boston Arena, Boston Garden, and the Eastern States Exposition Coliseum in West Springfield, Massachusetts, before settling into the brand-new Hartford Civic Center on January 11, 1975. A temporary move back to Springfield was necessitated three years later when the roof of the Civic Center collapsed under the weight of accumulated ice and snow.

The newly rechristened Hartford Whalers began their NHL tenure while still camped out in Springfield—they reopened the Hartford Civic Center on February 6, 1980, and called the building their home until April 13, 1997.

The Whalers' NHL run was never easy. The team recorded but three winning campaigns in their eighteen NHL seasons, never advancing to the Stanley Cup Finals.

Playing in the smallest market in the US, squeezed between New York and Boston and with little corporate support, the Whalers struggled, and when Peter Karmanos bought the club in 1994, many questioned his commitment to Hartford.

A spirited "Save the Whale" civic campaign ensued, but on May 6, 1997, Karmanos announced that the team would relocate to Raleigh, North Carolina, where they now play as the Carolina Hurricanes.

Decades after the team's departure, the Whalers' "Brass Bonanza" celebratory anthem is fondly remembered. The club played in an arena that was part of a shopping mall. Gordie Howe, Bobby Hull, Dave Keon, and Mark Howe all played for the team. The Whalers, like baseball's Brooklyn Dodgers, endure in the public imagination—and much has to do with their inventive and iconic logo.

THE NAME

The Whalers were officially launched at a Boston press conference on January 24, 1972. Of the name, team president Howard Baldwin said, "the whaling industry played an important part in the development of this area and is certainly as much a part of our heritage as the first Thanksgiving and the 'shot heard 'round the world.' Whalemen were known the world over for their teamwork and courage, a tradition we hope to emulate on the ice."

A year earlier the Whalers name had been considered and rejected by Boston's American Hockey League franchise, the Braves. (Other names in the mix for that team were Pilot Lights, Mariners, and Bosuns.)

The Whalers name was credited to Ginny Kelley, wife of new coach Jack Kelley, who came over from behind the Boston University bench.

"Boston" Whalers was deemed off limits in deference to the well-established boat manufacturers of the same name. The team instead opted for a regional designation, "New England," an appropriate move considering the fact that the Whalers had not yet secured a permanent residence.

The long, arduous negotiations that led to the Whalers becoming a member of the NHL forced the team to reconsider their "New England" moniker. The Whalers were regional rivals with—and former Boston Garden tenants of—the Boston Bruins. The Bruins, less than thrilled about sharing their market with a competitor, exerted pressure on the Whalers to make a name change—and even voted against the eventual WHA-NHL merger.

On May 23, 1979, the Whalers held a press conference in the Grand Ballroom of the Sheraton Hartford, announcing that the franchise would be named the "Hartford Whalers" when they entered the NHL later that year.

THE LOOK

The WHA New England Whalers' original logo was a complex affair. The focal point was a contemporary sans serif "W," bisected by a detailed depiction of a harpoon, encircled by the words "New England Whalers." A green and white roped border contained the entire thing. When the team announced its official name on January 24, 1972, they also announced that the team colors would be green and white.

The logo was designed by Charles Hoar Jr., with Whalers public relations director Art Dunphy spearheading the project. The end product was completed in March 1972, the result of a lengthy process that involved a review of more than a hundred variations.

The Whalers' first set of uniforms—white at home and dark green on the road—utilized the team's round primary logo as the central crest. A whimsical whale character, later nicknamed "Pucky," graced both shoulders of the sweaters.

The harpooned "W" soon took over as the team crest, a far more focused and far stronger icon. Yellow/gold was also added to the team's dark green and white color palette. This look would carry the Whalers through to the conclusion of the WHA's short but memorable history. The team's final game in these uniforms took place in Edmonton on May 8, 1979.

What came next is widely admired as one of the greatest and most beloved logos in sports history.

The mark was unveiled when the Whalers announced their new "Hartford" designation on May 23, 1979. The project to create a new identity was assigned to Jack Lardis

Associates, who in turn hired local designer Peter Good to create the logo.

Working in a pre-digital design world, Good sketched out a range of options that embraced what he described as "a modernist approach." His solutions were bold and devoid of needless detail. He explored the idea of incorporating a stylized harpoon, but was conscious of the fact that harpoons are, after all, weapons that kill whales—an unappealing notion.

He carried over the idea of the Whalers' existing green color, but made it brighter and more vivid. Good added a clean, blue color after exploring and then discarding an orange accent color, powered through a series of well-defined, tight comps that ultimately led to the finished product.

Good was part of a generation of designers who embraced a modern approach to logo design, characterized by spare aesthetics, clean lines, and direct visual messaging. Paul Rand, one of the most influential logo designers of all time, summed up the ideology behind this movement with these rather unsentimental words:

"The principal role of a logo is to identify, and simplicity is its means ... its effectiveness depends on distinctiveness, visibility, adaptability, memorability, universality, and timelessness."

Peter Good nailed it.

The elements within the mark are symmetrical and easy on the eye. A whale's tail sits atop the logo, with a "W" beneath. And there, nestled in between, tucked into the void of negative space, lies the letter "H" for "Hartford." Good's logo does a lot with a little, and the appeal is indeed timeless.

Working directly with team owner Howard Baldwin, Good's final logo resonated with fans from the moment it

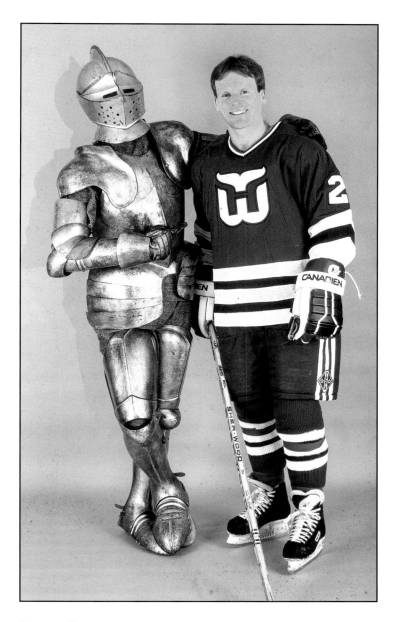

"Ironman" Doug Jarvis poses with a suit of armor in 1986.

The Whalers shifted to "better and bigger" navy blue in 1992.

was revealed.

Whalers' marketing director Bill Barnes described the mark as "progressive and upbeat," noting the fact that the whale was the "state animal" of Connecticut. "The tail is the most powerful part of the whale, which propels and protects him," he added.

The first set of Hartford Whalers uniforms were white at home and green on the road, and retained the "Pucky" character on their shoulders. In 1982, the Whalers adopted "Co-operalls" (officially CCM Pro Guards), the long pants that the Philadelphia Flyers had introduced to the NHL a year prior. The lightweight pants proved hazardous due to the lack of friction they afforded, causing violent crashes. They were soon banned.

The elegance of Good's logo was compromised in 1992, when the team shifted to a navy blue, green, and silver palette. The crest was outlined and backed with metallic silver, thus diminishing the subtlety of the hidden "H." General manager Brian Burke said, "I think we will look better and bigger. I think a uniform can make a huge difference in how a hockey club plays."

This look saw the Whalers through until the end of their tenure in Connecticut's capital city in 1997. Years after the Whalers passed into history, however, the logo endures. After disappearing from view for more than a decade, the NHL allowed licensees to produce merchandise containing the Whalers logo, starting in 2009.

And, in September 2018, the Carolina Hurricanes announced plans to wear throwback Whalers uniforms for select games, a full-circle visual treat for a whole new generation of fans who never got to see the originals in action.

KANSAS CITY SCOUTS
1974-1976

THE TEAM

Kansas City's fleeting tenure in the National Hockey League commenced on June 8, 1972, when the league conditionally awarded expansion franchises to KC and Washington, DC. The two new entries were to begin play in 1974–75 as the league's seventeenth and eighteenth teams. The NHL considered ten applicants in total, including three separate groups from the Kansas City area. KC's team went to a group fronted by thirty-seven-year-old real estate developer Edwin G. Thomson.

The new team was originally slated to play at a new 17,000-seat arena in Overland Park, Kansas, but those plans were scuttled when voters rejected a sales tax to help fund the facility. Acrimonious negotiations followed and, by the end of 1972, the franchise was in limbo, rumored to be headed to Cincinnati or elsewhere. The Kansas arena project collapsed in December 1972, but a deal was soon struck to build a facility on the site of the former Kansas City (Missouri) Stockyards.

A series of labor disputes delayed the completion of the team's new $22 million home, the Kemper Arena. The Scouts thus played their first eight games on the road—losing seven and tying one—before finally dropping the puck in KC on November 2, 1974, against the Chicago Black Hawks. They lost that night by a score of 4–3. The Scouts broke through for their first-ever victory the following night in Washington against the league's other new team, the Washington Capitals.

Long a minor league hockey stronghold, Kansas City seemed like an ideal candidate for an NHL franchise. The Central Hockey League's Kansas City Blues were locally televised and drew solid crowds. The Scouts, however, struggled to draw fans. A bad team, combined with higher NHL ticket prices, all set against the backdrop of a national recession, put the Scouts in a tenuous situation right from the get-go.

Perpetually undercapitalized, the Scouts stumbled through their first two seasons. The NHL floated the club a $300,000 loan in March 1976, directing team ownership to either get additional local financing or move to another city. Cleveland seemed a likely destination. Reports soon surfaced of a possible move to Toronto, with free agent Bobby Orr as the marquee attraction for a newly relocated franchise. With options and time running out, the league seriously considered terminating the franchise altogether. Finally, on July 26, 1976, Scouts ownership announced that they were selling their interests to a Denver-based group, who would move the team to Colorado.

After two troubled years, the Kansas City Scouts were transformed into the Colorado Rockies. Denver proved to be but a temporary home for the nomadic franchise, as the Rockies picked up and moved to New Jersey in 1982, where they now play as the New Jersey Devils.

THE NAME

Fans of Kansas City's brand-new team did not have to wait long for a nickname.

On June 9, 1972—the day after the NHL granted a team to KC—franchise officials announced that the new entry would be called the "Kansas City Mo-Hawks."

Chuck Manne, a member of the ownership team, relayed the news at a reception held at the Glenwood Manor Motor Lodge in Overland Park, Kansas. "It may not be legal," Manne said, noting the potential for objections by the Chicago Black Hawks. The name was selected with a regional approach in mind.

The nickname was intended to pay tribute to both Missouri and Kansas, combining "Mo" for Missouri, with "Hawks"—a contraction of Jayhawk—a name long associat-

Cyrus E. Dallin's "The Scout."
Originally sculpted for San Francisco's
1915 Panama-Pacific Exposition, the
citizens of Kansas City raised $15,000
to purchase it. It has overlooked
Kansas City's Penn Valley Park since
its dedication in 1922.

ed with Kansas and its residents.

The Mo-Hawks moniker lasted less than a month.

Not surprisingly, on July 5, 1972, lead owner Thompson said that the new name would be scrapped. He noted that the owners of the Chicago Black Hawks "helped us [get] the franchise so we're happy to go along with their wishes and not use the word 'Hawks' in our nickname."

A Name the Team Contest was then held, and it attracted 15,000 entries, which were eventually narrowed down to three finalists: Scouts, Tornadoes, and Crowns.

On June 4, 1973, the new team was announced as "Scouts," a tribute to "The Scout," Cyrus E. Dallin's bronze depiction of a Sioux scout on horseback that has overlooked Kansas City from Penn Valley Park since its dedication in 1922.

James R. Maxwell was declared the winner of the contest, and was awarded a new Ford automobile for his efforts.

THE LOOK

The Scouts' logo featured a depiction of the "Scout" statue, enclosed in a circle, accompanied by a stylized "KC." The team's colors were royal blue, red, and yellow gold. Gary Sartain, a graphic artist at Kansas City–based Hallmark Cards, created the visual identity.

The team's uniforms were highlighted by an abundance of stripes—across the shoulders, sleeves, and hems of the sweaters. When the Scouts made their debut at Toronto's famed Maple Leaf Gardens on October 9, 1974, the *Toronto Globe and Mail* proclaimed their uniforms to be "gaudy." Kansas City played but 160 games in royal blue, red, and yellow gold before carrying those colors with them to Colorado for another six seasons.

The Scouts wore blue uniforms with numerous red and gold stripes.

LOS ANGELES KINGS
1967-PRESENT

THE TEAM

Decades before the National Hockey League even considered its ambitious wave of expansion, Los Angeles was indeed home to professional hockey. Dating back to the Second World War, the Los Angeles Monarchs were members of the Pacific Coast Hockey League up until 1950. Eleven years later, in the same league—now known as the Western Hockey League—Los Angeles welcomed the relocated Victoria Cougars and renamed them the Blades, who played out of the Los Angeles Sports Arena.

Jack Kent Cooke, described in a *Sports Illustrated* article of the time as "silver-haired and suave," was a Canadian self-made millionaire who had relocated to Beverly Hills. Cooke was part-owner of the NFL's Washington Redskins and had recently purchased the NBA's Los Angeles Lakers when he turned his attention to the NHL. Cooke met with the league at the St. Regis in New York, presenting them with his plans for a brand new $7 million arena. He must have impressed the league, as Cooke was awarded an expansion franchise for Los Angeles the very next day, February 9, 1966, beating out competing LA bids from Dan Reeves, who owned the Blades and NFL's Los Angeles Rams, Buffalo Bills owner Ralph Wilson, and TV producer Tony Owens.

"I don't think I've ever been happier," Cooke said after winning the bid. "I was born in Canada, every boy there has one dream, not to become Prime Minister but to become a professional hockey player. Since I'm a little too old to play, I did the next best thing."

For an expansion fee of $2 million and an additional $1 million of indemnity to the Blades for taking over their territory, Cooke was in for the 1967–68 season, on the condition that he build that new arena. He quickly secured a former golf course in Inglewood, about 10 miles outside of Los Angeles, for his new column-clad circular arena which he immediately dubbed The Forum.

Cooke didn't waste time causing a stir with the league's old guard when he signed Red Kelly—a player still under contract with the Toronto Maple Leafs—to be the head coach of his expansion Los Angeles Kings. The Leafs appealed to the league, insisting this should count as an expansion draft choice. An agreement was made when the league required the Kings to send their 15th pick in the draft to the Leafs as compensation.

The Los Angeles Kings played their first game on October 14, 1967, against the visiting Philadelphia Flyers in front of just 7,035 fans at the Long Beach Arena. It was a rough start for the Kings, who scored into their own net just 42 seconds into their franchise's history. Things turned around fast, however, as they overcame the early setback to win their NHL debut, besting the Flyers, 4–2. Two months later, on December 30, 1967, the Kings moved to Cooke's "fabulous" Forum, debuting the arena to 14,366 fans with an opening ceremony emceed by actor Lorne Greene with the game broadcast nationally in color. Unlike the season opener, the Kings would lose to the Flyers on this night, 2–0, disappointing the sellout crowd by failing to score a single goal.

Success was hard to find in Los Angeles, as the team struggled at the gate and on the ice. The seasons in which the team excelled were snuffed out by quick first-round exits in the playoffs at the hands of underdogs. That all would change forever on August 9, 1988, when the Kings stunned the hockey world with the acquisition of arguably the greatest player of all-time, Wayne Gretzky, from the Edmonton Oilers. Gretzky led the Kings to five-straight playoff berths, culminating in their first trip to the Stanley Cup Finals in 1993, a five-game loss to the Montréal Canadiens.

Just under twenty years later, the Kings would finally get their crown, sneaking into the last spot of the playoffs before rolling right through everyone they faced on their way to

Rogie Vachon in the Kings' original "Forum Blue" (not purple.)

becoming the 2012 Stanley Cup Champions. And then, just two years later, they did it again.

THE NAME

With retired hockey legend Maurice "Rocket" Richard and the Stanley Cup both on hand, a contest was launched at the Beverly Hilton Hotel on April 13, 1966, to help determine the name of Los Angeles' new hockey team.

After receiving 7,649 entries—some of which included names like the Cobras, Lancers, Knights, and Panthers—the team announced that the club would be known as the Los Angeles Kings on June 3, 1966.

"Kings is distinctive, I don't recall another team being called 'Kings,'" Cooke told the *Los Angeles Times*. "We were looking for a name that would be symbolic of leadership in hockey—that we intended over the years to build a hockey dynasty and we wanted a name that would be properly representative of that. I feel that Kings is the most appropriate name," adding "we're starting out as the 'Kings of the NHL' and we intend to live up to that distinction."

Thirty-two of the 7,000-plus contest entries submitted the eventual winning name of Kings. The first person to do so was Harry Mullen of Pasadena, who was given a color television, portable radio, and a pair of 1967–68 season tickets for his entry. The thirty-one others to submit the "Kings" name were each given four tickets to one Kings game.

"I don't think I've ever been as puzzled or, honestly, as frustrated, by anything as I was about naming the team," Cooke explained to the *Valley News*. "We had at least eight names that appealed to us and we considered all of them very carefully and from all aspects. But the process of elimination involved such things as copyright clearance, a name that had previously been associated with a failure in sports here, some beautiful sounding Spanish names that didn't quite measure up to what we wanted and, of course, a lot of excellent names that are currently in use by other sports organizations."

THE LOOK

In a color scheme befitting their royal lineage, the Kings spent their first twenty years wearing "Forum Blue" (purple) and "Forum Gold" (yellow) with a simple crown on their chests as they skated around their fabulous new Forum. The Kings had no white uniform during this time, going against tradition. Cooke, admiring this aura of royalty in his new arena, simultaneously switched the colors of his Los Angeles Lakers. The use of the nonsensical name "Forum Blue" rather than the more accurate "purple" for the team colors is said to be due to Cooke's simple distaste for the word *purple*.

Quickly into their first season, the Kings began lobbying the league to allow their collection of expansion team players to wear names on the back of their jerseys to help fans get to know who's who. This was a practice already growing in use in Major League Baseball but, in 1968, was not yet allowed in the NHL. When baseball owner Charlie O. Finley bought the Oakland Seals up the coast, he also expressed interest in bringing player names to the NHL and, in 1970, the league agreed. The Kings joined the Seals, Rangers, and Penguins as the first teams to wear names on the back of their jerseys for the 1970–71 season, and before the end of the decade it was a rule that all uniforms must include the player's name.

The Los Angeles Kings showing off both "The Great One" and their brand-new black and silver uniforms on August 9, 1988.

Another less successful innovation spawned by both the Kings and Seals that same season was the use of colorful skates. Just a few weeks after Finley's Seals got the approval to wear white skates, Cooke's Kings announced they too would ditch black in favor of "Forum Blue" and "Forum Gold" skates. Players hated them, the league wasn't a fan of the non-traditional look, and the colorful skates were given the boot shortly thereafter.

In the summer of 1988, the Kings did the unthinkable . . . yes, they changed their uniforms. Unveiled on August 9, 1988, owner Bruce McNall welcomed the large media gathering with a little humor: "The reason we're here, and the moment you've been waiting for, the introduction of our new team colors and uniforms! May we have our model please?" At that moment NHL legend Wayne Gretzky, who had been acquired earlier that day in what has been called

The infamous "Burger King" uniform, worn by the Kings sporadically over the course of three months in 1996 as part of the NHL's inaugural third jersey program.

"the trade of the century," walked onto the stage and donned the Kings very fashionable new silver and black jersey. The crown on the chest replaced with a silver shield with "KINGS" across it in streaked italic black letters, a small crown remained below the wordmark.

Cooke's old purple and gold were gone in favor of the much more modern look, similar to those worn by the NFL's Los Angeles Raiders. The *Philadelphia Inquirer* noted the inspiration for the colors were actually the Hull Olympiques, a major junior hockey club in Québec who were coincidentally owned by Gretzky, though the new look had been designed and approved several months before the trade. The Kings quickly shot up to the top of NHL merchandise charts but it's likely more in part due to their addition of "The Great One" than it was the new uniforms.

In January 1996, the Kings were one of five teams to test out the league's unorthodox new alternate jersey program in which clubs were given a non-traditional design that incorporated elements of a team's history. Los Angeles thus returned to using purple and gold—but on a white jersey with a black sash across the front. A giant purple and gold king's head was placed in the upper corner of the chest which fans quickly dubbed the "Burger King uniform." Gretzky, speaking to press after the game, said he "liked the crest" and that "it's a little more creative than what we've been wearing," while goaltender Kelly Hrudey said, "It's difficult to recognize players," adding "it was hard to pick out the numbers." Tradition and player opinion typically win out in these cases, and after four months the new tops were turfed, never to be worn again.

Purple officially returned to the Kings on June 20, 1998, when a star-studded ceremony including TV's Tiffani-Amber Thiessen and Lou Diamond Phillips unveiled the new look at Universal Studios Hollywood. Now featuring a large coat-of-arms on the chest, the uniforms were purple and black with "LOS ANGELES" written across the waist. The coat of arms crest combined both local California flavor, as well as the team's name which included elements such as a lion wearing sunglasses. The original crown logo was updated considerably and placed on both the home and road jersey's purple shoulders. It took twenty months of development—involving several focus groups and consulting with players about design and the weight of the jersey itself—before they landed on this design.

Of course, it didn't take too long for fans to begin to miss the old black and silver so commonly associated with "The Great One." In 2009, the Kings introduced a new alternate uniform featuring the black and silver, the logo a highly simplified version of the one originally worn from 1988 to 1998, now simply featuring "LA" in large white letters above a small crown.

Two years later, on August 30, 2011, the Kings announced that purple was gone for good and this alternate uniform was coming on as their full-time home jersey, to be joined with a white version for road games. Team executive Luc Robitaille said fans had been asking for the black and silver to return for some time. The fans must've known something, because the switch back to black and silver worked, as the Kings won their first-ever Stanley Cup Championship that very season.

A return to black and silver full-time in 2011-12 was rewarded with the Kings being crowned Stanley Cup Champions for the first time in the franchise's 45-year history.

MINNESOTA WILD

2000-PRESENT

THE TEAM

The Minnesota North Stars' move to Dallas in 1993 left an undeniable void in this traditional hockey hotbed, and efforts to obtain a replacement began soon after the Stars' relocation to Texas. The (original) Winnipeg Jets came very close to moving to Minnesota in 1995, but negotiations for a new arena collapsed, as did the deal to return the National Hockey League to the Twin Cities. The following year, the Hartford Whalers seriously eyed a move to Minnesota, but opted to transfer to Raleigh, North Carolina, instead.

Focus now shifted to obtaining an expansion franchise. The NHL signaled its intention to add four new teams to supplement their existing twenty-six entries, and in January 1997, the Twin Cities sent a delegation off to NHL headquarters in New York to state their case. Competition was stiff—Houston and Atlanta were considered the frontrunners. Other applicants besides the Twin Cities included Oklahoma City (Oklahoma), Hampton Roads (Virginia), Hamilton (Ontario), Nashville (Tennessee), Columbus (Ohio), and Raleigh-Durham (North Carolina), the latter of which would land the Whalers a few months later.

The winning bids were announced on June 17, 1997—Minnesota emerged victorious, along with Nashville, Columbus, and Atlanta. Minnetonka businessman Bob Naegele Jr. and his group of investors were officially admitted to the NHL on June 25, 1997, at a cost of $80 million. Their new entry would begin play in 2000, but an arena was needed to host the fledgling team. Funding for a new facility in downtown St. Paul was eventually secured and, in June 1998, ground was broken for a new arena, soon dubbed the Xcel Energy Center, on the site of the old St. Paul Civic Center.

The arena and the team—the Minnesota Wild—made their regular-season debut on October 11, 2000. As construction crews frantically put the finishing touches on the arena, 18,827 fans celebrated the return of NHL hockey to Minnesota with appropriate pomp and circumstance. Team chairman Naegele announced that the Wild were retiring jersey number 1, in honor of the fans. "No player will ever wear that number," he said, "because you—the Wild fans—will always be number one with us." A chorus of local children sang the team's official "State of Hockey" anthem, which included the lyrics "On the ice we cut our teeth; we took our knocks in the penalty box; our mother was the referee."

The crowd loudly chanted nasty remarks about Norm Green, the despised owner who moved the North Stars to Dallas seven years earlier. St. Paul mayor Norm Coleman dropped the ceremonial first puck. Finally, the Wild and the Philadelphia Flyers played to a 3–3 tie, and NHL hockey was officially back in Minnesota.

The Wild predictably scuffled along over the course of their first several seasons. They made their first playoff appearance just three seasons into their existence, in 2002–03, making a surprising run to the Western Conference Finals before losing to the Mighty Ducks of Anaheim. St. Paul hosted the NHL's All-Star Weekend the following year. The Wild broke the 100-point barrier in 2006–07 and won the Northwest Division Championship in 2007–08. The team enjoyed a series of solid seasons over the next decade, but has yet to hoist the Cup, much less score an appearance in the Finals.

THE NAME

After the NHL officially awarded the franchise, officials of the new team formally solicited suggestions from the public. More than 13,000 responses rolled in, including a range of 3,000 potential names that included Gnats, Frozen Ears, Ninja Muskies, Fighting Smelt, and Flying Walleye. Over the course of two months these were culled down to six finalists: White Bears, Voyageurs, Northern Light, Blue Ox, Freeze, and Wild.

Team CEO Jac Sperling noted that the finalists were all "uniquely Minnesota names." He added, "In the end we believe that whichever of these six names is chosen will continue to reflect the great traditions of this state, result in a name that captures the imagination and excitement of NHL hockey and a name that every Minnesotan, hockey fan or not, can look to with pride."

The final six names were met with a distinct lack of enthusiasm, to say the least. Robert Whereatt, writing in the *Minneapolis Star Tribune*, noted that Blue Ox was less than inspiring. "The image is of a slow, clumsy, dumb animal," he said, adding that "an ox is a castrated adult bull, neutered to reduce its aggressiveness, the very essence of good hockey." Of "Wild," he said, "Grammarians will march out of the new hockey palace, protesting the morphing of a noun from an adjective."

Popular sentiment leaned heavily toward the reviving the familiar North Stars moniker. Some fans proposed Fighting Saints, St. Paul's World Hockey Association club of the early '70s.

Things were made official on January 22, 1998, during a 30-minute ceremony at the Aldrich Arena in Maplewood. More than 3,500 fans were there to see Minnesota native and former North Star Neal Broten skate around the rink, holding the Stanley Cup aloft, trailed by twenty-six youngsters, each wearing the sweater of a then-current NHL team. At last, a giant puck dramatically descended from the rafters, revealing the nickname and logo of the new team: the Minnesota Wild. Steppenwolf's classic rock anthem "Born to Be Wild" boomed, fireworks filled the arena, and fans cheered. Team CEO Sperling provided insight into the name: "We think it best represents what Minnesota hockey fans hold most dear. Our rugged natural wilderness, the premier brand hockey that's native to Minnesota and the great enthusiasm of all of our hockey fans."

THE LOOK

The Wild's first logo, unveiled along with the name, was described as "organic" and "naturalistic." Rendered in colors that were designated with regional appeal in mind—Minnesota Iron Range Red, Minnesota Forest Green, Minnesota Harvest Gold, and Minnesota Wheat—the word *Wild* was scrawled in jagged letterforms and enclosed in a green circle with the state name "Minnesota" along with "NHL Hockey," spelled out in caps.

Created by what was described as an eight-person team, CEO Sperling noted, "It's like something you see hanging from Granny Smith's northern Minnesota motor lodge. It's organic. It looks natural and it's very Minnesota to me. It says 'BOOM' and I think that 'W' is a pretty interesting letter." Lead owner Bob Naegele Jr. said, "it could be cattails and rushes in a marsh you see out duck hunting,"

The team revealed their home sweaters at an event held at the John Rose Oval at the Roseville Skating Center on November 18, 1999. More than 3,000 fans saw Naegele (a former high school and college goaltender, garbed in full goalie gear) and Broten don the new team's white jerseys, which featured a brand-new logo, later described by the team as a "Minnesota Wilderness pictogram including a wild animal, the North Star, evergreen trees, a red sky, the sun and/or moon and a stream."

John Millea, writing in the *Star Tribune*, likened it to "the head of a beast that might be a bear. Or maybe it's a mountain lion? A wolf? A very angry gofer? Who really knows?"

"It's a wild picture," said Wild CEO Sperling. "People will see what they want to see. It's intended to be a wild animal." He called out one small detail within the new logo: a star, streaking across the sky, forming the eye of the beast. A north star. "We've kind of paid homage in a little way to what's come before us."

The logo was created by New York's SME. Their website described the look in detail:

> After developing 10 different concepts for the Wild's icon, we conducted hundreds of one-on-one interviews with fans and leadership to tell a distinct visual story. The resulting multi-functional logo, known as the "Wild Animal," depicts a forest landscape inside the silhouette of a nondescript animal head. The "eye" of the "Wild Animal" is the north star, in tribute to the departed Minnesota North Stars. The logo's slightly jagged lines denote strength and motion, while skillfully portraying a pictorial dusk scene from the wilderness, replete with a meandering river and trees. Regarded as one of the most intricate and clever identities in sports, the icon seamlessly fits into one cohesive package, comprised of multiple uniforms, wordmarks, a secondary icon and mascot.

Green was the dominant color, with team officials noting the fact that the Dallas Stars' primary hue was now black. The team's original script logo was relegated to the sleeves of the sweaters, in the form of a patch.

David Haney, the NHL's director of creative services at the time, now says that he views the Wild's "animal logo" as "probably the most successful expansion branding and design project of my tenure." In an interview with the authors, Haney said, "It aggregates to a great narrative and a great expression of hockey and Minnesota. It's a great depiction and representa-

THE WILD ANIMAL

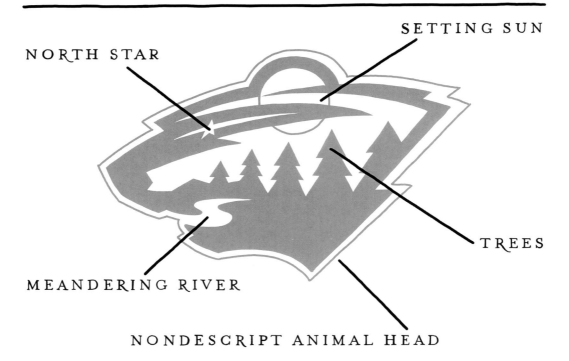

SETTING SUN

NORTH STAR

MEANDERING RIVER

TREES

NONDESCRIPT ANIMAL HEAD

tion of an idea. You look at it and you keep seeing new things."

The Wild introduced a third sweater in 2003, with the primary "wild animal" logo placed in a circle and surrounded by the team name. A traditional lace-up collar was included which, along with minimal embellishment, contributed to a time-honored look. A green alternate sweater came along in 2009, featuring an elegant script "Minnesota" wordmark angled upward, accompanied by wheat-colored trim. The NHL described the decidedly retro look as one that "harkens back to historic Minnesota teams of the past including Minneapolis and Saint Paul teams of the 1930s and

1940s." In a subtle touch, the "north star" element was brought over to dot the "I" in the state name wordmark.

On April 4, 2017, the Wild honored the franchise that arrived in Minnesota fifty seasons prior, as the team donned 1967 North Stars sweaters during pregame warmups. The North Stars competed in the NHL for 26 seasons. Two decades into their own existence, the Wild have firmly ingrained themselves into Minnesota's robust hockey culture. Their look has been consistent throughout, fronted by their unique logo; chock full of regional references, a hint of mystery, and a thoughtful tribute to the team's long-departed ancestors.

MONTRÉAL CANADIENS
1917-PRESENT

THE TEAM

The Canadiens were charter members of the National Hockey Association (NHA), a circuit that was formed in the wake of two snubs.

On November 25, 1909, the Eastern Canada Hockey Association (ECHA)—the nation's dominant league—held a meeting at Montréal's Windsor Hotel and immediately disbanded. A dispute involving the Montréal Wanderers team and their proposed move to a smaller arena caused the ECHA to dissolve itself and form a new circuit, the Canadian Hockey Association (CHA). This new league rebuffed the Wanderers, along with a team from Renfrew, Ontario, represented by twenty-four-year-old J. Ambrose O'Brien, who along with his father, Michael J. O'Brien, also owned clubs in Haileybury and Cobalt, both located in northeast Ontario.

Wanderers player-manager Jimmy Gardner approached the younger O'Brien with a plan. Frozen out of the CHA, they would form their own league. The new circuit, the National Hockey Association, was founded on December 2, 1909. The league's first four members were the Wanderers and O'Brien's Renfrew, Cobalt, and Haileybury teams.

Two days later, on December 4, 1909, the NHA introduced a fifth member—a new team based in Montréal, which would be stocked with French Canadian players. The team, intended as a natural rival to the Anglophonic Wanderers, was named *Les Canadiens*. Jean-Baptiste "Jack" Laviolette, described by the *Ottawa Citizen* as "probably the most famous French-Canadian player in the game," was brought aboard as general manager, coach, and captain.

The CHA folded on January 15, 1910, after only a handful of games were played. The NHA is the direct predecessor to today's National Hockey League, and the Montréal Canadiens are now the world's longest continuously operating professional ice hockey club.

O'Brien's claim to the Canadiens name was challenged by Montréal's Club Athlétique Canadien (CAC), an organization that promoted a range of sports—including professional wrestling. A lawsuit ensued and, in November 1910, just prior to the team's second season, a settlement was reached by which the CAC, headed up by George Kendall Kennedy, gained control of the hockey club.

LA PRESSE

MONTREAL LUNDI 6 DECEMBRE 1909

UN NOUVEAU CLUB CANADIEN

Jack Laviolette a été chargé de former une équipe qui fera partie de la National Hockey Association. --- Les deux ligues professionnelles se feront la guerre.-- Le National et les Shamrocks restent fidèles à la Canadian Hockey Association. --- 47 parties seniors pour Montréal.

HOCKEY

L'admission dans la National Hockey Association d'un club Canadien-Français ayant Jack Laviolette comme gérant, est le dernier développement dans la situation du hockey. Le nouveau club portera le nom de Canadien, et

sera le rival du National. M. T. C. Hare, de Cobalt, est le bailleur de fonds du Canadien. C'est lui qui a fourni la garantie de $1,000. Il déposera de plus aujourd'hui dans une banque, un montant de $5,000 pour garantir le salaire des joueurs. Afin de donner au Canadien toutes les chances possibles pour mettre une bonne équipe sur la glace, les autres clubs de la National Hockey Association ont résolu de ne pas engager de joueurs canadiens-français

avant que Laviolette ait trouvé tous ses hommes.

La fondation du Canadien privera le National de trois bons joueurs, car ce dernier comptait sur les services de Laviolette, Pitre et Poulin, qui porteront maintenant les couleurs du Canadien.

Jack Laviolette, qui a été chargé par un sportsman de Cobalt, d'organiser une équipe de hockey canadienne-française à Montréal.

Tout comme sa rivale, la National Hockey Association se composera donc

(Above) Montréal's La Presse *newspaper the morning of December 6, 1909, announces the birth of Les Canadien. (Right) A newspaper ad for their first-ever game on January 5, 1910, against the Cobalt Silver Kings.*

ASSOCIATION NATIONALE DE HOCKEY
Patinoir "JUBILEE" HOCKEY
MERCREDI SOIR 5 JANVIER | COBALT vs CANADIEN

La joute commencera à 8 heures p. m. La fanfare jouera de 8 à 8.30 heures, et le demi-temps. Billets en vente à la patinoire Jubilée. Les ordres par téléphone ou autrement ne seront acceptés qu'après 6 heures, le mercredi soir. Prix d'admission 35c. Sièges réservés 50c, 75c, $1.00. Loges $2.00. Tél. Est 6742.
51—5 E

The Canadiens hoisted their first Stanley Cup on March 30, 1916, with a victory over the Pacific Coast Hockey Association's Portland Rosebuds. "Flying Frenchmen Lift Stanley Cup" read the headline in the next day's *Montreal Gazette*, words that would be often repeated throughout the course of the twentieth century.

The club was reorganized as "Le Club de Hockey Canadien" in 1916 and, on November 26, 1917, the Canadiens became charter members of the NHL, which succeeded the NHA.

On November 29, 1924, the team played its first game at the newly opened Forum, a $1.5 million hockey palace, which was located at the corner of Sainte-Catherine and Atwater Streets. More than 9,000 spectators were on hand to witness the match against the Toronto St. Patricks, a 7–1 victory for the home team. The Canadiens moved into the Forum on a full-time basis two years later, and the facility continued to serve as their home until 1996.

A Stanley Cup victory in 1924 was followed up by back-to-back Cup wins in 1930 and 1931. The Great Depression hit the Canadiens particularly hard. In April 1935, the Associated Press reported that the club was considering a sale to a syndicate that was interested in moving the franchise to Cleveland. "Montreal is obviously losing interest in professional hockey," said co-owner Joe Cattarinich. Several months later, the Canadiens were sold to a trio of local businessmen, led by stockbroker Ernest Savard, for the bargain basement price of $165,000. Savard and his partners effectively served as a front for the Canadian Arena Company, owners of the Forum and the Montréal Maroons. The Canadiens stayed put and the Maroons went belly up after the 1937–38 season.

Maurice Richard made his Canadiens debut in 1942, and the team won the Stanley Cup a year later—the first Cup win for the franchise in thirteen years. Richard, joined by his younger brother Henri and a star-filled roster that included luminaries such as Jean Béliveau, Doug Harvey, and Jacques Plante, won a record five-consecutive Cups, from 1956 to 1960.

Montréal dominated the NHL in the 1970s, winning four straight Cups starting in 1976. The team moved into a new arena in 1996, and celebrated its centennial in 2009 with appropriate pomp, a fitting observance for the 100th anniversary of the NHL's oldest and most successful franchise.

THE NAME

The Canadiens have been called *Les Canadiens* since the franchise was announced on December 4, 1909.

The December 6, 1909, edition of Montréal's *La Presse* featured a photo of Jack Laviolette, accompanied by an article heralding the arrival of the new entry, noting, "Le nouveau club portera le nom de Canadien."

The name of the team is attributed to Jimmy Gardner. According to a 1967 biography of Michael O'Brien, *O'Brien, From Water Boy to One Million A Year*, by Scott and Astrid Young, it was part of Gardner's pitch to Ambrose O'Brien to form a new league.

The scene takes place in the lobby of Montréal's Windsor Hotel on November 25, 1909:

> *Ambrose, why don't you and I start a league? You've got Haileybury, Cobalt and Renfrew, and we've got the Wanderers. And I think if a team of Frenchmen was formed in Montreal it would be a real draw. We'll call this team Les Canadiens.*

Red, white, and blue barber pole sweaters worn in 1911–12.

THE 1924-25 CANADIENS
CELEBRATED THEIR STATUS AS
DEFENDING STANLEY CUP CHAMPS
WITH THESE SWEATERS

The Canadiens' "Habitants" nickname also dates back to the earliest years of the franchise. *Habitants*, a reference to Québec's French farm settlers of yore, appeared in a headline in the December 23, 1910, edition of the *Ottawa Citizen*. The paper noted the fact that the local team would be taking on "Newsy Lalonde's Habitants in Montreal" the following week to open the season.

The shorter "Habs" started to appear in the pages of the *Montreal Gazette* in 1943. Habs began to be commonly included within newspaper headlines the following year and has continued to be applied to the team ever since.

THE LOOK

The Canadiens' sweater has been called *La Sainte-Flanelle*, or "the holy flannel sweater." Their crest—a "C" for Canadiens, encircling an "H" for hockey—dates back to the team's final season in the NHA. Their iconic red, white, and blue colours have been associated with the franchise since the very beginning; an item in the December 15, 1909, edition of the *Montreal Gazette* states, "the colours of the club will be the national blue, red and white, the playing costume being in the blue and white and the red being introduced in the Garnet sweater coat."

The crest and uniforms of the Montréal Canadiens are important cultural symbols of French Canada, and have been so for more than a century.

The team's first sweater was blue, which featured white bands across the chest and shoulders, with a large, rounded white "C," front and centre. This look was discarded after a single season, replaced by red sweaters with an Old English "C" contained within a Canadian maple leaf. These uniforms were trimmed in red and blue. The January 21, 1911, edition of the *Ottawa Citizen*

referred to the Canadiens as "red, white and blue hockeyists," still an apt descriptor more than a century later.

Season three, 1911–12, brought yet another uniform change, with white sweaters. The 1912–13 team took on a decidedly different appearance. The Canadiens skated in sweaters with blue and red horizontal stripes—a lot of them, in fact. The maple leaf was restored to the fronts, with the initials CAC nestled within, a nod to the Club Athlétique Canadien connection. These uniforms were the cause of controversy and confusion due to the Ottawa club's similarly striped appearance (they first did the stripy thing back in 1896.) For the January 5, 1913, game, the Canadiens, according to the *Citizen*, "changed their striped sweaters and played

in their old jerseys of white."

Spectators at games between the two clubs were puzzled. On January 28, 1913, the *Vancouver Daily World* reported, "The crowd at a recent game got the teams mixed and often cheered Canadiens instead of Ottawa. Some of the spectators, who didn't know the players, left the rink under the impression that Ottawa had won, but the victory was one for Canadiens."

On January 20, 1913, the *Montreal Gazette* reported that Ottawa would be asking the NHA to "force the Canadiens to discard their new sweaters of red, white and blue. The Ottawas have worn 'barber poled' uniforms for many years and until this season the Canadiens wore loud red sweaters with blue and white trimmings. There was so much confusion

when the teams first played at Montreal that the Canadiens went back to their old jerseys. Last night the Ottawas wore all white uniforms and Canadiens their 'barber poles.'" Montréal adopted a new, alternate red sweater for games against Ottawa for the balance of the season.

Finally, in 1913–14, the Canadiens began to take on their now familiar form. A new crest was introduced, consisting of a large elongated "C," with an "A" centred inside of it—again symbolizing the Club Athlétique Canadien designation. The sweater was red, and the crest was centred on a tall blue horizontal band, flanked by narrow white bands on top and bottom.

On March 10, 1916, the team was reincorporated as the Club de Hockey Canadien, a change that caused the "A" for "Athlétique" to be replaced by an "H" for "Hockey." Though it's been slightly revised over the ensuing century, this is the logo that the club still wears today.

There have been a couple of outlier sweaters along the way since, but examples are few and far between. On January 5, 1918, the team took the ice against Ottawa, clad in uniforms borrowed from the City League's Hochelaga team, the result of a fire at the Westmount Arena. In 1924–25, Montréal deviated from their usual look for the entire season, sporting sweaters with a crest of a globe with "CHAMPIONS" arched across the bottom, a salute to the team's Stanley Cup title of the previous season. The primary crest was relegated to the sleeves.

The most recent significant change to Montréal's livery took place in 1935, when they adopted a white sweater, which was worn on the road at first, then used at home for games against the similarly red clad Detroit Red Wings.

When the Canadiens celebrated their centennial in the 2008–09 and 2009–10 seasons, they brought several of their NHA uniforms back for select games. These throwbacks returned the Habs to the very roots of the franchise, born in the lobby of Montréal's Windsor Hotel in the waning days of the first decade of the twentieth century.

Goaltender Ken Dryden during a break in play in 1979, wearing a uniform nearly identical to what the Habs were wearing sixty years earlier and continued to wear forty years later.

MONTRÉAL MAROONS

1924-1938

THE TEAM

The Montréal Maroons participated in fourteen National Hockey League seasons, from 1924–25 to 1937–38, winning two Stanley Cups along the way. The NHL awarded expansion franchises to Montréal and Boston on October 12, 1924. The new Montréal team paid a hefty $15,000 fee to join up, $11,000 of which went to their new neighbours, the long-established Montréal Canadiens.

The new Montréal team was created to appeal to the city's English-speaking citizens, who were left without a club of their own when the Montréal Wanderers ceased operations in 1917. Wanderers founder James Strachan was named president of Montréal's new NHL franchise.

The team's first game was played in Boston on December 1, 1924; a 2–1 defeat. They opened up their home schedule with another loss two days later against the Hamilton Tigers, their first at Montréal's new Forum, which they would call home throughout the remainder of their history. Box seats were priced at $2.25, and general admission went for 50 cents. The team finished last in the league, but attendance was strong and better days lay ahead.

The team—originally nameless but now known as the Maroons—won the Cup in only their second season, defeating the Victoria Cougars of the Western Hockey League. Their second Cup victory came in 1935, with a win against the Toronto Maple Leafs.

The Great Depression took a heavy toll on the team's finances, as ticket sales took a nosedive. Two NHL teams in Montréal was no longer a viable scenario, and the Maroons suspended operations after the 1937–38 season.

Ownership attempted to sell the dormant franchise to interests in St. Louis in 1938, but the NHL refused to approve the arrangement. (The Missouri group put up no cash and did not offer up a long term plan for the club.) As such, the Maroons remained in a state of suspended animation. In 1945, a deal was struck to revive the franchise and move it to Philadelphia, but funding for a new arena could not be secured. Litigation surrounding this failed move continued until 1958, but in that time the Maroons passed quietly into hockey heaven.

THE NAME

The Montréal Maroons came into existence with no formal nickname. Officially known as the Montréal Professional Hockey Club, the team was commonly referred to as the "Montreals." Team president Strachan attempted to revive the Wanderers nickname of yore, but was rebuffed. A November 7, 1924, article in the *Ottawa Journal* stated, "Montreal's new team will be known as Montreal, and not as Wanderers, and thereby hangs a tale."

Strachan had sold the Wanderers—along with their name—to businessman Sam Lichtenhein back in 1911.

The article continues. "Recently Sam heard with interest that the name was to be revived. He pointed out blandly that he had proprietary rights on it, but is said to have amended the statement with the declaration that a monetary consideration would induce them to part with his interest in the cognomen. The price, of course, it is said, was a bit out of line considering the fact that Wanderers are only now an historic name in hockey. On that account the Montreal directors decided to use Montreal professionals as the name of their team."

Nature, of course, abhors a vacuum. A November 24, 1924, account in the *Montreal Gazette* noted that crowds of spectators "crashed the gates to see the Montreal maroons work out." Maroons (with a capital "M") would serve the club well for the duration of their tenure.

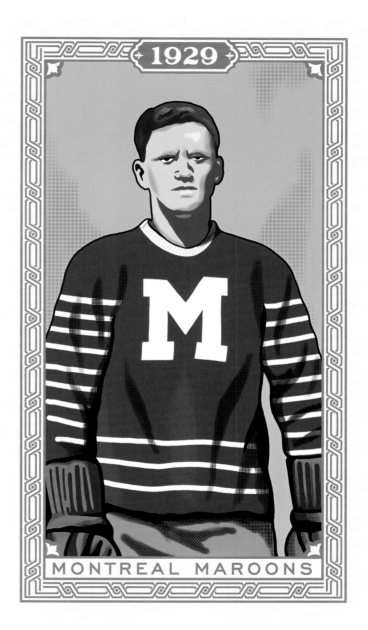

1929

MONTREAL MAROONS

THE 1924-25 MONTREALS SPORTED
THESE VERY PLAIN SWEATERS.

THE LOOK

The team's inaugural uniforms were no-nonsense affairs, stark and utilitarian. The November 21, 1924, edition of the *Gazette* reported, "...it was announced that the colours had been decided on as maroon and white. The jersey will have a maroon body, white arm bands, with a Montreal blazed across the front."

With a formal nickname firmly in place, the team rolled out a new look in 1925–26, just in time for their Stanley Cup victory. A large block "M," rendered in white, served as the crest for their maroon sweaters. White stripes rounded out the package. While the number of stripes fluctuated, the "M" remained as the core component of the team's visual package until they played their final game on March 17, 1938.

MONTRÉAL WANDERERS
1917-18

THE TEAM

The Montréal Wanderers were one of the four founding members of the National Hockey League, along with the Montréal Canadiens, Ottawa Senators, and Toronto Arenas. The Wanderers hosted the first of two official inaugural games on December 19, 1917. (Newspaper ads from that day indicate that the puck dropped in Montréal at 8:15 p.m., while the Canadiens at Ottawa game seems to have started 15 minutes later.) Ticket prices ranged from 50 cents to $1.55.

The Wanderers defeated Toronto that evening, 10–9. It turned out to be their only NHL victory.

The team began play as an amateur club in 1903, and won multiple Stanley Cups prior to the formation of the NHL. The 1906–07 Wanderers became the first team to engrave the names of their roster on the Cup, with twenty names etched inside the inner bowl.

Montréal was faced with a series of challenges in December 1917. Set against the backdrop of Canadian involvement in World War I, the team drew only 700 fans to their inaugural matchup with Toronto, and management had trouble attracting players, too. Owner Sam Lichtenhein threatened to withdraw from the league as his team lost three consecutive games following their opening night win.

Then, on January 2, 1918, the Montréal Arena—also known as the Westmount Arena—caught fire. The facility, which also played host to the Canadiens, burned to the ground. Newly homeless, the Wanderers ceased operations.

The Canadiens found a new home in Montréal, the Jubilee Rink. Hamilton, Ontario, offered to host the Wanderers, but Lichtenhein resisted, leaving the NHL with but three teams and dispatching the Wanderers off to hockey history.

THE NAME

The Wanderers nickname has been cited as a reference to the supposed fact that the team would wander across the entirety of Canada in their efforts to win the Stanley Cup. That angle is likely an apocryphal one.

When Montréal formed their team in 1903, "Wanderers" was already an established and popular moniker for British

VANCOUVER, B. C., WEDNESDAY, JANUARY 2, 1918.

FIRE DESTROYS MONTREAL RINK

Arena, Home of Professional Hockey, Burns in Early Morning — May Suspend N. H. L. Series.

MONTREAL, Jan. 2.—The Arena was destroyed by fire this morning, and in a short time the home of professional hockey in Montreal had been destroyed. Officials of the Wanderers Hockey Club announced that there will be no National Hockey League game tonight, and judging from unofficial talk of prominent professional league men, it would not be at all surprising if the fire results in the entire National League series being suspended indefinitely.

The Arena was the largest building of the kind in eastern Canada, and was of brick, built sixteen years ago. One side of the building was quickly destroyed by fire, and then the ammonia plant, used for making of artificial ice, exploded and blew down a fire wall. The fire started about 1:20 a.m., and in less than an hour the whole building had been destroyed. The fire leaped across the street and set six houses aflame.

The fire is reported to have commenced in the Wanderers dressing room.

soccer teams such as the Bolton Wanderers and the Wolverhampton Wanderers, whose names dated back to 1877 and 1879, respectively.

In those days, the name was adopted by teams without a permanent home stadium or arena.

THE LOOK

The Montréal Wanderers were noted for their white sweaters, which featured a bold band of scarlet across the midsection. A shield, outlined in white with a white block "W" set against that band, was also part of the look. Newspapers of the day frequently referred to the team as "Redbands" and "Redhoops."

The Montréal Wanderers wore a white sweater with red "hoops" as far back as 1904.

NASHVILLE PREDATORS
1998-PRESENT

THE TEAM

Nashville's efforts to actively target a National Hockey League team began in 1995. The city was planning a new downtown arena and the city—a decidedly untraditional hockey locale—offered up a $20 million relocation bonus to any team that would make the move to Tennessee.

In March 1995, team officials from the New Jersey Devils visited the Music City and discussed a possible shift. Later that year, the Florida Panthers and Winnipeg Jets also floated the idea of a potential move to Nashville. The following year brought forth rumors of a move by the Hartford Whalers.

Shifting strategy, Nashville city officials, in conjunction with Gaylord Entertainment, owners of the Grand Ole Opry—a Nashville country music institution—applied to the NHL for an expansion franchise. They traveled to New York and, on January 14, 1997, made a 45-minute presentation to the league. Although they were one of eleven groups to make a pitch, Nashville made a positive impression. The Tennessee capital was named as one of six finalists for an expansion franchise, and, on June 25, 1997, the NHL Board of Governors unanimously voted to award new teams to Nashville, Atlanta, St. Paul, and Columbus. Nashville's club was scheduled to begin play first, in 1998, followed by Atlanta the next season, with Minnesota and Columbus joining the circuit in 2000.

The new Nashville franchise was awarded to a group fronted by Wisconsin businessman Craig Leipold, who forked over a non-refundable $10 million deposit, which would later be followed by an additional $70 million.

The Nashville Predators made their NHL debut at home on October 10, 1998, where they lost to the Florida Panthers, 1–0, in front of a sellout crowd of 17,298. The team's inaugural season saw them finish with a record of 28–47–7, but they averaged more than 16,000 fans per home game.

The team traveled to Japan to open the 2000–01 regular season against the Pittsburgh Penguins. They qualified for their first playoff berth in 2002–03, losing a first-round matchup to the Detroit Red Wings. In 2005–06, the Predators won 49 games, including 32 at home. This was a team on the rise, and the following season, 2006–07, Nashville went 51–23–8 and finished with 110 points.

Despite the first real sniff of franchise success, attendance sagged, and rumors of a potential move began to circulate. An "Our Team Nashville" movement rallied support for the franchise and, late in 2007, new ownership pledged to keep the team in the Volunteer State.

In 2010–11 the Predators won their first playoff series in franchise history, topping the Anaheim Ducks. Another playoff series win, this time over Detroit, followed in 2011–12. Nashville went all the way to Game Seven of the Western Conference second round in 2015–16, before falling to the San Jose Sharks. The following season represented a franchise breakthrough, as the team advanced to their first-ever Stanley Cup Finals with series wins over Chicago, St. Louis, and Anaheim, before losing to Pittsburgh in six games. Nashville also hosted the NHL All-Star Game in January 2016, a banner year for the franchise, now in its nineteenth season.

THE NAME

Team officials surveyed Nashville area residents and sought the input of the NHL as they considered a nickname for the new club. Early speculation centered on a series of names that included Knights, Thunder, Explorers, and Phantoms.

Public conversation was influenced by bad feelings surrounding the NFL's Tennessee Oilers, who had recently relocated from Houston. One survey revealed that 83 percent of fans wanted them to change their name to something more location-specific, a situation that was later rectified when they were renamed the Tennessee Titans.

Majority owner Craig Leipold's wife, Helen, was an heir to consumer products giant SC Johnson. The name of one of their offerings was very nearly chosen to be the name of Nashville's NHL entry.

In his book, *Hockey Tonk: The Amazing Story of the Nashville Predators*, Leipold wrote, "My first choice was the Nashville Edge. I took Edge from the Edge shaving gel, one of my wife's most successful products at SC Johnson. We did some initial focus group testing, and Edge came back as a really strong name for a hockey team."

Commissioner Gary Bettman, however, had other ideas. "When he picked up that Helen's family owned Edge shaving gel, he called me and said in no uncertain terms, 'No, get rid of that idea.'"

On September 18, 1997, the *Nashville Tennessean* reported that the team had hired a marketing company to focus-test three finalists: Ice Tigers, Fury, and Attack. Three backup names were reported to be in the running: Copperheads, Hounds, and Stallions. Six days later, the same publication said that "Ice" had been dropped from the potential "Ice Tigers," and that a new name—Predators—had been added to the mix. Fury and Tigers apparently tested well, but there were trademark concerns.

When the team unveiled its visual identity on September 25, 1997, the nickname of the team was conspicuously absent. Team officials held an "Ice Breaker Bash" at the Nashville Arena two days later, and attendees were asked to vote on the name finalists.

The team was officially announced as "Predators" in front of a crowd of 1,500 at a November 13, 1997 event, held at Nashville's Wildhorse Saloon. The presentation in-

The Predators initially wore blue uniforms with metallic silver sleeves, as seen above during their inaugural 1998-99 season.

cluded a short video, which displayed the new name in conjunction with the previously released logo.

"This is probably the most researched name in team sports history," said majority owner Leipold. "We've gone one-on-one and probably talked to 20,000 people about this name," he added. "The fans told us they wanted a name with strength, speed, determination, and focus." Predators, he said, was the choice by a 2–1 margin.

THE LOOK

The still-to-be-named Predators' first visual identity was unveiled on September 25, 1997, at Nashville's First American Center. The mark featured the profile of a saber-toothed tiger, an animal that went extinct at least 12,000 years ago. The rare remains of a saber-toothed tiger were excavated during the construction of the downtown First American Center when it was being built, in August 1971.

The logo was created by Burlington, Vermont–based JDK Design, who worked in conjunction with Nashville agency Dye Van Mol & Lawrence. JDK was also responsible for the Buffalo Sabres' visual identity that was introduced the previous year. JDK designer Rich Curran, writing on his personal website, said:

From the start the project had rather interesting challenges, most notably bringing hockey to the deep south and conceptualizing a logo for a team named "The Edge" … through research I learned that the single largest sabre tooth tiger tooth was found during the excavation of the downtown Nashville First American building. That became the focus of my inspiration.

To bridge the two main challenges I pushed to create a mascot-based logo to give traditional team sports fans a connection point, and to use the tiger tooth as the expression of "The Edge." This direction was chosen and after much exploration and refinement we had an identity.

The Predators' logo consisted of five colors: navy blue, yellow-gold, metallic silver, orange, and "steel," a greenish blue. When it was introduced, the *Pittsburgh Post-Gazette* described the mark as "everything that a 1990s hockey logo should be, some mean-looking animal with really big teeth."

Nashville's first set of uniforms was unveiled at a February 12, 1998, event held at the CoolSprings Galleria shopping mall. The models included coach Barry Trotz and his assistant, Paul Gardner, as well as players from Nashville-area youth hockey teams. Predators team president Jack Diller said, "We took a prototype to a merchandising show in Atlanta and people from all over the country were there and gave us a very positive reaction."

Trotz, modeling the blue road sweater, said to the *Nashville Banner,* "You know, they say you dress for success. …I do like the dark colors and the silver. You get the dark shade with the light. It's like Chicago; they've had the same thing for like 100 years. For the next 100 years, when we're playing on the moon, it's still a classic jersey."

The team unleashed its first alternate sweater on November 21, 2001, a mustard-colored number featuring what the team called a new "animated" saber-toothed tiger logo. It was worn through the 2006–07 season.

Prior to the 2011–12 season, the Predators showed off a new, streamlined look. The team's color palette was simplified to blue, gold, and white. The logo and wordmark were refined and stripped of detail, and a new alternate mark was introduced, featuring three stars—borrowed from the Tennessee state flag—placed within a guitar pick. The emphasis was on the color gold—team CEO Jeff Cogen said, "It's about creating a dominant color, and blue is not a dominant color." This look accompanied the Predators as they embarked upon their first era of sustained success, the perfect "golden" hue for a new golden era.

NEW JERSEY DEVILS
1982-PRESENT

THE TEAM

The Devils' road to the Garden State was a circuitous one. They began life in 1974 as the Kansas City Scouts before moving on to Denver two years later—reborn as the Colorado Rockies—before finally landing in New Jersey.

The new Meadowlands Sports Complex, opened in 1976, was seen by many as a gold mine, wildly exceeding the loftiest expectations of the developers and promoters who were responsible for putting New Jersey on the pro sports map. Located only miles from midtown Manhattan, the development already served as host to the NFL's New York Giants, as well as the successful Meadowlands Racetrack. The NBA's New Jersey Nets settled in to the new $85 million Brendan Byrne Arena in October 1981, and, on May 27, 1982, the Rockies announced that they would be joining them.

The team was sold to a group headed by Houston Astros owner John McMullen, a New Jersey native and resident of Montclair, located approximately 10 miles from the Meadowlands.

The Rockies' shift to Jersey was a complex one; the total cost of the deal was more than $30 million. McMullen and company had to pay a reported $10 million transfer fee to the NHL, in addition to millions more to the Rangers, Islanders, and Flyers for infringing upon their territorial rights. Financial considerations were also paid to the Winnipeg Jets for moving from the Norris to the Smythe Division.

The team announced their new name—"Devils"—on June 30, 1982. Their regular-season debut took place at home against the Pittsburgh Penguins on October 5, ending in a 3–3 tie. The Devils' inaugural campaign saw them finish fifth in the six-team Patrick Division, but the franchise began to establish its presence in the New York metropolitan area, laying the groundwork for future success.

New Jersey finally broke through in 1987–88, making the playoffs for the first time since moving to the Garden State. They defeated the Islanders in the first round, four games to two, and followed that up with a seven-game upset of the Washington Capitals in the second round. Their Cinderella season finally came to a halt in the Wales Conference Finals, when they fell to the Boston Bruins in seven games, thus concluding the franchise's first winning season.

As the '80s gave way to the '90s, the team evolved into serious contenders, playing deep into the spring for five straight years; a run that culminated in a seven-game Conference Finals loss to the rival Rangers in 1993–94. Finally, in 1995, the Devils won it all, sweeping the heavily favored Detroit Red Wings in the Stanley Cup Final.

Two more Cup championships soon followed, in 2000 and 2003. Decades removed from their wandering origins, the Devils made one more move, in 2007, shifting their home ice some 10 miles southwest, to Newark's new downtown Prudential Center.

THE NAME

The agreement to bring NHL hockey to the Garden State included mandatory contractual language that "New Jersey" must be included in the team's official name.

A "Name That Team" contest, conducted by the New Jersey Sports and Exposition Authority, launched on June 7, 1982. Local newspapers were asked to poll their readers. Less than a week later the eleven most frequently suggested names were made public. Fans were asked to choose between Americans, Blades, Coastals, Colonials, Devils, Generals, Gulls, Jaguars, Meadowlanders, Meadowlarks, and Patriots. "I like Meadowlanders," said team owner McMullen, "but that's not too popular with the rest of my family."

More than 10,000 ballots were submitted, and "Devils" emerged as the runaway winner, with more than 2,400 votes. "Blades" finished a distant second.

The new moniker was officially announced at a June 30, 1982, press conference at the Brendan Byrne Arena.

"It's a great name because it combines the folklore of South Jersey with the Meadowlands," McMullen noted "Besides, Webster's Dictionary defines devil in a very interesting way: 'A person of notable energy, recklessness and dashing spirit.' I think that's an excellent way to de-

Washington's Sunday Star *tells the terrifying tale of New Jersey's "Horrific Leeds Devil" on the morning of January 24, 1909. Seventy-three years later this mysterious creature would become the inspiration for the state's first-ever NHL hockey team.*

scribe what we're going to have with this new franchise."

The folklore that McMullen alluded to involves the legend of the Jersey Devil—sometimes called the Leeds Devil—a kangaroo-like creature with the face of a horse that is alleged to have been haunting the Pine Barrens of South Jersey since the early eighteenth century.

The origins of the Jersey Devil legend are generally said to be centered on a Mrs. Leeds, who resided in the town of Estellville, located just west of Atlantic City. In 1735, faced with the unhappy news that she was expecting her thirteenth child, she is said to have exclaimed, "Let it be the Devil!" And, according to the legend, it was. The Jersey Devil was allegedly responsible for raiding farms, killing livestock, and terrorizing the locals. A January 1909 panic included the formation of armed posses, organized to hunt down and dispose of the creature. Local schools were closed. One newspaper account noted, "Attempts of farmers near Columbus to hunt down the creature failed today because hounds put on the tracks turned tail and headed home and could not be encouraged again to take the scent."

McMullen also said that he received letters and phone calls that objected to the chosen name because of negative religious connotations, but that local clergy were consulted before proceeding forward with the demonic nomenclature.

John J. Reinhardt Jr., an accountant at Middlesex General Hospital in New Brunswick and a resident of Old Bridge, New Jersey, was deemed to be the winner of the naming contest, which netted him two season tickets for the new team's inaugural home campaign.

Eight decades later, this powerful local mythology reso-nated mightily with the state's hockey fans as the name of their new NHL team.

THE LOOK

The Devils unveiled a logo at the same June 30, 1982, press conference during which they announced their new name. The trademark, described as a "preliminary version," was created by advertising agency Keyes, Martin & Co. of Springfield, New Jersey, who delivered the goods on 48 hours' notice.

The logo, which featured a white "N" and a red stylized "J" bedecked with horns and a tail, was originally enclosed in a green circle. (This was soon refined.) The letters were bulked up a bit and straightened out slightly, and were joined into a single red "NJ," outlined in green and surrounded by a white circle, also outlined in green.

On June 15, 1982, the *Journal-News* of White Plains, New York, reported, "There's a rumor that [John] McMullen likes the Boston Bruin colors." His wife, Jacqueline, who is credited by many with the green and red color scheme, apparently overruled him. In October 1982, the *Philadelphia Inquirer* noted, "The woman who designed the New Jersey Devils' Christmas-type uniforms … is the wife of owner John McMullen."

For some, this palette was a polarizing one. A month later, the *Bergen Record* reported, "[the] Devils' road uniforms have been reviled in every city in the league. The bright red and green would be more appropriate in a Saks Fifth Avenue Christmas display than on the ice." And, in a seemingly clairvoyant comment, the article went on to say, "Red and black would be much more chic."

The color red was a no-brainer, and green was chosen to

The Devils quickly won three Cups after switching to black in 1992.

represent both the Pine Barrens and the Garden State itself.

Much like the logo, the Devils' first set of uniforms was temporary. When the team played its first exhibition game on September 17, 1982, against the Washington Capitals in Hershey, Pennsylvania, they wore red practice uniforms with only a number and no names on the backs of the sweaters. Things were soon righted, however, and the team spent its first decade clad in traditionally grounded red and green livery.

On June 10, 1992, the Devils announced that they were ditching green for black. Regardless of the color shift, their primary logo remained intact, and the team continued to feature white sweaters at home and red on the road.

Team general manager Lou Lamoriello presided over an informal press luncheon at the Meadowlands Arena that day, and distributed color renderings of the new look as a team employee modeled the uniforms.

The tweak was designed to spur sales of licensed merchandise, as well as to provide a more aggressive look. The *Asbury Park Press* noted, "Traditionally, sales of Devils merchandise went up around the Christmas season ... but lagged the rest of the year."

This look accompanied the Devils as they evolved into a model organization that has hoisted multiple Stanley Cups, a winning set of uniforms for this once-Nomadic franchise.

NEW YORK AMERICANS
1925-1942

THE TEAM

Madison Square Garden played host to New York's first National Hockey League entry, the Americans, for seventeen mostly losing seasons (1925 to 1942). The Amerks were a distant second to their Garden co-tenants, the Rangers, in the hearts and minds of Big Apple hockey fans, but helped pave the way for the Blueshirts during an era when the NHL was just starting to make its presence felt in the United States.

On April 12, 1925, the NHL voted to expand to New York. The new team was born from the ashes of the Hamilton Tigers roster, a franchise that had finished the previous season with the league's best record. Hamilton's players went on strike at the conclusion of the regular season, refusing to participate in the Stanley Cup Playoffs without increased compensation. NHL president Frank Calder came down hard, fining and suspending the entire roster. As such, the fiscally challenged Hamilton franchise went under, and the Tigers' players were sold to the league's new Gotham entry for $75,000.

The Americans were operated by sports promoter Thomas Duggan and the notorious "Big Bill" Dwyer, who was later described by the *Cincinnati Enquirer* as running "what the government termed a $20,000,000 bootlegging operation."

NHL hockey made its New York debut on December 15, 1925, when the Americans lost to the Montréal Canadiens by a score of 3–1 in front of a huge crowd of 17,000. The team generated lots of local enthusiasm that first year, but finished out of the money.

The Great Depression and the end of Prohibition combined to make life difficult for Dwyer and the Americans. Rumors of a merger with the Ottawa Senators swirled in December 1933, but the discussed combination never came to fruition. The team's debts piled up, and the NHL took over the troubled franchise in October 1936. The league installed Mervyn "Red" Dutton at the helm, and the Amerks defeated the rival Rangers in the first round of the playoffs in 1937–38, a high-water moment for the perennially beleaguered Americans.

The team's last gasp came in 1941–42. Less than two weeks into the new season, Dutton announced that the team would henceforth be called the "Brooklyn" Americans, despite the fact that they would still call Manhattan's Madison Square Garden their home. The Amerks did, however, shift their practices to the Brooklyn Ice Palace, located at Atlantic and Bedford

Avenues. "We have definitely transferred our allegiance to Brooklyn," said Dutton, citing the desire for a fresh start.

The Japanese invaded Pearl Harbor a little more than three weeks later, vaulting America into World War II, and the team went on to finish the season at the bottom of the league standings.

On September 25, 1942, the league unanimously decided to suspend the Brooklyn franchise for one year, with the expectation that Dutton would try and secure financing for an arena in the borough after the war ended. The new facility never came to be.

In 1943, Dutton was called on to serve as acting president of the NHL after the sudden death of Frank Calder. The war dragged on, and Dutton carried the torch for his phantom franchise while steering the league.

Clarence Campbell was then named NHL president at a September 4, 1946, meeting and, with the war over, Dutton revived his efforts to reboot the Americans. The prospects for a new arena in Brooklyn were bleak, and the Rangers—eyeing the potential economic benefits of the postwar era—had no desire to share their building ever again. Several months earlier, Madison Square Garden executive and former Rangers boss Lester Patrick told the *Montreal Gazette*, "The Amerks franchise is owned by Madison Square Garden. Dutton has no financial interest in it and the Garden has found that two teams are unprofitable in Manhattan. If someone—Dutton or another group—had a rink in Brooklyn, the Americans might be revived. But I don't see any possibility of that."

Many years later, Dutton described the September 4, 1946, league meeting to legendary Canadian sportswriter Trent Frayne. As the discussion turned to reviving the Americans franchise, Dutton said, "I looked around the room and nobody was looking at me. I got the message. 'Gentlemen,' I said to the governors. 'You can stick your franchise up your ass.' I gathered my papers and left."

And, with that, the New York/Brooklyn Americans officially ceased to exist.

Legend has it that Dutton was so bitter about the Rangers' efforts to force the Americans out of business that he put a curse on them, allegedly saying, "the Rangers will never win the Cup again in my lifetime." Red Dutton passed away at the age of eighty-eight in 1987, with the Rangers forty-seven seasons removed from their last Stanley Cup Championship—and seven seasons before they finally lifted Lord Stanley's Cup again.

THE NAME

There is no "aha moment," no backstory, no formal announcement on why the Americans were so named. We can, however, speculate.

Team founder Thomas Duggan was a Montréal native who was connected with the group that built the Montréal Forum, the new home to the Canadiens. Perhaps "Americans" would serve as the perfect bookend to the already legendary Canadiens? Or, just maybe, Americans would be a fine moniker for the NHL's second US-based team, after Boston.

Whatever the case, newspapers referred to the team as the "New York Hockey Club" right through the summer and fall of 1925. The *Brooklyn Eagle* called them the "New York Giants" two weeks before they made their debut, and other publications called them the "Texans," in honor of Madison Square Garden honcho Tex Rickard, who would go on to

1932

NEW YORK
AMERICANS

NEW YORK AMERICANS

found the Rangers the following year.*

An interesting "what if?" involves the Americans' redesignation as the Brooklyn Americans in 1941. The team planned on becoming the Brooklyn Dodgers the following season, a campaign that never occurred. The Dodgers name was, of course, attached to the baseball club that still carries it in Los Angeles, and was also the name of a NFL team in 1941.

Red Dutton said, "When we've shown ourselves capable of playing the same kind of championship game as the base-

ball and football teams we'll more than likely adopt the name of Dodgers."

THE LOOK

The Americans' sweaters were among the most audacious in the history of the National Hockey League. The *New York Times*, covering the fledgling team at its Niagara Falls, Ontario, training camp, told readers, "These uniforms are going to please the eyes of New Yorkers. They are red, white, and blue and there are many stars and stripes here and there to give a pleasing and decided suggestion of Uncle Sam."

In the late 1920s, the Canadiens listed their colors as "red, white and blue," and the Toronto Maple Leafs designated theirs as "blue and white." The official colors of the New York Americans were "stars and stripes."

Tex Rickard, a savvy and legendary promoter, likely had something to do with the flashy outfits, recognizing the PR value that they'd bring to the new team.

The Americans began to distance themselves from their original look in the mid-'30s, adopting a shield-like crest that featured an interlocking red "NY" quite reminiscent of the New York Yankees' famed mark.

The Amerks went with a stark varsity-style "A" on their sweaters toward the end of their existence and, at the end, wore the borough name *Brooklyn* displayed diagonally in New York Rangers style, along with a sleeve emblem featuring interlocked American and Canadian flags. The franchise's final game took place on St. Patrick's Day, 1942, an 8–3 loss to the Bruins at the Boston Garden.

* That team was actually named for Rickard.

THE AMERICANS WORE A RANGE OF UNIFORMS
OVER THE COURSE OF THEIR 17 NHL SEASONS.

NEW YORK ISLANDERS
1972-PRESENT

THE TEAM

Long Island gained a National Hockey League franchise on November 9, 1971, when the league voted to add two expansion clubs. New York and Atlanta were awarded teams, which would begin play in 1972–73. This ballooned the circuit to sixteen entries, up from only six in 1966–67.

New York's second franchise was created to fill the Nassau County Veterans Coliseum, a sparkling new arena located in the affluent Long Island suburbs, just east of New York City. The rival World Hockey Association planned on placing their own team, the New York Raiders, there, but the NHL fast-tracked things, forcing the Raiders to move to Madison Square Garden.*

The New York Islanders' entry into the NHL cost some $10 million, $4 million of which went to the New York Rangers to help salve the wounds of having had their territorial rights infringed upon. The group that purchased the new team was fronted by forty-one-year-old Roy Boe, who also owned the American Basketball Association's New York Nets.

The Isles made their debut at home on October 7, 1972, a 3–2 loss to their expansion mates, the Atlanta Flames. The team's inaugural season was horrible, but the fans responded positively with an average attendance of nearly 12,000 per game.

While the initial results were disappointing, general manager Bill Torrey, the team's first hire, was already sowing the seeds for what would soon become one of the greatest dynasties in the history of the NHL.

The Islanders won four consecutive Stanley Cups between 1980 and 1983. They tore through the league, winning five straight conference championships and nineteen straight playoff series before giving way to the NHL's next great dynasty, the Edmonton Oilers.

The team remained a contender for the next several seasons before falling on hard times at the conclusion of the decade. The 1990s and early 2000s were an era of transition and great change for the club, who cycled through multiple ownership

---

* They failed miserably. That team was renamed the New York Golden Blades after a single season before being relocated twice, first to South Jersey and eventually to San Diego.

1979-80   1981-82
1980-81   1982-83

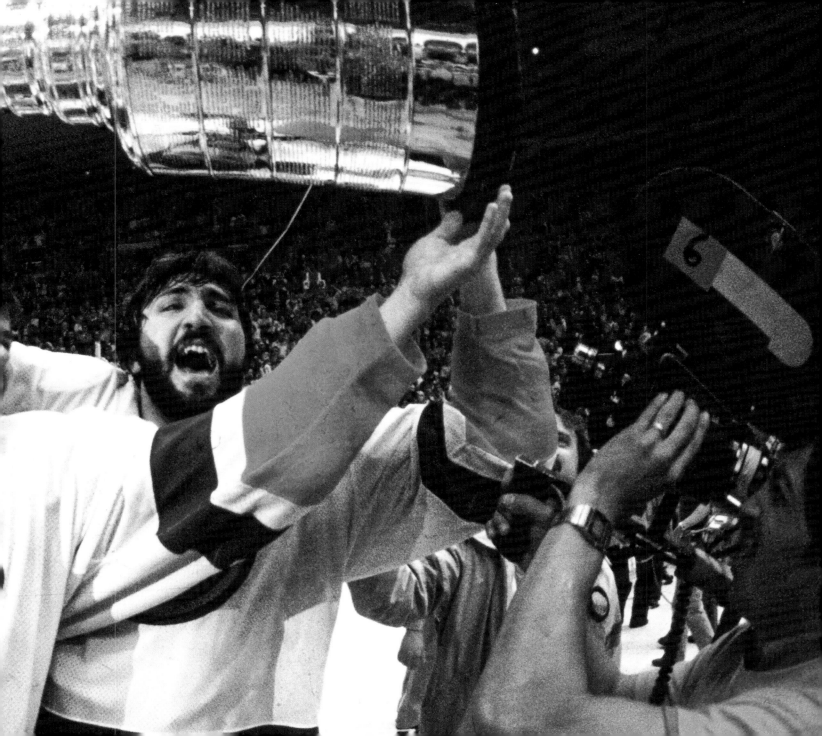

groups and management configurations.

A proposed overhaul of the aging Nassau Coliseum went nowhere. Attendance nosedived and, by the end of the 2000s, the Islanders were rumored to be bound for Kansas City. In October 2012, the team announced that it would be relocating to Brooklyn's new Barclays Center—an unpopular move with the Isles' suburban, automobile-centric fan base. Location aside, the facility was not built with hockey in mind. Obstructed-view seats, bad ice, and a very visible off-center scoreboard greeted the already unhappy fans. The Islanders hovered at or near the bottom in league attendance in Brooklyn, and it soon became apparent that the venue was not destined to be the club's long term home.

On December 20, 2017, the Isles disclosed plans to build a new $1 billion, 18,000-seat arena at Belmont Park—on the Nassau-Queens border—closer to their long-standing fan base. With that facility not set to open until 2021, the Islanders sought temporary refuge when they decided to play a portion of their home schedule on familiar ice—at the newly downsized, refurbished Nassau Coliseum; a return to the place where the franchise was born and where a mighty dynasty once held sway.

THE NAME

The New York Islanders first pronounced themselves "Islanders" at a February 15, 1972, press conference held at Burt Bacharach's Dover House in Westbury, Long Island, located near the team's new arena. Owner Roy Boe and his wife, Deon, chose the name, surprising many who were expecting the team to be called the "Long Island Ducks" after the successful minor league hockey club that was based in Commack, from 1959 to 1973.

Boe eschewed the idea of a formal Name the Team Contest, citing a compressed timeframe, but suggestions were plentiful.

A couple of weeks before the formal announcement Boe told the *Bergen Record*, "we've received at least 100 letters suggesting nicknames. Some are really something." Noting that he was looking for a name that reflected the team's Long Island home, people suggested monikers such as Ospreys, Expressways, and Polluters.

"I feel a name grows on you," he told the *Record*. "Like the Nets. When we first named the basketball team that after they had been the New Jersey Americans, frankly, I didn't like it. It didn't sound good to me then, but now it sounds good."

The "New York" designation was created with an appeal to a broad fan base in mind—after all, the Islanders had coughed up $4 million to be part of the Rangers' territory. Surely there were new fans waiting to be picked off.

THE LOOK

The Islanders unveiled their logo and color scheme at the same February 15, 1972, press conference where they revealed their name. Long Island adman John Alonga created their primary visual identity, a round logo that was centered around a stylized "NY," with the "Y" cleverly merged into a hockey stick. A map of Long Island, the team's new home, sat beneath, and the team's color palette embraced the official colors of Nassau County—orange and blue—a look that was rooted in the region's distant past, having been settled by the Dutch and their House of Orange-Nassau.

Owner Deon Boe reportedly wanted to drape the team in green and black. A successful clothing designer, she de-

Mercilessly mocked upon their introduction in 1995, the Isles' "Fish Sticks" uniforms have since gained a cult following.

signed the red, white, and blue New York Nets uniforms made famous by Long Island's own "Doctor J," basketball legend Julius Erving.

Alonga was quoted as saying that the job was a fast mover. "They had a press conference scheduled for a Monday and they told me the Thursday before," he noted. His cre-

ation saw the team through its first quarter-century, from modest beginnings to a great dynasty, and beyond. What happened next is the stuff of legend.

The Islanders embarked upon a total brand refresh, which was announced on June 22, 1995. Their primary logo, created by New York design firm Sean Michael Edwards

(SME), embraced a white-bearded fisherman, hockey stick in hand, ready to do battle.

Years removed from their Stanley Cup dynasty and facing the reality of being number three in the crowded New York NHL market behind the recent and future Cup champs, the Rangers and Devils, the Isles went all in. This was an era of change across the sports identity landscape, and the league took notice of the energy and dollars that were being generated by the likes of the San Jose Sharks and Mighty Ducks of Anaheim.

SME's new Islanders identity shed the traditional royal blue and orange in favor of a more aggressive combination of navy blue, orange, silver, and "Atlantic green," which was, in reality, teal, that staple hue of so many sports rebrands of the 1990s. The look was made complete by a bold, wavy striping pattern with skewed player names and numbers that evoked an underwater experience.

The logo was leaked to the media in advance of the formal unveiling, and reactions were less than kind. During a game at the Coliseum, one Islanders fan hung a banner which read, "fish sticks are for dinner, not our logo." Gary Miles, writing in the *Philadelphia Inquirer*, said, "Jeers to the Islanders for adopting a fisherman holding a hockey stick as their new logo. A fisherman? Now that will strike fear into the hearts of opponents. Maybe he'll hit 'em with his pole. Maybe he'll throw some chum at them. Even the old logo, the "NY" with the map of Long Island, was better than that. At least it didn't look like an ad for fish sticks."

David Haney, the NHL's director of creative services at the time, remembers the Isles' change as occurring "at the nexus of the sports licensing boom of the era." It was, he now says, "an effort to develop a more attractive look and improve licensed product sales." While the intentions were good, he says that the results were, in retrospect, "not supported by enough research."

The Isles maintained this polarizing look for but two seasons before new ownership decided to restore the team's comfortable, traditional logo. The wavy, aquatic sweater striping soon disappeared as well, replaced with straight stripes that bore a close resemblance to the uniforms of the club's glory years. Navy blue was discarded in favor of the team's original royal blue, thus completely obliterating any traces of the "fish sticks" era.

A small but meaningful tribute to the dynasty years was added in 2010–11 in the form of four orange stripes on the hockey stick within the primary logo, signifying the club's four straight Stanley Cup Championships. (The original logo featured a seeming random three taping stripes on the Y/stick.)

In March 1998, the Islanders donated some 1,500 items bearing the abandoned fisherman logo to the Gloucester, Massachusetts, chapter of the American Red Cross. T-shirts, replica jerseys, computer mouse pads, and the like—all featuring the grizzled seafarer—fittingly found their way home to the community where frozen fish stick conglomerate Gorton's—whose logo seemingly inspired the Isles—has been headquartered since 1849.

NEW YORK RANGERS
1926–PRESENT

THE TEAM

The Rangers were not New York's first National Hockey League team, nor were they the first to call Madison Square Garden home. That distinction goes to the New York Americans, who made their debut in 1925–26. The Americans were a box office sensation and, sensing opportunity, the Madison Square Garden Corporation—led by famed boxing promoter George Lewis "Tex" Rickard—quickly zeroed in on a second team for the Garden.

The NHL conditionally granted Rickard an expansion franchise at the league's semi-annual meeting on April 17, 1926. Formal approval was granted on September 25 of that year and, just like that, the New York Rangers were born.

Playing steps away from Broadway during the prime years of the Roaring Twenties, the new team was an immediate success. They attracted an enthusiastic celebrity following and, led by coach Lester Patrick, won the Stanley Cup in only their second season, 1928. They won a second Cup in 1933, but bumped along through the years of the Great Depression at a .500 clip.

The Rangers took home a third Stanley Cup championship in 1940, their last until they broke through again in epic fashion in 1994.

The team has played at two different Madison Square Gardens—the first, located on Eighth Avenue between 49th and 50th Street, and the second, which opened in 1968, between Seventh and Eighth Avenue from 31st to 33rd Street.

THE NAME

"Rangers" was firmly established as their sobriquet even before the NHL agreed to add them to the league's family of franchises. Named for Tex Rickard, the "Tex's Rangers" nickname was coined by George Daley, sports editor of the *New York Herald Tribune*. The team even conjured up an elaborate backstory, as outlined in a game program from their very first season:

"Tex" Rickard, original owner and inspiration for "Rangers" name.

They started in Texas—rounding up cattle rustlers and bad men whose trigger fingers were ever itching for the draw. A few of the gang migrated North, joined the Mounties and helped to clear the range of Louie Riel's mob and other troublesome bands of Indians. Regardless of which side of the border they patrolled or what uniform they wore, they were always the Rangers, steel-muscled and steady-nerved—hell-bent on the performance of their duty. Now come their descendants, on a more peaceful mission, to the Garden—they have swapped their horses for a set of steel blades, exchanged their rifles for hickory sticks, their quest being for hockey honors rather than unfortunate lawbreakers—but the same old fighting spirit remains and will be carried onto the ice with the
RANGERS.

The informal nickname "Blueshirts" was applied to the team right out of the chute, with *The New York Times* leading the charge as early as 1927. Alternately, "Broadway Blue Shirts" began to become popular with sportswriters in the late 1930s.

THE LOOK

The New York Rangers' core colors have been blue and red since their inception. The club's primary logo—a shield with a slashing diagonal panel, containing the team name—also dates to the very beginning of the franchise.

Original Ranger Frank Boucher, who later coached the 1940 Stanley Cup Championship team, wrote a memoir

The 1938 New York Rangers, wearing blue uniforms with diagonal lettering, a look which still feels very familiar more than eighty years later.

many years later in which he tells what is probably an apocryphal tale of an early, unused logo:

In fact, our first team crest was that of a horse sketched in blue carrying a cowboy waving a hockey stick aloft. The horse was rearing, with the word TEX'S in a crescent at the top of the emblem with RANGERS looped below. But Rickard didn't like the idea and before the season opened our insignia was changed to the present diagonal splash of the word RANGERS.

THE RANGERS WORE THESE UNUSUAL SWEATERS FOR ONE SEASON, 1946-47.

The team's first game took place on November 16, 1926, before of a crowd of 13,000 at Madison Square Garden, against the Montréal Maroons. The *Times* described the uniforms in that first matchup. "The color scheme was a dark blue, with red and white stripes."

The team's blue sweaters featured a diagonal representation of the word *Rangers*, a team staple throughout their history, with but a couple of exceptions.

Sans serif letterforms gave way to italicized serifs in 1941–42, and the now familiar drop shadow was added soon after.

In 1946–47, the Rangers became the first team to regularly televise their home games. In a move seemingly designed to coincide with this development, the team wore uniforms featuring an arched "Rangers" over player numbers. These lasted but a single season. In 1976–77, the franchise streamlined their look in a big way, placing their primary shield logo front and center for the first time in team history. Contemporary, bold striping and chunky sans serif uniform numbers rounded out the new look.

The design of the uniforms was credited to Edd Griles of the New York firm People & Properties. Griles, described as a "life-long Ranger fan," also worked as editor and creative director of *Goal* magazine and as executive producer of NHL Films.

New general manager John Ferguson instituted the change, saying that "we want to project a new image... those wider stripes make an athlete look taller." Indeed, the uniform striping was radically modernized, a total and clean break from a half-century of tradition.

Above: September 20, 1976: Phil Esposito and John Ferguson examine the Rangers' new uniforms. Below: Luc Robitaille, Mark Messier, and Adam Graves model new "Lady Liberty" third jerseys, January 10, 1997.

Ferguson was fired at the conclusion of the 1977–78 season. The shield jerseys were directly associated with him, and were widely disliked by the fans. Thus it came as no surprise when, in July 1978, new team GM Fred Shero announced that he was scrapping the look instituted by his predecessor. Aging superstar Rod Gilbert, effectively forced into retirement by Ferguson in late November 1977, was instrumental in convincing the team to return to the traditional look.

On July 18, 1978, the *Times* stated, "Gilbert contended that Ferguson's uniforms had the team crest on the chest, and that made it uncomfortable for the Rangers to move their arms."

Shero touted Rangers tradition at his introductory press conference, and no visual symbol was more associated with Rangers tradition than their traditional sweaters. Back they came, and have remained there ever since, albeit with slight tweaks and the addition of a third jersey in 1996, as well as a series of one-offs.

John Ferguson went on to run the Winnipeg Jets as they entered the NHL in 1979–80. He instituted uniform change there, too, nearly replicating the Rangers style that he implemented a few seasons earlier.

The Rangers' visual DNA runs deep and connects the original Broadway Blueshirts of the Roaring Twenties to the current day. Embraced by the team's loyal fan base, they are NHL Original Six classics that have stood the test of time.

OTTAWA SENATORS I
1917-1934
OTTAWA SENATORS II
1992-PRESENT

THE TEAM

They didn't belong to a league and they certainly weren't making any money, but that didn't stop a small group of Ottawa hockey players from getting together to form the Ottawa Hockey Club in 1883, the team that would eventually become the National Hockey League's original Ottawa Senators.

The amateur club spent their first twenty-four years bouncing around from league to league, appearing in tournaments, and occasionally challenging for the Stanley Cup—including playing in the first-ever Stanley Cup Finals, a 3–1 loss to Montréal on March 23, 1894. Ottawa would capture multiple Cups, from 1903 through 1906, a period during which the team was dubbed the "Silver Seven." The Sens turned pro along with the Eastern Canada Hockey Association in 1907, joined the National Hockey Association (NHA) in 1909, and along with the Montréal Canadiens and Montréal Wanderers split off from the NHA as founding members of the NHL in 1917.

Ottawa's first game in the newly formed NHL was on December 19, 1917, at home in front of 6,000 fans against the Montréal Canadiens. Things got off to a rocky start for the club, as a contract dispute between players and ownership delayed the game by 15 minutes and, even then, a few Sens players refused to suit up until the second period. The Habs took advantage of their short-staffed opponents, scoring three early goals in the opening frame, en route to a 7–4 win.

By the late 1920s, the Senators were playing in a league which was quickly expanding to major cities across the United States, though the town they called home had a population of just over 100,000. A ninth Cup win in 1927 wasn't enough to correct significant financial losses due to low attendance and increased travel costs to new expansion cities. The team was forced to play several "home" games in cities such as Detroit, Atlantic City, and Boston between 1927 and 1930. A bid by future Red Wings owner James Norris to purchase and move the club to Chicago in 1931 was vetoed by the Black Hawks, leaving the team with few options other than to suspend operations for an entire season. They made a formal announcement on September 26, 1931, hoping to save up enough cash to stay alive. Toronto was seen as a potential destination during the suspended season, but Leafs owner Conn Smythe asked for too much in return for sharing his newly built Maple Leaf Gardens.

Ottawa returned for the 1932–33 season and were greeted by crowds as low as 3,000 for some games. The original Senators played their final home game on March 15, 1934, against the New York Americans, where a crowd of 6,500 tossed an assortment of fruits and vegetables—such as lemons and parsnips—onto the ice throughout the game. Three weeks later, on April 6, 1934, the team announced they were relocating to Missouri for the following season, where they'd play just one season as the St. Louis Eagles in 1934–35 before suspending operations once again ... this time permanently.

For the next two decades, Senators owner T. P. Gorman kept the memory of the Senators in Ottawa alive by starting an all-new senior league team in a Québec league immediately following the NHL's exit from the city. The new "senior" Senators retained the name and uniforms and hung around until the end of the 1953–54 season, when the advent of television and the birth of CBC's *Hockey Night in*

Canada kept just enough fans away from the arena to end the team's second life.

Thirty-five years later, in 1989, real estate developer Bruce Firestone of Terrace Investments—along with Cyril Leeder and Randy Sexton—launched a bid which they called "Bring Back the Senators." A presentation was made by Firestone and his group to NHL president John A. Ziegler and future commissioner Gary Bettman at the Breakers Hotel in Palm Beach, Florida, on December 4, 1990. Other groups presenting that day represented the cities of Hamilton, Ontario; Houston, Milwaukee, Seattle, and two separate groups from the Tampa Bay area. Firestone and his team, which included an appearance by the Ottawa Fire Department Marching Band, spent 65 minutes selling Ottawa's passion for hockey, its history, and the promise of a brand-new arena to be built for the club in nearby Kanata, Ontario. Firestone's group won the bid, along with one of the two Tampa Bay bids, bringing NHL hockey back to Ottawa in time for the 1992–93 season.

Opening night back in Ottawa was on October 8, 1992, at the Ottawa Civic Centre, a junior hockey rink comically unsuited for the NHL. Much like Ottawa's previous debut in the NHL, game one was against the Canadiens. Owing entirely to the tiny arena, only 10,449 fans were on hand as Olympic silver medal–winning figure skater Brian Orser danced around the ice decorated with a series of columns hanging from the rafters, and local teenage pop star Alanis Morissette sang "O Canada." Despite the fact the two were completely independent and separate franchises, the new Senators also raised nine Stanley Cup banners commemorating those won by the original team some sixty to ninety

Ottawa Hockey Team. N. H. Ass'n. World Champions and Stanley Cup holders 1911.

The 1911 Stanley Cup Champion Ottawa Senators in their famous black, red, and white horizontally-striped "barber pole" uniforms.

NO 27

FRED LAKE OF OTTAWA CLUB

Ottawa flipped their horizontal stripes 90 degrees to appear vertically for just one single season in 1909.

years earlier. Frank Finnigan, the last surviving member of the original Senators and who had been very involved in the bid to bring the team back before his death ten months earlier, had his original number 8 retired. This time Ottawa came out on top, beating the Habs by a score of 5–3. The opening-night victory was the only highlight in an otherwise terrible season, as the Senators would go on to finish that year with a record of 10–70–4.

In their nearly thirty years back in the league, the Senators have since settled into their new home arena in Kanata, won a President's Trophy for finishing first overall during the regular season, and even made an appearance in the 2007 Stanley Cup Finals. Though they've made a few runs deep into the playoffs, they've yet to match the success of their great grandparents a century ago by taking a sip from the most sought-after mug in the world, Lord Stanley's Cup.

THE NAME

As life began for the young Senators, the team went through several different unofficial nicknames. When first established in 1883, they were simply the Ottawa Hockey Club. By the end of their first decade, they had begun using multiple names interchangeably, such as the Generals and Capitals.

For a spell in the early 1900s, the team had adopted the name Ottawa Silver Seven, and, after winning the 1903 Stanley Cup, players were given silver nuggets by the club as a way to get around rules preventing any compensation for the then-amateur team. According to Paul Kitchen's book, *Win, Tie or Wrangle,* former player Harry Westwick recalled in a 1957 interview that "one of the players said 'we ought to call ourselves the Silver Seven' and the name caught on right there," a reference to the seven players per side that took the ice at the time. The Silver Seven name lasted for three years until the team lost possession of the Stanley Cup in 1906.

While the first recorded use of the name "Senators" in relation to the team was in an *Ottawa Journal* article back in 1901, it wasn't until the 1912–13 season that the Senators name caught on for good. A *Globe & Mail* article on December 30, 1912, is the first time the pro club is referred to as such, the name used

OTTAWA CELEBRATED STANLEY CUP
VICTORIES WITH UNIFORM PATCHES
IN THREE DIFFERENT SEASONS.

in reference to the senators serving in the Canadian parliament who call Ottawa, the capital city of Canada, home.

After the original Senators moved to St. Louis in 1934, the name was used by a local senior league team from 1935 until 1954, and then by a tier-two junior league team in the 1980s. When Firestone announced he was launching a campaign to "Bring Back the Senators" at the Château Laurier Hotel on September 6, 1989, he couldn't imagine the team going by any other name . . . nor the legal headache he was about to encounter. While Firestone sat on stage preparing for his announcement, the junior team made their move. "As I was getting ready to give my first public speech on resuscitating the Senators in front of 350 guests, a process server handed me a lawsuit, claiming the name" Firestone remembered in his book *Don't Back Down.*

Joe Gorman, who inherited the rights to the name from his father and had given permission to Firestone to use it in June of that year, shared his thoughts with the *Ottawa Citizen*. "Anyone who claims the name is foolish. The name is in the public domain. Our family was the last to use the name when we were in the Québec league in 1951 until these guys [the junior team] asked me eight years ago for permission."

"If we have to fight we will, but I can't see why this can't be resolved. Why can't the two organizations coexist? The real value of the name doesn't relate to the junior team, the name goes back to the NHL and the Gorman family," said Dave Morrow, legal advisor to Firestone's group. "The name 'Ottawa Senators' has been used since the early part of this century up to the present day in connection with hockey. It is the *only* appropriate name for an NHL expansion team in Ottawa. Terrace Investments Limited is the owner of the name 'Ottawa Senators'"

Fortunately, things were quickly settled between the two, and the agreement gave Firestone ownership of the name for his NHL team while allowing the junior team to retain the right to continue using the name, slightly modified to the "Ottawa Junior Senators."

"The selection of 'Ottawa Senators' for the name of a new NHL franchise in Ottawa was one of the most important decisions for us to make about the team," the Sens explained in their 1990 presentation package to the NHL. "When naming a new baby, parents often attempt to perpetuate the qualities of a successful ancestor or famous personage. The situation with naming a team is similar: values and family connection matter. To hockey fans in Canada and the United States, the name 'Ottawa Senators' conjures up images of legendary hockey stars and history."

THE LOOK

Ottawa's use of black and red dates all the way back to their first organized hockey game, wearing black and red sweaters at the 1884 Montréal Winter Carnival Tournament. A temporary switch to blue and gold followed a year later. After a brief hiatus due to the lack of a decent arena, the team reorganized in 1889, partnering up with the Ottawa Amateur Athletic Association (OAAA) who provided them sweaters in their organization's colours of white with black stripes, with the OAAA's logo featuring a red triskelion (it's like a wheel with legs) placed on the sweater.

The team's famous "barber pole" sweaters, a series of alternating black, red, and white horizontal stripes—with no logo whatsoever—made their debut for the 1896–97 season.

Aside from wearing plain white tops with an "O" on the front in 1900 and 1901, the Senators kept this iconic look relatively unchanged until the end of their first run in the NHL in 1934. Some of the slight alterations over the years included a one-year switch to vertical stripes in 1909, an addition of a patch showing the crossed flags of Canada and the United Kingdom at the onset of the first World War in 1914, and the commemoration of their Stanley Cup victories by wearing "World's Champions" patches the season following their victories. A logo was finally added to the front of the sweater in 1929, when a large blank "O" was placed onto the barber pole stripes. This "O" would remain on their jerseys until the team left for St. Louis.

While the barber pole look is certainly synonymous with the Ottawa Senators still to this day, in the early twentieth century it was a far more common look throughout hockey. When the Senators were slated to face the Pacific League champion, and similarly barber pole–clad Seattle Metropolitans in the 1920 Stanley Cup Finals . . . well, there would be a problem. As was custom at the time, the opening game's home team was responsible for finding a new look to avoid a confusing uniform matchup. In a pinch, the Senators switched to a plain-white sweater with a red "O" on the chest, paired with new white socks with narrow black and red stripes. Ottawa wore this new look throughout the Cup Finals.

"Some of the spectators were confused in the early stages of the match and could not restrain themselves when the barber-poled visitors charged in on the Ottawa goal," the *Ottawa Citizen* noted on March 23, 1920, "but it did not take long to make them familiar with the different settings and toward the finish of the big struggle there were repeated roars of applause every time a white-jerseyed athlete secured possession of the puck."

Sixty years later, when Firestone announced his bid to revive the Senators name on September 6, 1989, he did so with a new logo and uniform on hand. "Ottawa" was laid out in black lettering with the two "T"s positioned to form the Peace Tower clock from Canada's Parliament buildings, complete with its clock face, green roof, and the Canadian flag flying above. A jersey was also presented to original Ottawa Senator Frank Finnigan, showing this logo on a white jersey with black and red shoulders and striping around the waist.

Designed by David O'Malley, the owner of a local company known as Aerographics, the Peace Tower logo was just one of dozens presented to the team. Many others, all of which in black and red, included various combinations of stylized "S"s, renderings of the Peace Tower, and maple leaves. According to reports, fans spent more than $1 million on T-shirts and other merchandise featuring this original logo before, to their surprise, an entirely new logo suddenly appeared two years later.

On May 17, 1991, seventeen months before playing their first game, Ottawa hockey fans woke up to find the profile of a Roman senator inside black and gold circles with red frills greeting them on the front page of that morning's *Ottawa Sun*. The new look (leaked to the paper) led to a negative fan response, with many feeling duped by the club, tricked into buying two sets of merchandise before the team even took the ice.

An anonymous NHL spokesman told the *Ottawa Citizen* that the league had actually rejected the Peace Tower logo as a full-time primary logo "because it was too local to Ottawa and didn't emphasize sports," later adding it was "too collo-

capital city would focus on a Roman theme for their logos and uniforms, rather than something more patriotic to Canada or even local to Ottawa. Senators CEO Randy Sexton tried to explain, speaking with the *Citizen*.

> *The Roman Senate was made up of generals, leaders and magistrates. Men of vision and courage, men who put themselves behind their communities. That is what we are looking for in our hockey players, men who put the team before themselves, men who put their community before themselves.*

The logo was designed by Senators graphic artist Tony Milchard who said he looked to the Chicago Blackhawks logo as a source of inspiration.

"The Blackhawks emblem projects an image of power and determination but it was a tough challenge matching something to 'Senators,'" he told the Canadian Press at the time. "We figured the senate does originate in Rome. We needed an image. Rome was known for its great armies. A Roman general was striking and colourful and quite aggressive. It was the perfect image for the team"

Slight changes were made to the logo in 1996, as the club replaced its English-only team name with a series of laurel leaves to help with their bilingual fan base. A new third jersey came with a redesigned logo in 1997, the roman warrior head now facing the viewer placed on a red jersey with a large black swoosh across the front. This would eventually replace the original black jersey as their full-time road uniform.

On August 22, 2007, the Senators moved away from

quial for a permanent hockey crest." Despite the rejection of the logo by the league, the Senators still sold merchandise featuring it, not once mentioning to purchasing fans that it was never meant to be anything more than a campaign logo to bring back the team.

The Senators made their first official look officially official at Ottawa's Congress Centre a week later, on May 23, 1991. With former NHLers Ted Bully, Peter Lee, Tim Higgins, and Fred and John Barrett on hand as models, the five ex-players took the stage to Gary Glitter's "Rock and Roll Part 2," wearing the new home white and road black uniforms. The new logo that had leaked earlier that week was on the chest and a new alternate logo featuring an "S" with a roman numeral for 1894, the year of the original Senators first game, was placed on each shoulder.

Many fans were confused as to why a team in Canada's

their original two-dimensional logo with an updated version of the third jersey mark unveiled a decade earlier. This new logo, designed by Ottawa's Acart Communications, was "redrawn with bolder, crisper, lines" with the eyes of the "Roman warrior now staring more sharply and directly at the viewer" new "chiselled, tough, and angular" facial features. The new uniforms accompanying this change also brought back a familiar old look to each shoulder, a black "O" with two large red and black stripes behind it, a nod to the original Senators uniforms from the 1930s. In over a century of hockey, the Senators have changed uniforms, logos, and leagues; they've suspended seasons, relocated, died, and were revived. But one thing has always remained: the black, red, and white.

PHILADELPHIA FLYERS
1967-PRESENT

THE TEAM

The financial disaster that was the 1931 Philadelphia Quakers was no need for concern when the National Hockey League awarded local banker Bill Putman an expansion team for Pennsylvania's largest city, on February 9, 1966. The City of Brotherly Love was one of six cities to get a new team that day, as the league immediately doubled in size with their first expansion since forty years earlier, in 1926.

Taking the ice at the Philadelphia Spectrum for their inaugural season in the NHL's brand new West Division—a division made up entirely of expansion clubs—the 1967–68 Flyers finished the season in first place, clinching the first-ever Clarence S. Campbell Bowl as a result. They couldn't ride that success into the playoffs, however, losing in seven games during the first round to the St. Louis Blues. Despite the early disappointment, the Flyers were still able to be the first of the new expansion teams to reach the ultimate summit, capturing the Stanley Cup with two consecutive championships, in 1974 and 1975.

In the many years since their twin champagne celebrations, the Flyers have managed to reach the Finals multiple times, coming awfully close before running into the Wayne Gretzky–led Edmonton Oilers juggernaut on two occasions in the 1980s, the Detroit Red Wings in 1997, and Chicago Blackhawks in 2010, but never again were they able to win the Cup.

THE NAME

With the promise of a new color television to whoever could come up with the winning choice, Putman announced a Name the Team Contest in the summer of 1966.

"We received 11,216 ballots," Putman announced, interrupted by the loud construction equipment building their new home arena, The Spectrum, across the street from the team-naming party on August 3, 1966. "They included 500 different names and the fans showed both enthusiasm and imagination."

Ice-Picks, Acmes, Philly-Billies, and Greenbacks were some of the more creative names submitted, with special prizes for creativity given out to the fans who came up with Croaking Crickets, and Scars and Stripes. The most common names were the Lib-

Bernie Parent with the Flyers' original orange uniform, the Stanley Cup patch was worn briefly in the fall of 1974.

erty Bells and Quakers, but Putman was not a fan of the latter name despite its place in Philadelphia's professional sports history, having also been used by the baseball's future Phillies for seven seasons the 1880s, in addition to the NHL team. "I was superstitious about Quakers," he revealed. "They in the NHL record book four times: fewest goals in one season, fewest wins, longest losing streak, and most shutouts against!"

With more than 100 ballots suggesting it, the club went with Philadelphia Flyers as their name. "We think it fits the action and speed of the game," Putnam explained at the time. Nine-year-old Alec Stockard was chosen as the winner of the contest. The Narberth, Pennsylvania, boy suggested the alternate spelling of "Fliers" on his ballot, but still took home that brand new color TV set.

THE LOOK

Before the logo was conceived, the team revealed their color scheme of orange and black at the team naming party by way of three models, described only as "leggy" in the newspaper accounts of the time. The women showed off the new colors with an orange sweatshirt paired with black mesh stockings. Yes, the color scheme happened to match those worn by the original Quakers, but this was only by coincidence; they were said to be chosen in tribute to the University of Texas Longhorns, Putnam's alma mater.

The task of designing the Philadelphia Flyers logo was given to Mel Richman, Inc., a Philadelphia-based advertising and graphics design firm who in turn entrusted the project to designer Sam Ciccone. "We wanted to come up with something with motion," Tom Paul, a sales manager at Mel Richman, Inc., said in Jay Greenberg's book *Full Spectrum*. "We

wanted it to refer to Philadelphia and the sport of hockey."

With those goals in mind, Ciccone added four wings to a stylized "P," so as to give it the impression of flight, adding a single orange dot inside the "P" to represent a hockey puck. While several options were presented to Flyers owner Ed Snider, it was clear to those around him that the "winged-P" design was his preferred design.

The uniforms were likewise designed by Ciccone, and included long, thin stripes down each arm, meant to give the look of wings on the players. "Like the logo, the concept of the uniform was speed and motion," Ciccone said in *Full Spectrum*. With a base color of orange, the Flyers uniforms featured white arms trimmed in black, the winged-P logo on the chest, and black pants. The width of the wings would expand and contract over the years, but the same basic design concept has remained throughout. Ciccone had also designed "Freddy Flyer," a cartoon character of a hockey player wearing a Quaker-style hat and a Flyers logo on his shirt. Freddy was used much like a mascot would be today, depicted in some of the club's early advertising and on children's merchandise.

For the 1981–82 season, the Flyers became the first NHL team to adopt the "Cooperalls" style of long pants worn in place of the traditional short pants and socks, extending from the player's waist right down to their skates. Flyers coach Pat Quinn explained the team's switch to the new style, which was very common throughout junior hockey at the time, "because the girdle provides better protection and it's lighter in weight." One season later, the Flyers were joined in wearing Cooperalls by the Hartford Whalers, but after much criticism from journalists who deemed them untraditional, the pants were banned from the NHL on June 22, 1983, the league citing a desire for "uniform uniforms" in their decision, forcing the Flyers to go back to the short pants in 1983–84.

As Meat Loaf once sang, "Two Out of Three Ain't Bad," and while the Freddy Flyer character didn't last long, Ciccone seems to have nailed it in his other two designs for the team. Quality design is quality design, and the fact that the Flyers have never once changed their logo and only moderately tweaked their uniform is a clear testament to just how great Ciccone's original designs were. Outliving the artist himself, the Flyers have now taken the ice with that same emblem, those same uniforms from the 1960s, for more than fifty years.

Alternate uniforms have added metallic colors to the Flyers' look over the years, silver (above) from 2002–2007 and gold (left) for their 50th season in 2016–17.

PHILADELPHIA QUAKERS
1930-31

THE TEAM

The Quakers represented the City of Brotherly Love for a single season, 1930–31. The team moved from Pittsburgh, where they previously played as the Pirates. Facing financial headwinds in the Steel City, the Pirates sought a temporary reprieve with a one-year transfer of the franchise to Philly, but the Quakers were an abject failure, winning but 4 of the 44 games they played before folding up the tent at the conclusion of the season.

The front man for the Quakers was former lightweight boxing champion Benny Leonard, described in the team's game program as "one of the most popular sports figures ever to come into Philadelphia, where he has probably more friends than any other athletic luminary in the world."

National Hockey League governors approved the move on October 18, 1930, and the team, dubbed "Quakers," made their regular-season debut at home on November 11, when they were beaten by the New York Rangers, 3–0. The Quakers home was the Arena, located at 45th and Market Streets in West Philadelphia. Five thousand fans—their largest home crowd of the season—witnessed the team's debut. Newspaper ads for the game promised "free skating after the game until midnight," and tickets were priced from 75 cents to $2.50.

The Quakers' financial situation was as bad as their on-ice product, and the franchise—along with the Ottawa Senators—was suspended for the 1931–32 season. Pittsburgh interests continued to promote the idea of a new arena and a restored team, but after several years of fits and starts the franchise was formally terminated by the NHL on May 7, 1936.

THE NAME

The team announced their new name at an NHL board meeting in Toronto on October 18, 1930. Before they were an NHL team, the Quakers were a religious order, one of whose members, William Penn, founded the city of Philadelphia in 1682. Various Philadelphia sports teams adopted the Quakers nickname, starting in the 1880s and 1890s. The University of Pennsylvania's teams are still called "Quakers," and the MLB team now known as the Philadelphia Phillies was informally referred to a "Quakers" in the late nineteenth century.

THE LOOK

The Quakers were Philadelphia's orange and black NHL team decades before the Flyers came into existence. For their lone campaign, the Quakers wore flashy orange sweaters with a series of thin horizontal black stripes cascading down each arm. The name "Quakers" was rendered diagonally in black script across the front of the jersey.

An orange and black game-worn Philadelphia Quakers sweater.

THE TEAM

Pittsburgh's hockey roots date back to the late nineteenth century. In the early 1920s, the city hosted the amateur champion Yellow Jackets—the core of which took the ice in 1925 as the National Hockey League's first Steel City entry, the Pirates. This team skated for five seasons before moving eastward in 1930, across the state to Philadelphia, victims of the Great Depression.

Pittsburgh was then home to several popular minor league franchises over the following decades, including the American Hockey League's (AHL) Hornets. When rumblings of a future NHL expansion began brewing in earnest in the early 1960s, Pittsburgh was considered to be prime real estate. In early 1963, Toronto Maple Leafs president Stafford Smythe cited Pittsburgh as the the leading candidate for a potential franchise.

On February 9, 1966, the NHL announced a plan to double the circuit to a dozen total teams. Pittsburgh, along with Los Angeles, Minneapolis-St. Paul, St. Louis, Philadelphia, and San Francisco, was conditionally awarded a franchise.

Pennsylvania state senator Jack McGregor and his law school classmate, attorney Peter Block, headed up Pittsburgh's new ownership. They assembled a syndicate of twenty-one investors who put up a total of $2 million for the entry. The new team would play in Pittsburgh's Civic Arena, a retractable roof facility that opened in 1961.

McGregor relayed the genesis of the Penguins franchise in comments made to the *Pittsburgh Tribune-Review* upon Block's death in 2015. "We were in a car together driving to Harrisburg, and he started complaining to me that Pittsburgh was not as good a sports town as it was cracked up to be. I said, 'What do you mean?'" Block, a hockey fan, knew that the NHL was pursuing a major expansion, and opined that Pittsburgh needed a big-league hockey team in order to truly be considered a top tier sports town. Their vision was rewarded on October 11, 1967, when the Penguins played the first home game in franchise history, a 2–1 loss to the Montréal Canadiens.

The Penguins scuffled through their early years. Their first playoff berth was realized in their third season, 1969–70, but their first real postseason success came in 1974–75. That season, they beat the St. Louis Blues in the first round before blowing a 3–0 series lead and losing in the quarterfinals to the New York Islanders. More seriously, less than two months later, the team found their offices padlocked by the Internal Revenue Service. Ownership was $6.5 million in debt and forced to declare bankruptcy. "What we need around here is an Arab with $5 million who played hockey at Yale," declared Charles W. Strong, director of the Civic Arena. The Pens appeared to be headed for contraction or relocation to Seattle, but a new ownership group purchased the franchise for $3.8 million and was able to keep the team in Pittsburgh.

The Penguins selected Mario Lemieux with the first pick in the 1984 draft, a franchise-turning event that resulted in 12 playoff appearances in 13 seasons, including back-to-back Stanley Cup victories in 1991 and 1992.

The team continued to be a contender for the balance of the decade, but renewed financial troubles forced the franchise to file for bankruptcy—yet again—in November 1998. The recently retired Lemieux was a major creditor, having deferred millions of dollars in salary over the years. He converted those funds into equity and assumed control of the team the following year, thus saving the franchise for a second time. A rebuilding period ensued, but the Penguins, led by homegrown stars Sidney Crosby and Evgeni Malkin, won the Stanley Cup in 2009 and moved into the new Consol Energy Center in October 2010. They again won back-to-back Cups in 2016 and 2017 to close out the franchise's first half-century.

THE NAME

Local sentiment was strong for the new NHL team to be designated "Hornets," just like the AHL team that it was supplanting, but team co-founder Peter Block was said to be adamant in his opposition to using the moniker. In *Pitts-*

PENGUINS GM JACK RILEY HATED THE TEAM NICKNAME SO MUCH THAT HE BANNED IT FROM THE CLUB'S FIRST SET OF UNIFORMS.

burgh Penguins: The Official History of the First 30 Years, Block was quoted as saying, "The Hornets were a minor league team. I knew we were going to get some bad players (in the expansion draft), and I didn't want to be called just another minor league team." Besides which, the Hornets' name was property of the Detroit Red Wings, owners of a minor league club of the same name.

General manager Jack Riley and coach Red Sullivan, both proud sons of the Emerald Isle, suggested "Shamrocks."

Senator McGregor's wife, Carol, chimed in with the alliterative "Pittsburgh Penguins." She envisioned the team in black and white uniforms, skating at "The Igloo," which was the nickname of the team's future home, the Pittsburgh Civic

Arena. Her proposed name won the day, but consensus and publicity were both required.

The *Pittsburgh Post-Gazette*, in conjunction with the Hockey Club of Pittsburgh and Mellon National Bank, launched a Name the Team Contest on January 23, 1967. The winner was to receive a 25-inch color television set and two season tickets to the new entry's inaugural campaign.

A committee consisting of Block, his co-founder McGregor, and board member Dick George were tasked with selecting the winner, even though the fix was seemingly in. When the dust settled, more than 26,400 entries had been submitted, with 356 different names suggested, ranging from Aardvarks to Zeniths. Pussycats, Crickets, Pioneers, Pipers, and Golden Triangles were among the names that fell short.

On February 9, 1967, team officials announced that the franchise would be called "Penguins." A total of 716 individuals suggested the name, and the contest winner was later declared to be Emily Roberts of Belle Vernon, Pennsylvania.

"It seemed natural," Block said. "The penguin lives on ice; hockey players make their living on ice." Logic, nepotism, and alliteration emerged victorious, and Penguins soon hatched in Western Pennsylvania.

THE LOOK

The Penguins' first logo was designed by Bob Gessner, a Pittsburgh sports artist whose other creations include the University of Pittsburgh's script "Pitt" logo and the Pittsburgh Pirates' smiling character that launched in 1967. In 1961, Gessner created a new logo for the Pittsburgh Hornets.

Gessner was said to have received $1,500 for his new Penguins mark, which featured a portly, scarf-wearing, skating penguin, hockey stick in gloves, backed up by a triangle, symbolic of Pittsburgh's downtown Golden Triangle. The whole thing was contained in a circle, along with the city and team names.

In 2010, Gessner told the *Pittsburgh Tribune-Review*, "What I can't say is why I put a scarf on the Penguin originally. The owners were just concerned with getting a logo that included a Penguin. Right away I thought that scarf made him look like an ice skater rather than a hockey player. They asked me for something else, something more aggressive, and I went along with it because I agreed."

GM Jack Riley, no fan of the Penguins name, was assigned the task of picking the team's colors—he chose Columbia blue, navy blue, and white. Riley, a Toronto native, was supposedly inspired by the colors of the Toronto St. Michael's Majors, a fabled junior club. The inaugural set of uniforms reflected his disdain for the team name, with just the city name "Pittsburgh" rendered diagonally in a fashion similar to the New York Rangers' sweaters, both at home and on the road.

The second season brought forth a new set of uniforms, the first to feature the skating penguin logo, whose trailing scarf had now been removed.

In January 1980, the club announced that they were changing the team colors to black and gold, the official colors of the city of Pittsburgh as well as the NFL champion Steelers and MLB champion Pirates. United in black and gold, the Penguins would take their place alongside their Steel City sports brethren in a display of civic pride and solidarity. The Boston Bruins, however, had strenuous objections.

The Bruins filed a formal complaint to the NHL, citing their long-standing use of the colors. On January 26, 1980, Penguins

team vice president Paul Martha told the *Pittsburgh Press*:

> Boston officials have expressed their position in this matter. They claim they have been wearing black and gold uniforms since their inception in the NHL in the 1920s. But I have documented proof that the old Pittsburgh Pirates ... wore black and gold uniforms and at that same time Boston was wearing brown and yellow, before they changed.

Two weeks earlier, Martha told the same publication:

> The change to black and gold uniforms is certainly in our plans. Exactly when is yet to be determined. It will be this year. The philosophy is that black and gold has become Pittsburgh ... We figure we owe it to our fans to change to the black and gold. They have asked for the change in an overwhelming way and we wish to make that change as soon as possible.

NHL commissioner John Ziegler denied Boston's protest, and the Penguins made their debut in black and gold on January 30, 1980, at home against the St. Louis Blues. Ironically, the

Luc Robitaille enjoys a penguin's favorite treat, courtesy of teammate Jaromir Jagr in 1995.

Pens ordered the uniforms from the Boston Bruins' pro shop.

On June 11, 1992, less than two weeks after the team's second straight Cup victory, the Penguins officially unveiled the first major logo change in franchise history. The new identity, created by Pittsburgh-based Vance Wright Adams and Associates Inc., showcased a contemporary, stylized penguin silhouette, rising out of the familiar triangle. "We've spent a long time thinking about this change," said majority owner Howard Baldwin, "and in the long run we feel that it is best for the club."

A short video, released soon after the new look made its debut, discussed the design process and pointed out the fact that the team reviewed 20 to 25 different uniform designs. While the original plan was to wear four different uniforms—two each at home and on the road—the Pens ended up with a conventional home/road combination that included a road look featuring a diagonal "Pittsburgh," reminiscent of their original 1967 togs.

As the millennium came to a close, the Penguins again shook up their look. They brought back the old skating bird on a third jersey in 1999, replacing the long-standing yellow gold color with a more subdued and trendier "Vegas Gold." Three short years later, in 2002, the team announced that it would be restoring the old logo as their official symbol, effectively replacing its replacement, which was long derided by many fans as too slick and corporate-looking.

Things came completely full circle in 2014, when the team unveiled their "Pittsburgh Gold" third jerseys, which bore a close resemblance to what the Pens wore while winning Stanley Cups in 1991 and 1992. Vegas Gold was shown the door in favor of the old yellow gold hue in 2016–17, the club's 50th season, a change that coincided with yet another Cup victory—the fifth in franchise history.

PITTSBURGH PIRATES
1925-1930

THE TEAM

On November 7, 1925, National Hockey League moguls voted to award an expansion franchise to Pittsburgh, a city with an established and thriving hockey tradition. The core of the new team was composed of players from the Pittsburgh Yellow Jackets, champions of the United States Amateur Hockey Association.

The team's first game took place in Boston on Thanksgiving Night, November 26, a 2–1 victory over the Bruins. They opened up their home schedule on December 2, at Pittsburgh's Duquesne Garden, with an overtime loss to the New York Americans, also by a 2–1 count.

The Pirates enjoyed a successful maiden campaign, advancing to the league semifinals where they lost to the Montréal Maroons, the eventual Stanley Cup Champions. The team stumbled in year two, and poor attendance began to take its toll on the franchise. Rumors of relocation to Cleveland, Philadelphia, or New Haven swirled throughout the opening months of 1928. The Pirates were then sold to a group led by famed boxing champion Benny Leonard, but the team continued to struggle both at the gate and on the ice. October 1929's epic stock market crash and the beginning of the Great Depression only added to the Pirates' woes.

Lack of a suitable arena and heavy financial losses sent the Pirates packing at the conclusion of the 1929–30 season, across the Commonwealth of Pennsylvania, to Philadelphia. The move was intended to be for but a single season with the hopes that a better facility could be built in Pittsburgh, but the team never returned. The league officially terminated the franchise on May 7, 1936.

The epic expansion of 1967 restored NHL hockey to the Steel City in the form of the Pittsburgh Penguins.

THE NAME

Pittsburgh's new team adopted the name of baseball's Pittsburgh Pirates, a move that doubtlessly sought to capitalize on the success of the hardball Bucs, who had won the World Series only a month prior to the new hockey team's debut.

Conjecture holds that the hockey team's ownership worked out a financial arrangement with their baseball counter-

A Pirates jacket patch from 1928 shows their Harding blue and gold color scheme.

parts to employ the name. Newspapers variously referred to the new NHL entry as "Yellow Jackets" as the inaugural season neared, but when the team took the ice for their first game on November 26, their sweaters read "Pirates."

THE LOOK

The Pirates originally utilized the Yellow Jackets' old color scheme of black and gold, which were also the official colors of the city of Pittsburgh. In fact, the NHL Pirates wore the black and gold years before football's Steelers or baseball's Pirates ever did.

The new team's first uniforms were gold, with two black horizontal stripes across the gut, topped by black script letterforms that spelled out "Pirates," with an upward-tilting block letter "P" beneath. The coat of arms of the city of Pittsburgh, based on that of William Pitt the Elder, was showcased on each sleeve.

The *Boston Globe*, reporting on the team's first game, dryly said, "[t]he two teams appeared in uniforms, the predominating color being yellow. Before the start for some reason or other the band played only 'God Save the King.'"

The troubled franchise was sold in October 1928, and the papers reported that a change in style would help usher in the new era. "Heretofore the skaters wore Pa Pitt's colors—black and gold," reported the *Pittsburgh Post-Gazette*, "but another color scheme, to be selected later, will be noted when the players skate onto the ice for their season's opener November 15."

On October 28, 1928, the *Pittsburgh Press* noted, "the old yellow and black colors have been abandoned and they have given way to brighter hues. The new colors will be Harding blue and light gold. The shoulders of the jerseys will be gold in the body of Harding blue with golden stripes. The stockings will be the same color combination."*

The November 11, 1928, edition of the *Press* provided additional, granular detail. "When the skaters make their initial appearance on the ice Thursday at 8:30, the fans will see the flashiest uniforms in the league. Blue and gold striped, with solid gold shoulders—with 1-inch blue and gold strips across the jerseys and 'Pirates' inscribed across the front."

The Pirates took the ice for their swan song season of 1929–30, clad in new colors yet again—this time orange and black. They wore orange sweaters with a bold diagonal black striping pattern across the front, accompanied by a crest featuring the head of a Pirate, flanked top and bottom by the city and nickname of the team. This attention-getting ensemble provided lots of visual sizzle, but the team won but five of their 44 games and then departed for Philadelphia, never to return.

---

* Harding blue presumably referred to the favorite color of former First Lady Florence Harding.

QUÉBEC ATHLETICS
1919-20

THE TEAM

Québec's first National Hockey League entry played for but one season, 1919–20. Québec was one of the NHL's four charter members, along with the Montréal Canadiens, Montréal Wanderers, and Ottawa Senators. That Québec team, the Bulldogs, traced their roots back to 1878, when they began play as an amateur outfit. They later joined the pro ranks and won back-to-back Stanley Cup Championships in 1912 and 1913.

The financially challenged Bulldogs could not field a team in the newly formed NHL, and their players were dispersed to the remaining clubs, the three of which were supplemented by the Toronto Hockey Club, added as a temporary replacement for Québec.

Operating under a new charter, the Québec franchise—officially the Quebec Athletic Club—reclaimed many of their old players and finally made their NHL debut at home, on December 25, 1919, losing to the Canadiens by a score of 12–5.

The team played 24 games in their lone NHL season, winning only four. They were led by hockey's first superstar, Joe Malone, who led the league with 39 goals, including a seven-goal game against Toronto on January 31, 1920.

The team's final game in the "Ancient Capital" took place on March 10, 1920, with a 10–4 win over the Ottawa Senators, played on what was described as a "slushy sheet of ice."

The Québec franchise was sold to the Abso-Pure Ice Company and relocated to Hamilton, Ontario, the following season, where they were reborn as the Hamilton Tigers.

THE NAME

The official team name was "Quebec Athletic Club," which was designated as such at the league's annual meeting on December 6, 1919.

The old Bulldogs nickname specifically referred to the Quebec Hockey Club, the established entry that released their claim to an NHL franchise after having failed to operate a team following the formation of the new league. Despite this, many newspapers referred to the new NHL team as "Bulldogs." Others called the team the "Athletics," which made sense considering the official designation.

THE LOOK

The Athletics were garbed in blue and white, the same colours sported by their illustrious Bulldog predecessors. Their sweaters featured broad stripes of blue and white with no lettering or graphics at all—a bold, minimal look.

Notably, on December 27, 1919, Québec players "wore crepe bands" on their arms in tribute to Joe Hall, a former Bulldogs legend who was playing for the Montréal Canadiens in the Stanley Cup Finals when he passed away the previous spring, a victim of the global flu pandemic.* This memorial tribute was one of the first, if not *the* first, in NHL history.

---

* Crepe, a lightweight silk fabric, was the material of choice for bereavement at this time.

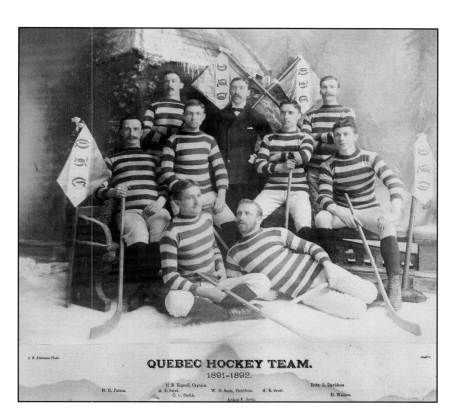

The amateur 1891-92 Quebec "Bulldogs" wore blue and white striped sweaters.

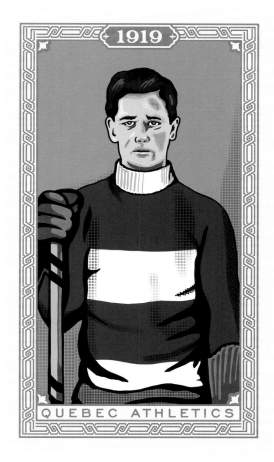

QUÉBEC NORDIQUES
1979-1995

THE TEAM

Long before Les Nordiques were even a thought, *La Vieille Capitale* was home to the National Hockey League. The Québec Athletics played just a single season in the NHL back in 1919–20, before they were sold off and moved to Hamilton. Before the Athletics, there were the Bulldogs, who bounced around various early leagues in the 1900s and 1910s—even clinching back-to-back Stanley Cup championships in 1912 and 1913. Québec City was then home to the American Hockey League's (AHL) Aces for nearly fifty years before the Flyers-owned farm club was relocated to Virginia in 1971. Having been home to two different teams for nearly seventy years, it was clear the city was no stranger to professional hockey.

In 1971, a new major professional hockey league was formed—the World Hockey Association (WHA)—created to compete directly with the NHL. League president Gary Davidson was awarded one of the twelve original franchises to play out of San Francisco, but when he was unable to secure sufficient funding, he began to look for an out before the club played a single game. On February 11, 1972, a group of Québec business owners bought the San Francisco franchise for $215,000, and immediately relocated it to Québec City.

"The [AHL] Aces were run by Philadelphia men, we never had Québec ownership of our teams before," said Jean-Marc Bruneau, one of the team's several owners in response to concerns about Québec City having just lost a team a year earlier. "We never had enough French players and the good ones we had were soon gone to the NHL. Our fans lost loyalty to the team." Ensuring that local loyalty wouldn't be a problem with the new team, French-Canadian hockey hero Maurice "Rocket" Richard was hired to be the team's first head coach.

Québec lost their first game in the WHA, a 2–0 defeat on the road at the hands of the Cleveland Crusaders, on October 11, 1972. Two days later, the Nordiques played their home opener against the Alberta Oilers, with fans receiving miniature hockey skate pins featuring the Nordiques logo, as well as a 45 RPM record of the team's theme song "Les Nordiques" ("C'est notre équipe à nous"). Local songstress Ginette Reno performed the Canadian national anthem for the 10,441 fans before the game, after which the Nordiques thrilled the home crowd by shutting out the Oilers, 6–0. Richard noticeably struggled in his

new role as bench boss, at one point forgetting his team was on a power play and sending out the wrong line. Just three days later, the Nordiques announced Richard would be taking time off to recover from "nervous strain," saying he was depressed, very quiet of late, and had lost weight. On October 18, 1972, the "Rocket" resigned from his role after just two games behind the bench. The strain of coaching was just too much for the famously fiery player.

After seven seasons, it was clear the Nordiques were a success in a failing league. After months of back-and-forths, it was announced on March 30, 1979, that the Nords would move to the NHL along with the Edmonton Oilers, New England (Hartford) Whalers, and Winnipeg Jets for the 1979–80 season. A dispersal draft was held to transfer players who still had their rights owned by NHL teams, which was certainly a blow to the Nordiques roster. An expansion draft was then held to fill the remainder of the rosters.

NHL hockey returned to Québec City for the first time in fifty-nine years on October 10, 1979, when a sellout crowd packed the Colisée to watch the Nordiques battle the Atlanta Flames. Fans were greeted by two marching bands stationed outside the arena and a Bavarian band set up inside the arena's main lobby. NHL president John Ziegler was on hand to drop the puck for the ceremonial face-off, and the Royal 22nd Regiment played both national anthems. Québec's Réal Cloutier scored a hat trick for the home side, with all three goals coming in the third period. That was all the scoring the team could muster, though, as the Flames won, 5–3.

The Nordiques were plagued by historically terrible seasons in the latter part of the 1980s and early 1990s, resulting in a series of first overall draft picks. In 1991, top pick Eric Lindros announced he would refuse to join the team if drafted; the Nordiques picked him anyway and Lindros made good on his promise, holding out for an entire year before being traded to Philadelphia. Québec started to show improvement in the standings but could never make a run for it in the playoffs. The team finished first overall in the Eastern Conference in 1995, but were trounced by the eighth-seeded New York Rangers in six games during the first round. Those would end up being the final games for the Québec Nordiques.

In February 1995, during negotiations to acquire $125 million in funding from the province for a new arena and aid their financial woes, Nordiques president and part-owner Marcel Aubut was approached by Comsat Video Enterprises, owners of the NBA's Denver Nuggets, about purchasing and relocating the team to Denver. Québec premier Jacques Parizeau rejected the team's request for the arena money in May, instead offering to buy-out Aubut's shares for $12.9 million and providing $15.5 million in debt relief over three years. The team refused the offer, and a public relations battle ensued with the province saying they could do no more to help the team, having just announced the closure of nine hospitals due to cuts to its health budget. The public sided with the government, and a save the team protest organized at the Québec parliament building attracted just 300 fans.

With the prospect of more than $22 million in projected losses over two years awaiting the Nordiques, the team felt they had no other option. On May 25, 1995, the team announced the sale of the franchise for $75 million to Comsat, who would move the team to Denver for the 1995–96 season. The league's Board of Governors unanimously approved the relocation request, making it official on June 21, 1995. Just to rub a little extra salt in the wound, the team—now playing as the Colorado Avalanche—would win the Stanley Cup during their first season in Denver.

THE NAME

Broadcaster and former Montréal Canadiens player Gilles Tremblay unveiled the results of the Name the Team Contest at the Au Vatel restaurant in Québec's Charlesbourg neighbourhood on March 29, 1972. An eleven-member panel had narrowed down the 475 different names sent in from more than 1,400 entries to Les Nordiques ("The Nordics"). The runner-up name was Laurentians, a reference to a nearby mountain range. Sixteen people had submitted the name Nordiques, and Québec City's Michel Lebrun was chosen as the winner, receiving a pair of 1972–73 season tickets, as well as a trip to watch the team's inaugural game. "After consultation with two advertising experts it was determined that 'Les Nordiques' was an excellent choice," the team said to the L'Action Québec newspaper at the time.

It applies well to the Québec franchise since "La Vieille Capitale" is one of the most northern cities among all the teams in the WHA. It also identifies Québec and the region since the Belisle Dictionary of the French Canadian language states that "the people of the North are the Canadians who live on the shore north of the St. Lawrence."

The word "Nordiques" implies an idea of vigour, of energy and strength because the Nordic countries have always been considered the most advanced of the world. French writer Xavier Marmier once declared "the nature of the North has a special charm," and Canada being one such country we believe this name will also evoke an idea of charm and attraction.

There would be no English version of the name, as the club insisted the name remain the same in both French and English coverage of the team, "in order to preserve the French character of the team."

THE LOOK

Québec's *Le Soleil* newspaper says the team briefly considered purple, while the artist says he originally pitched a double-blue look. But when the Nordiques unveiled their team logo and colours on June 26, 1972, the good ole bleu-blanc-et-rouge was their ultimate decision. Designed by Roger Gingras, a local seventeen-year-old who was also the son of a team shareholder, the logo featured the letter "N" in red in the shape of an igloo, and a hockey stick rested on the side of it with a blue hockey puck on the stick. A young, sideburn-clad man recalled the design process in the 1972 National Film Board of Canada documentary *Just Another Job*:

> My initial drawings were in blue but this wasn't what they wanted, so finally I made it in blue, white, and red. I had initially chosen blue primarily to be different from what had been done, also because we're in Québec and Québec's colour is blue but I was told to work in blue, white, and red, it felt more French Canadian.

> Blue, white, and red? Well, it's for the other generation, it's an establishment, everybody likes it and it's been seen before. It's like a flash of colour, everyone sees it and they immediately think it's their colours. In Montréal, we have always had a winning team, everybody has seen and followed them in their childhood, so keeping the same colours you make

> everybody feel at home, they feel it's their team, they see with their own eyes the colours they used to see on TV before.

Québec's original uniform featured Gingras's logo on a light blue jersey with bold red shoulders and waist striping paired with red pants. Red was reduced the following season, and the blue was darkened considerably throughout the uniforms.

On September 18, 1975, the team unveiled a uniform very similar to what we most commonly associate with the Nordiques: a light blue jersey with the team logo on the front in white with red trim, a single stripe at the waist and cuff of each sleeve and a total of eight fleur-de-lis symbols—six around the waist and one on each shoulder. Red was nowhere to be found aside from the edging surrounding the team's logo. "We will keep this uniform for several years," Nordiques general manager Maurice Filion correctly predicted at the time.

The new blue uniform with white stripes and the fleur-de-lis created an overall design that was very similar to Québec's provincial flag, the *Fleurdelisé*, a white cross on a blue field with a white fleur-de-lis in each quadrant. "Think about the advertising impact for everyone in Québec that our sweaters will provide during the 10 televised games we play outside the province," Georges Caron, a team councillor who also designed the now-iconic uniform told *Le Soleil* at the time. "Let's wait and see if these initiatives will bring back any of the expected rewards."

Upon their move to the NHL in 1979, the Nordiques retained the same uniform style, and for the 1980–81 season, switched the logo on their road blue jersey from white to red, a design they would wear for the remainder of their time in Québec.

Following several seasons among the worst-selling teams in the league, the Nordiques announced they'd be drastically changing their logo and uniforms on March 30, 1995, for use beginning in the fall of 1996. (The team just missed the league's deadline to make the change for the upcoming 1995–96 season.) The new look was purple with black and teal stripes and came with a logo featuring a husky dog facing the viewer on a triangle, with the team name written be-low. A fleur-de-lis remained on each shoulder, but was no longer worn around the waist. The team had considered several different concepts and spent tens of thousands of dollars on the project before signing off on the radical redesign that would have fit in quite perfectly with what the rest of the league was doing around the time. Of course, this uniform and logo would never take the ice in an NHL game, as the Nordiques would relocate to Denver to become the Colorado Avalanche only two months later.

SAN JOSE SHARKS
1991-PRESENT

THE TEAM

In 1990, when George and Gordon Gund, owners of the Minnesota North Stars, were turned down in their request for $15 million to renovate the team's home arena, they started to look elsewhere. The Bay Area, where the Gunds once owned the disaster that was the California Golden Seals, was the largest market currently without a team in the National Hockey League. It also just happened to have a shiny new arena on the way in San Jose. Naturally, that caught their attention.

The Gunds were faced with a few complications: the league did not want to lose Minnesota as a market, nor did they want to lose out on the potential for millions in expansion fees that a Bay Area team would surely provide. There was also Howard Baldwin, the former owner of the Hartford Whalers, who had the exclusive rights to operate an NHL team out of the new San Jose Arena. Needless to say, this was going to take some creative maneuvering to make everyone happy.

On May 9, 1990, at a meeting of the Board of Governors in Rosemont, Illinois, a solution to achieve this goal was approved by the league. Baldwin, along with Morris Belzberg, would purchase the North Stars for $38 million to keep the team up north, the Gunds would get Baldwin's rights to the arena and immediately receive an expansion franchise for an expansion fee of $50 million from the NHL. The new team would begin play in the 1991–92 season and would be granted the rights to 30 players under contract to the North Stars. In turn, the North Stars would get to join San Jose in an expansion draft in 1991, despite the fact the club was nearly a quarter-century old. Each team would draft 10 players from the other 20 NHL clubs.

If you follow the Gunds' adventure through the NHL, it began with the Golden Seals, who relocated them to Cleveland and merged them with the North Stars before finally taking half the North Stars down with them to San Jose to become the Sharks. One could certainly make the argument the Sharks were the de-merged Cleveland Barons, and therefore could have been a continuation of the original Seals franchise. Of course, neither the league nor the Sharks officially acknowledge this potential for a linked history between the two Bay Area teams. For the record, the Sharks are considered an entirely separate and new franchise that began its life in 1991.

San Jose Sharks draft picks Ray Whitney and Pat Falloon show off the team's home and road sweaters ahead of their expansion season.

The Sharks' debut in the NHL came on October 4, 1991, a 4–3 loss on the road to the Vancouver Canucks. The same two teams met up again the following night—this time in California—at the old and dated Cow Palace for the Sharks' home opener. The sellout crowd of 10,888 were given hats with a rubberized shark fin, Bay Area baseball legend Willie McCovey took part in the opening ceremonies, and there was an amusing laser show which included a shark gobbling up bigger and bigger fish until it finally snacked on a hockey player—all to the tune of the theme from the movie *Jaws*. But all that pomp couldn't stop the Canucks, who beat the Sharks, 5–2, for their second win in as many days.

After moving into the new San Jose Arena in 1994, the Sharks surprised the hockey world by knocking out the mighty Detroit Red Wings in the first round of the playoffs in just their third season. The next two decades saw the Sharks consistently field strong teams—including Hockey Hall of Famer Teemu Selänne and Hart Trophy winner Joe Thornton—but they just couldn't get through the playoffs. It wasn't until 2016 that they found their way into the Stanley Cup Finals, winning the Clarence S. Campbell Bowl before falling to Sidney Crosby's Pittsburgh Penguins in six games.

The continued success the Sharks have seen in the stands year after year since their debut has proven that, despite what may have happened with the Golden Seals back in the 1970s, the Bay Area was indeed now a viable hockey market.

THE NAME

A contest garnering over 5,700 entries suggesting a staggering 2,300 different names, referencing everything from sea creatures to computer parts to Oakland A's slugger José Canseco. The team announced the fifteen names that received the most votes from fans. Blades came in first, with Sharks second, and others (in alphabetical order) being Breakers, Breeze, Condors, Fog, Gold, Golden Gaters, Golden Skaters, Grizzlies, Icebreakers, Knights, Redwoods, Sea Lions, and Waves.

On September 6, 1990, the team announced "San Jose Sharks" was the team's choice. About a year later, they revealed that it had narrowly beat out two other strong contenders—the Seawolves and the Stingrays—though the Blades was the most popular entry submitted by the fans. "We were considering several alternatives for a name prior to the sweepstakes," Sharks executive VP of business operations Matt Levine said at the time," but the creativity shown by many of the entrants was of great benefit to us. Sharks are relentless, determined, swift, agile, bright and fearless. We plan to build an organization that has all those qualities."

"Club management was looking for something that would appeal to children and adults. It needed to be a name that would inspire graphic logo applications for uniforms and merchandise," read an October 1991 edition of *San Jose Sharks* magazine. The information included that "the neighboring Pacific Ocean is home to seven different varieties of sharks and several area institutions provide great amounts of time and money to shark research, preservation, and education."

Allen Speare, an attorney from San Jose, was chosen as the random winner, receiving a trip for two to the 1991 NHL All-Star Game in Chicago. Three-hundred other smaller prizes—such as commemorative pucks and Stanley Cup videos—were distributed randomly to some of the others who entered the contest.

THE LOOK

With hockey legend Gordie Howe, co-owner George Gund, and a few hundred lucky media and fans in attendance, the San Jose Sharks unveiled their original logo, uniforms, and color scheme at an on-ice press conference held at a local skating rink, on February 12, 1991. Pacific teal, representing the ocean waters, was announced as the primary color, bringing back a hue not seen in the NHL since the California Golden Seals skated 'round these parts about fifteen years earlier. Additional colors included black, gray, and white, which represented the colors of a shark.

The entire process took twelve months, which included multiple focus group tests, a Design the Logo Contest, and a uniform company suggesting they switch to royal blue instead of teal.

Two logos were unveiled alongside the new uniforms.

San Jose's original logo featured a shark on a triangle destroying a hockey stick. The Sharks would use this logo from 1991-92 through 2006-07.

The primary consisted of a shark just absolutely destroying a hockey stick bordered by a triangle, and an alternate showing just a fin ominously peeking out above the waves. Both were designed by Terry Smith, an artist for JRS Enterprises, based out of nearby Sunnyvale, California.

"It was a little more difficult than I anticipated," Smith told the *San Jose Mercury News*. "Essentially a shark is a cigar and I was trying to give a cigar personality." Smith said he had made nearly forty different designs before settling on the now familiar mark, which was ultimately selected by both team and league officials.

"During the development process, we sought to have the logo communicated as the shark is in the water—determined, focused, swift, and fearless," Levine told the Associated Press. "We think it has those qualities."

Howe, known as "Mr. Hockey" who, at the time, was also the league's all-time leading scorer, had been picked to model the new teal uniforms, a shade he certainly never wore during his nearly 30 seasons as a player. "The crest you wear on your chest is what catches everybody's eye," Howe said. "And if this crest doesn't catch your eye, you'd better check your pulse."

"I'm a fisherman, so I like it," Howe added. "I'm scared of those suckers."

A wordmark spelling out the team's name with jagged lettering resembling the teeth of a shark was designed by Mike Blatt of Lafayette, California, and had been unveiled several months earlier accompanying the announcement of the team's name.

With such a refreshing design hitting the league, Sharks merchandise immediately shot to the top of the NHL's sales charts. For 1991, Sharks merchandise alone was responsible for more than a third of all NHL items sold. By the end of the year the team was third overall in all of pro sports behind only the NFL's Los Angeles Raiders and MLB's Chicago White Sox. Soon, teams all around the sports world were redesigning their logos and uniforms, trying to duplicate the Sharks' success.

"From the beginning, the Sharks logo was designed to sell merchandise," Smith would tell the *San Francisco Examiner* during the team's rise up the revenue charts. "Other logos count on the team to sell the merchandise; we counted on the merchandise to sell the team."

As successful as the Sharks look was in the early 1990s, after sixteen years an update was necessary. Coinciding with the NHL's switch to a new Reebok uniform system, the Sharks unveiled their new logo on July 24, 2007.

The new look was certainly based off the original logo—and with good reason, as the team brought back Terry Smith to refresh his original creation. The biggest change was to the shark, who got a much more aggressive look overall and a new coat of teal splash over its body, a change suggested by several Sharks players during the 30-month design process.

"If you look at the old mark, you wouldn't even know teal was in there," Smith told the *San Jose Mercury News*, noting the original logo's near total lack of the team's most famous color.

Several other variations of the new logo were unveiled alongside the tweaked design featuring the shark in various different poses in and out of its triangle.

SEATTLE KRAKEN
2021-22

THE TEAM

The city of Seattle's history with professional hockey dates back to the early twentieth century, even before the establishment of the National Hockey League, when the Seattle Metropolitans—named for the Metropolitan Building Company—joined the Pacific Coast Hockey Association (PCHA) for the 1915–16 season. The Mets, as they were commonly called, were famous for their barber pole sweaters featuring alternating horizontal stripes of red, green, and white, with a large red "S" with "SEATTLE" stitched inside. Hockey history was made in Seattle when, on March 26, 1917, the Mets defeated the Montreal Canadiens 3 games to 1 to clinch the Stanley Cup Championship, the first time the Cup had been won by an American-based team.

Following the disbandment of the Mets in 1924, the city was served by teams such as the Western Hockey League's Seattle Totems, as well as the major junior Seattle Breakers (later the Thunderbirds). But while those clubs may have kept the spirit of hockey alive in the Pacific Northwest, none were eligible to compete for Lord Stanley's Cup.

There were attempts to relocate the Pittsburgh Penguins to the city in 1975, an expansion bid in 1990 was withdrawn as they were just about to present to the league's Board of Governors, and a last-minute council vote in Glendale, Arizona, was all that kept the Phoenix Coyotes from moving up north in 2013.

Ultimately, the city of Seattle would have to wait nearly a full century for the opportunity to once again compete for hockey's ultimate prize. Renovations carefully got underway at the Key Arena to both preserve its historical architecture and bring it up to the standards of a twenty-first century NHL arena. A very successful ticket drive was then launched that hit 25,000 deposits within its first 75 minutes. It was getting more and more apparent that the NHL could no longer ignore the viability of the Emerald City as a potential future market.

On December 4, 2018, the league made it official and announced an expansion team had been awarded to Seattle and their ownership group of David Bonderman, Jerry Bruckheimer, and Tod Leiweke for a fee of $650 million, to begin play in the 2021–22 season.

THE NAME

A kraken is a mythological sea creature, with its origins in Scandinavian folklore. Legend says the kraken lives in the Northern Atlantic off the coasts of Norway and Greenland, terrorizing any seafaring vessel which may have had the misfortune to journey past. How it ended up as the name of a hockey team in Seattle likely originates with the 2006 Bruckheimer-produced film *Pirates of the Caribbean: Dead Man's Chest*; throughout the film, Captain Jack Sparrow is hunted by the mysterious kraken, repeatedly destroying any ship he happens to be on.

The potential name proved popular on social media. In January 2018, the club registered thirteen domain names, giving fans a peek into names the club was considering: the Cougars, Eagles, Emeralds, Evergreens, Firebirds, Kraken, Rainiers, Renegades, Sea Lions, Seals, Sockeyes, Totems, and Whales. Throwing back to the Metropolitans name was considered, but NHL commissioner Gary Bettman was reluctant to change the name of the league's Metropolitan Division. Ultimately, the team said they considered over a thousand names before weeding those down to a final five, which were then tucked away safely in a time capsule at the Seattle Space Needle, not to be opened until 2062.

On July 23, 2020, with only construction workers from their Climate Pledge Arena in attendance (standing six feet apart from each other due to the COVID-19 pandemic), the team announced they would be known as the Seattle Kraken.

"There is longtime folklore in Seattle and the Pacific Northwest of this mystical Kraken creature that lives just below the surface of the seas, which really captivated people for many years," Kraken part owner Andy Jassy told ESPN.com. "That mystique, that intensity, and that power that people have long talked about with the Kraken is what we expect our NHL team to play with."

THE LOOK

Designed in a partnership with Adidas, the Kraken unveiled their logo, colors, and uniforms—along with the name—on July 23, 2020. The team's primary logo shows an "S," a nod to the original Metropolitans logo, in three varying shades of blue—Deep Sea Blue, Shadow Blue, and Ice Blue with the tentacle of a kraken creeping up the side. The only red (known officially as Red Alert) to be found anywhere on the logo is from the eye of the nautical nemesis. A secondary logo combining the Space Needle with an anchor was added to the set, to be worn on the shoulder of the team's uniforms.

At home, the Kraken wear a Deep Sea Blue jersey with the club's primary logo on the chest, with the striping at the waist done so in order to resemble the design of the ferries that can be found on the nearby Puget Sound.

ST. LOUIS BLUES
1967-PRESENT

THE TEAM

On February 9, 1966, the National Hockey League awarded franchises to St. Louis, Los Angeles, Minneapolis-St. Paul, Philadelphia, Pittsburgh, and San Francisco. The St. Louis franchise was conveyed on a conditional basis, as the league sought a satisfactory applicant to front the new team and purchase the St. Louis Arena from its owner, Chicago Black Hawks boss Arthur M. Wirtz.

Less than three weeks later, and with still no traction, the league threatened to pull the franchise and award it to Baltimore. One applicant—a group headed up by insurance executive Sidney Salomon—emerged, and were officially awarded the franchise on April 5, 1966. The NHL thus doubled in size, from six teams to twelve, and St. Louis returned to the circuit for the first time since the old St. Louis Eagles folded after a single season, in 1935.

Salomon and Co. spent $2 million to purchase the new franchise, $4 million for the arena, and $2.5 million more to renovate the thirty-eight-year-old building.

The new team was an immediate success, representing the all-expansion West Division in the Stanley Cup Finals during each of their first three seasons (though being swept each time). Aging goaltending legends Jacques Plante and Glenn Hall manned the net for the Blues in those early years as the team captured the imaginations of local hockey fans.

The 1970s, however, found the franchise in perilous shape. Competition from the World Hockey Association, escalating costs, declining revenues, and a dizzying carousel of coaching and front office changes contributed to a tumultuous decade. The Blues pared their staff down to only three employees after the 1976–77 season, and the team was sold to St. Louis' Ralston Purina Corporation.

The company soon lost interest in the money-losing Blues, and the team was once again put up for sale. In early 1983, Ralston officials announced that they had received an offer from a Saskatoon-based group to purchase the franchise, with the intent of moving it to Saskatchewan, but NHL owners overwhelmingly voted down the proposed transfer. Saskatoon's remote location and diminutive size were factors, as was the absence of a suitable arena to host the team. After many months of legal wrangling, the club was sold to a group headed up by investor Harry Ornest, who pledged to keep the Blues in St. Louis.

Stabilized, the Blues ran off an enviable streak of 25 consecutive playoff appearances between 1979–80 and 2003–04. On January 26, 1995, the Blues played their first home game at the brand new $135 million Kiel Center. A total of 20,282 fans witnessed Missouri native Jack Wagner, star of TV's *Melrose Place*, sing the national anthem, followed by a 3–1 Blues win over the Los Angeles Kings. The advent of the new millennium saw the Blues tally a franchise record 114 points, which also netted the Presidents' Trophy for the league's top record in 1999–2000. They were, however, stunned by San Jose in the first round of the playoffs.

Finally, on June 12, 2019, after 42 playoff appearances and 72 series, the Blues hoisted the Stanley Cup skyward for the first time in their half-century of NHL play when they defeated the Boston Bruins in a decisive Game Seven. The victory marked an improbable run, which saw the Blues buried in last place in the league standings in early January, 37 games into the regular season.

The Blues' first Cup victory set off a celebration for the ages, arriving exactly 19,481 days after St. Louis was awarded an NHL franchise.

THE NAME

When the syndicate headed by Sidney Salomon was officially awarded a franchise on April 5, 1966, he immediately announced that the team would be named "Blues."

Suggestions, he said, included Apollo and Mercury, nods to the fact that NASA's ten manned Gemini space capsules were made in St. Louis in 1965 and 1966, in anticipation of the Apollo program (which successfully landed astronauts on the moon a few years later).

Salomon said that he was inspired by the thought of composer W. C. Handy and his famous tune "St. Louis Blues."

"No matter where you go in town there's singing," said Salomon. "That's the spirit of St. Louis. I thought of the man on the wharf on the Mississippi riverfront singing."

The day after the franchise became official, the *St. Louis Post-Dispatch* wrote, "About 10 minutes before Salomon, his son, their attorney, James Cullen, and their public relations director, Tom Chapman, appeared before the NHL's Board of Governors, the elder Salomon suddenly thought of the designation for the then unnamed St. Louis team they were seeking. 'The name struck me as a natural,' Salomon told the *Post-Dispatch* from New York this morning, just prior to his return here. 'And when we announced the name, we got a tremendous reaction.'"

In 1969, *Sports Illustrated* further quoted Salomon on the birth of the Blues name:

> The committee had asked us to say a few words to the press…. It was a Monday night and, being an ex-sports-writer, I knew news would be pretty scarce for the next day. I said, "Gentlemen, we only have two or three minutes, but it would be to our advantage if we could name this team right now. Nobody else has come up with a name, and those fellows out there need something to write about."
>
> We started kicking names around fast—mostly space names, like Mercurys and Apollos … Nothing

clicked. It was time to go outside. Then it hit me. I said, "What about the Blues—the St. Louis Blues?" It had a great identity with the city and it gave us an instant theme song…We all liked it, but then our lawyer, Jim Cullen, said, "Sid, you could be asking for a lawsuit. I think we should clear it with the [W. C.] Handy estate first."

"Tom," I said, "if that's the way your mind reacts, then we've got to use the Blues. The publicity surrounding a lawsuit like that would be priceless."

THE LOOK

When the Blues were officially launched on April 5, 1966, team owner Salomon said the club was planning to employ an insignia depicting a clarinet in a banner of blue, thus emphasizing the name of the new franchise.

His vision soon gave way to an alternate one. Lynn Patrick, the first head coach of the Blues, is generally credited with having created the team's famed bluenote logo.

In 2016, Lynn's son, Dean Patrick, told the *Post-Dispatch*, "The Salomons came up with a name, the Blues, but they said, 'We've got to come up with colors and logos and everything'… they were thinking W. C. Handy, the St. Louis Blues, they were thinking music. Dad just drew a musical note with a wing at the top."

Patrick noted the fact that his father had most recently coached the Los Angeles Blades of the Western Hockey League, a team whose colors included the same gold color that would accompany the obvious blue for St. Louis. "There weren't any teams that wore those colors and he thought it

was a pretty uniform," he said.

Alternatively, on February 28, 1967, the *Post-Dispatch*, under a headline that read "Musical Note to Be Hockey Blues' Symbol," said "The flying musical note was designed by Sid Salomon III and will appear on all club stationery and the team's uniforms."

Origin stories are often shrouded in mystery, and the bluenote is no exception. Going back even further, on August 30, 1966, the *Post-Dispatch* published a photo of Coach Patrick and the younger Salomon modeling a pair of jerseys that the team intended to wear when it began play the following year. A simpler, nascent bluenote logo, nestled beneath the city name "St. Louis," sat atop a large "Blues." Salomon sported the home white and Patrick wore the proposed road blue, and both featured the number 35—recognition of the fact that the team did not intend to issue uniform numbers higher than 30 when the inaugural squad hit the ice. The sweaters were twilled up by Chesterfield, Missouri–based R. J. Liebe Athletic Lettering Company, and put together by Rawlings.

Hidden from view for a half century, one of the two original prototype sweaters resurfaced in 2016, just in time for the Blues' golden anniversary.

Whatever the case, the Blues' now familiar winged bluenote, simple and iconic, has continued to serve as the focal point for the club's visual brand throughout the franchise's entire history.

In 1970–71 the Blues took the ice in blue and yellow skates but, with a handful of outlier exceptions, the team has employed a steady, solid look since its inception.

In 1984, new owner Harry Ornest and his wife, Ruth,

For three seasons in the mid-1980s, St. Louis players wore uniforms with "BLUES" arched over their famous bluenote logo.

spearheaded a series of revisions to the uniforms; goalie Mike Liut and defenseman Rob Ramage modeled the new look for the media.

The traditional blue and yellow colors were adjusted, and red was added into the mix as an accent color. The word *Blues* was added as well, arched across the uniforms with a smaller bluenote underneath. "St. Louis" was tucked inside the note logo. "We feel the red trim makes the logo 'pop' more," said Mrs. Ornest. She created the look with assistance from her husband, family, members of the team's front office, and Rawlings, who manufactured the uniforms.

She told the *Post-Dispatch*: "Until Harry mentioned changing the uniforms, I was satisfied with what we had, but the colors disturbed me. They weren't quite strong enough. But if we were going to change the colors, we might as well change the whole thing. I think we've given it a little more pizzazz."

Already roiled by franchise instability and tumult, the Blues' fan base was not happy with the changes.

Ron Cobb, writing in the September 30, 1984, edition of the *Post-Dispatch*, discussed the uniform changes with Ruth Ornest.

"I know the fans are far more comfortable with the old logo, and anything new is somewhat unsettling… It's like changing furniture or putting a new painting in a room. We felt the colors definitely weren't strong enough. The new colors are sharper and will televise better."

Fans especially disliked the addition of the word *Blues* above the treasured logo. "But we have the bluenote," she said. "Harry really wanted the name 'Blues' added, and I really didn't disagree. What do I know about uniforms except colors? But I think the name is important. We're not a note, we're the Blues... We felt the note alone didn't tell you what team we are. If the team is on the road and you're a new fan. How can you tell what team it is?"

"We didn't abandon the note," she added. "It's still there."

This look was discarded when the Ornests sold the team several years later.

Sports branding powerhouse Sean Michael Edwards (SME) was brought in to tweak the Blues' on-ice look in 1994. They added an alternate trumpet logo, which was featured on the sleeves of the sweaters. The uniform trim was now diagonal; a visual representation of a musical staff. Red was emphasized as well.

Again, the team's new visual package was not well received. A few short years later, on January 31, 1998, the Blues took the ice in new, more traditional alternate uniforms, trimmed in navy blue. The bluenote logo was refined as well. The uniforms, designed by Buck Smith of Fleishman-Hillard, became the club's new permanent look the next season.

Blues superstar and future Hall of Famer Brett Hull told the *Post-Dispatch*: "This is unbelievably good-looking ... these are classy and I feel like a hockey player. They're back to where they should be... the St. Louis Blues and not the St. Louis Reds."

Hockey legends Brett Hull and Wayne Gretzky model the Blues' very red, very infamous musical staff uniform in 1996. The design lasted just three seasons.

ST. LOUIS EAGLES
1934-35

THE TEAM

The St. Louis Eagles played but a single season in the National Hockey League, 1934–35. They arrived in Missouri via Canada's capital city of Ottawa, where they enjoyed a lengthy and successful run as the original Senators.

The Senators were charter members of the NHL and won multiple Stanley Cups but, similar to other franchises, succumbed to the fates of the Great Depression. Their small market could not support an NHL franchise, and team ownership voted to transfer the Senators to St. Louis at a May 12, 1934, meeting, held in Chicago.

St. Louis offered both a larger population and a huge modern arena, a facility that later played host to the city's second NHL franchise, the St. Louis Blues.

The new St. Louis team trained in Ottawa, then opened up the regular season at home on November 8, 1934, against the defending Stanley Cup Champion Chicago Black Hawks. Admission prices ranged from 55 cents up to a top ticket of $1.75.

The team struggled to attract paying customers and, by December 1934, rumors began to swirl that the team would be disbanded. High travel expenses added to their fiscal woes. By the time the red ink dried at the conclusion of the season, the Eagles were hemorrhaging money and selling off key players.

On October 15, 1935, the NHL Board of Governors voted to purchase the Eagles franchise for $40,000. The team was eliminated, and the league went from nine to eight teams. Thirty-two years later, St. Louis rejoined the circuit when the Blues were formed.

THE NAME

Team president Redmond Quain officially designated the new club as "Eagles" in comments made on October 17, in Ottawa. The name was selected by the team's board of directors, with "Blue Streak" receiving the second-highest number of votes.

THE LOOK

An October 18, 1934, item in the *St. Louis Post-Dispatch* described the on-ice look of the Eagles: "This season the Eagle players will be clad in white jerseys which will be trimmed around the neck, sleeves and waist in blue and have a red Eagle and the city name "St. Louis" written across the front of the sweater."

A rare game-used example of this sweater, worn by defenseman Frank Finnigan, resides at the Hockey Hall of Fame in Toronto.

1934

ST. LOUIS EAGLES

TAMPA BAY LIGHTNING
1992-PRESENT

THE TEAM

As the National Hockey League entered the final decade of the twentieth century, with no national television contract in the United States in place, a plan was put into action in which the 21-team league would add seven new expansion franchises before the year 2000. Without any teams in the southeastern US, several suitors lined up looking to fill this massive void on the NHL's map. Among this group were two strong, simultaneous bids based out of the Tampa-St. Petersburg area. The first was headed by future Carolina Hurricanes owners Jim Rutherford and Peter Karmanos from Compuware, Inc., and the other was led by legendary Hockey Hall of Famer Phil Esposito.

Rutherford's group held a 20-year lease on St. Pete's cavernous Florida Suncoast Dome (now a MLB stadium known as Tropicana Field) and proposed having the team play there. Esposito's plan called for a brand-new hockey arena—known as the Tampa Coliseum—to be built next door to Tampa Stadium, home of the NFL's Buccaneers. Esposito really got things going for his side when he organized a game at the Suncoast Dome between the Los Angeles Kings and Pittsburgh Penguins, on September 19, 1990. A staggering 25,582 fans attended the preseason contest, shattering what was then the NHL's all-time single-game attendance record.

On December 6, 1990, with the NHL looking to add two teams for the 1992–93 season, both groups made 20-minute presentations on why they should run a prospective Tampa-St. Pete team to the NHL's Board of Governors at the Breakers Resort in Palm Beach. Other groups representing the cities of Hamilton, Miami, Ottawa, San Diego, and Seattle also made their pitches. The league made their decision that afternoon, and Esposito's Tampa bid was accepted—along with a group from Ottawa—for expansion fees of $50 million each, to be paid in installments over the next year. Rutherford and Karmanos, surprised at losing to Esposito's group, were encouraged to come back and try again another time.

"All of you are very good friends of mine," Esposito told the ballroom full of NHL executives after winning the bid. "It's great to be back with you lunatics." Within an hour of the league's decision, Esposito ditched his suit and tie for a more celebratory black, blue, and silver Tampa Bay Lightning T-shirt.

Lightning president Phil Esposito at the massive Florida Suncoast Dome in 1990, later the home of baseball's Tampa Bay Devil Rays.

Plagued by problems in their first year, the Lightning missed expansion fee payments and had issues negotiating an arena lease and securing approval to use the land for a new arena. With time running out, the Lightning looked to the Suncoast Dome to host their team until the new arena was ready. Due to a combination of mounting pressures from the league to hurry up and pick their home, as well as considerable concerns with the cost of maintaining an ice surface in the Dome, the Lightning announced on April 22, 1992, that they would instead play their first two seasons at the Expo Hall on the site of the Florida State Fairgrounds; a minuscule venue by NHL standards with a seating capacity of just over 10,000.

"Wow, what a bolt!" exclaimed the next day's headline on the *St. Petersburg Times*, as Lightning finally struck the league on opening night, October 7, 1992, in front of 10,425 fans at the Expo Hall. The pregame show included laser lights, fireworks, and figure skaters as excited fans looking to get the game underway began chanting "Hock-ey! Hock-ey!" It would turn out to be a very memorable debut for the Lightning, as Chris Kontos tallied four goals on the way to a 7–3 rout over the defending Stanley Cup finalist Chicago Blackhawks.

It didn't take long for the team to realize a venue of just 10,000 seats wasn't going to cut it in the NHL, and the Lightning announced they'd be leaving Expo Hall a little earlier than they originally hoped, shifting to the Dome after just one season. The newly renamed Thunderdome allowed for a larger capacity, which set in motion numerous NHL attendance records during their three seasons there. In 1996, the Lightning moved to downtown Tampa into their "forever home," the Ice Palace—now the Amalie Arena—where they still play today.

In 2004, in just their 12th season, Lord Stanley finally went electric when the Lightning defeated the Calgary Flames in seven games to win the first Stanley Cup for both the team and the southern United States.

THE NAME

No contest, no focus groups, no polling. Heck, there wasn't even a franchise yet when Phil Esposito announced his hopeful NHL team would be known as the Tampa Bay Lightning, on September 12, 1990—nearly three months before the NHL granted their group the team.

"It was during a thunderstorm," Esposito recalled at the time to the *St. Pete Times*. "We were all sitting around here a few months ago and all of a sudden there was a bolt of lightning. I kept saying 'look at the light,' and somebody said 'that's a great name for a hockey team.'"

A very appropriate name for a team in the Tampa Bay area, as it is commonly referred to as the "Lightning Capital of the World."

"I think everything about the name really exemplifies the Tampa Bay area as an electrifying place to be and live, and I think the name expresses the fast-paced action of the game of hockey," Esposito told the *Tampa Tribune*, before adding that he also enjoyed that the name didn't end in the letter "S."

There was no need to hold a Name the Team Contest, though the club did consider it, "we thought seriously about it but then we thought that we really couldn't come up with anything better [than the Lightning]."

THE LOOK

Prior to getting the franchise, a blue, black, and silver word-mark logo was unveiled by Esposito—alongside the team name—on September 12, 1990, featuring a large letter "L" in the shape of a lightning bolt. This logo was used only during the first few months of the season ticket drive and was replaced just six months later.

The first real Tampa Bay Lightning logo made its debut on March 25, 1991, at a press conference attended by several NHL officials in Tampa. A silver and black circle with a single, large white lightning bolt striking through it, "Tampa Bay" scrawled over the top in a blue cursive font, and "Lightning" italicized below.

"It's a sharp-looking design," NHL VP of marketing Steve Ryan said at the unveiling. "I think it's going to be one of the hottest, fastest-selling items that the NHL will have to offer."

The league had earlier rejected a design submitted by the team that December and responded with their own collection of fourteen acceptable designs drawn up by various agencies hired by the league. The Lightning deemed all of the NHL's counter-logos unacceptable, but instead worked on a compromise by mixing parts of three of those designs to assemble what would eventually morph into the final, approved logo.

Originally, the Lightning uniforms were described as being black with a large "V" shaped design running down the entirety of the front and back of the jersey, Esposito noted that he wore this prototype jersey at an old-timers' tournament in Stockholm, in mid-August 1990, to great acclaim.

"It was dynamite, all the guys loved them and we knew it was good because the wives loved them too. You know it's a good-looking sweater when the wives like them, and they

were all asking if they could get one!"

Of course, these uniforms were never worn, let alone introduced by the team. Instead, Lightning fans would have to wait until June 4, 1991, to see what their club would wear when they took the ice for their inaugural season.

The plan originally called for Esposito, along with his brother Tony—himself a Hall of Fame goaltender—to roller-skate into the ballroom at Tampa's Sheraton Grand Hotel while modeling the new home and road jerseys. Instead, the team shoehorned the unveiling into an announcement of new investors, one of whom was Angus Montagu, 12th Duke of Manchester, who was presented a brand new Lightning jersey with "THE DUKE" and the number 1 on the back. In hindsight, the number 28—symbolizing the amount of

Tampa Bay wore a thunderstorm on their third jerseys, 1996 to '99.

months he served in prison after being convicted of fraud for failing to pay the team—may have been more appropriate.

At home, the Lightning's jerseys were white with black shoulders, alternating blue and black stripes along the waist and on the arms and the team's primary logo on the chest. The road jersey was black with white shoulders and the same striping patterns. A unique feature was the addition of several thin stripes located under each player's arm, visible only when a player raised their arms to celebrate a goal.

"We wanted to be a little different, so after a lot of arguing we finally decided on this," Esposito said of the underarm stripes. "That's something no other NHL team has and we really like it. We really think these uniforms are unique."

Black was chosen as the team's primary color thanks to a future division rival.

"I played in Boston [with the Bruins] all those years with that black sweater and I loved it," Esposito said. "It makes you look tougher! They made me feel stronger. I guess it was just mental, which this game really is." The Lightning would wear this logo and uniform set for their first 12 seasons including a Stanley Cup Championship in 2004. A more modernized version of the bolt logo was unveiled on August 26, 2007, at a fan event known as IceFest. With a countdown from five, a 25-foot tall depiction of the new logo was unveiled on the side of the parking garage next to the team's home arena. The logo removed the redundant word *Lightning* and made the "Tampa Bay" font more clear. It came with tweaked uniforms in the same color scheme as the originals, but with the shoulder and waist stripes eliminated.

"We wanted to keep many traditional, quintessential Tampa Bay details," J. J. Stelter, a senior designer at Reebok, told the *St. Pete Times*. "We were looking to have a little more of an evolution story."

Less than four years later, the Bolts went in an entirely new direction when they unveiled a very traditional-style logo, color scheme, and uniforms on January 31, 2011, in a ceremony which included original owner Phil Esposito and 2004 Stanley Cup–winning captain Dave Andreychuk showing off the new look.

Switching to blue as their primary color and eliminating black entirely, the new logo, designed by New York's SME, was reduced to a simple single-color lightning bolt and circle. "Tampa Bay" was added above the logo for road games only.

Tampa Bay general manager Steve Yzerman said the uniforms were given a "timeless" look "which also happen to be worn by some of the most respected and admired teams in sports," he told the *Tampa Tribune*.

Fan reaction at the time was mixed, with many mourning the shift away from black. An olive branch was extended to the fans with the announcement that black would be added after all as a trim color on player numbers in time for the first game in 2011–12.

TORONTO MAPLE LEAFS
1917–PRESENT

THE TEAM

No team in Canada can lay claim to the passion that the Toronto Maple Leafs evoke in sports fans throughout the country. Whether the emotion is positive or negative, a Canadian hockey fan simply cannot have a neutral opinion of the blue and white; you either love them or hate them, the two poles defending their fervour with religious zeal.

So much of the overall history and identity of the club is ingrained in Canadian culture. The maple leaf was adopted as the name and logo of the team four decades before the country made it the focus of its national flag. Tim Horton, the founder of a massive network of coffee shops bearing his name, known the world over as a Canadian institution, spent twenty seasons patrolling the Maple Leafs blueline during a Hall of Fame career; his number 7 now hangs from a banner, retired high above the Leafs' home ice. The Tragically Hip, one of Canada's all-time great rock bands, tells the story of Stanley Cup hero Bill Barilko scoring the winning goal to clinch a Cup win for the Maple Leafs before perishing in a plane crash a couple of months later, in their song "Fifty Mission Cap." It's no surprise that any game the team plays throughout the country, home or on the road, a legion of fans follows, loud enough to cause one to briefly wonder—just which of these teams is the home team again?

The Toronto Maple Leafs officially began their life more than a century ago, in the inaugural 1917–18 season of the National Hockey League. But depending on your definition of what constitutes a single franchise, the Maple Leafs could arguably be traced as far back as the National Hockey Association's (NHA) Toronto Blueshirts in 1911.

The birth of Toronto's NHL franchise was one filled with controversy. Fuelled by a desire to rid themselves of Blueshirts owner Eddie Livingstone in 1917, the four remaining NHA teams led a mass exodus out of the league to form today's NHL. Much to his chagrin, the new league put a team in Toronto for that first season, using identical uniforms and largely the same roster as Livingstone's NHA Blueshirts. While the club was officially known as the Toronto Hockey Club, local newspapers regularly referred to the team as the Blueshirts. It probably didn't help Mr. Livingstone feel any better that this new team then immediately went on to win the Stanley Cup in that first season. Ouch.

Livingstone tried to legally win back ownership of the team but failed, and the franchise passed from owner to owner as they struggled to find their own identity in that first tumultuous decade.

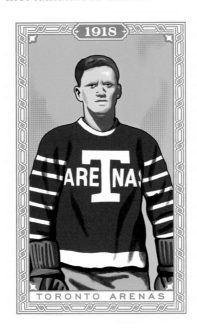

1918

TORONTO ARENAS

In the century since their establishment, the club has changed its name numerous times, and switched their colours from blue-and-white to green and then back to blue again—all the while winning a baker's dozen Stanley Cups and cementing their place in Canadian culture. Despite the team going more than fifty years without a Cup victory, their overall championship tally is still good for second most in league history, as the organization has continued to play before a packed house nearly every night for the past quarter-century.

THE NAME

Originally taking the ice as the nameless Toronto Hockey Club during their inaugural NHL season in 1917–18, a new ownership group known as "the Toronto Arena Company" took over the team and proceeded to name the team after themselves, putting the Toronto Arenas out on the ice at To-

ronto's Arena Gardens for the 1918–19 season. Terrible performances by the team right out of the gate turned off most locals—who responded by staying away—resulting in a suspension of operations midway through the season. This left the league with just two teams and the immediate end of the regular season, forcing the two other clubs—Ottawa and Montréal—into a championship series to determine who would represent the NHL in the Stanley Cup.

Coming to the rescue of the struggling franchise, the Toronto Arenas were purchased in the fall of 1919 by Fred Hambly, who sought and received permission to rename the team the Tecumseh Hockey Club, a moniker previously used by one of Toronto's NHA entries back in 1912; the team was named for Tecumseh, a nineteenth-century Native American Shawnee warrior and chief who had allied with the British Canadians to fight the American invasion of Ontario during the War of 1812. In the end, the NHL's Tecumseh Hockey Club would last no more than 24 hours; ownership of the team changed hands once again before the weekend was up to a group who ran the St. Patricks Ontario Hockey Association (OHA) senior amateur team.

The St. Patricks ownership group grabbed the reins and quickly renamed the team after their OHA club, branding the club the Toronto St. Patricks and dropping the blue and white in favour of a new green and white colour scheme. The OHA's St. Patricks had originally chosen their name to appeal to Toronto's growing Irish population in the 1800s, a surge so significant that it led to the city, at one point, being tagged with the nickname "Little Belfast." The new owners hoped by directly reaching out to the Irish community it would help end Toronto's struggle with attracting large crowds to their games.

The St. Pats would immediately turn things around, setting attendance records while also capturing a Stanley Cup Championship in 1922. Unfortunately, the good times were short-lived, and within a couple of years the team was struggling yet again. And, not surprising, interest from the public and attendance waned.

By 1926, most of the investors involved with the St. Patricks wanted out and the group was even eyeing an offer from Philadelphia to move the team to the United States. J. P. Bickell, who owned 40 percent of the shares, preferred to stay in town and recruited Conn Smythe, who had recently worked with the New York Rangers to help buy out the other shareholders and run the team. Smythe raised $160,000 with the help of 14 others to purchase the remaining shares and keep pro hockey in Toronto.

"If Toronto lost its NHL franchise it might be a long time before we got another," Smythe recalled in his 1981 autobiography *If You Can't Beat 'Em in the Alley*. "Bickell assured me if I could match the Philadelphia offer, they'd give me the edge."

After taking control of the St. Patricks in February 1927, Smythe's first order of business was changing the name of the team to the Maple Leafs right in the middle of the season. The Maple Leafs name had been in use by the local pro baseball team since the 1880s, but Smythe wasn't looking at the ballclub when he picked the new name.

The St. Pats wore a patch celebrating their 1922 Stanley Cup win in 1922–23.

The maple leaf had been used as a symbol of pride by Canadians as far back as the 1700s. Originally adopted by French Canadians along the St. Lawrence River, the first mayor of Montréal, Jacques Viger, described it as "the king of our forest, the symbol of the Canadian people" in 1834. The maple leaf was adopted by both the provinces of Ontario and Québec in their coat of arms, and eventually by the country upon confederation in 1867. Its status as a Canadian symbol was cemented with the composing of the popular patriotic song "The Maple Leaf Forever" in the 1860s, quickly gaining status as Canada's unofficial national anthem. When Canada joined the First World War in 1914, many soldiers wore the maple leaf on their uniform badges.

"I had a feeling that the new Maple Leaf name was right. Our Olympic team in 1924 had worn maple leaf crests on their chests, I wore it on my badges and insignia during the [First World War]," Smythe explained. "I thought it meant something across Canada, while 'St. Patricks' didn't—a name hatched originally merely in an attempt to attract the Irish population in Toronto."

From that wealth of patriotism in the heart of Constantine Falkland Smythe, the Toronto Maple Leafs were born.

THE LOOK

Toronto's first season in the NHL saw the club borrow the same logo and uniforms as the NHA's Toronto Blueshirts, a simple white block letter "T" on a blue sweater with a white collar and cuffs. The change in ownership came with the new name "Arena Hockey Club" for 1918–19, sweaters were simply altered to add the word *Arenas*, also in white, around the "T."

In 1919–20, the Arena Hockey Club became the Toronto St. Patricks, trading the familiar blue and white for the green and white colours of the OHA senior club of the same name. The St. Pats bounced back and forth between three different looks in their six and a half seasons, with some years wearing a white sweater with a green horizontal band and others in an all-green top with the team name arched across the chest. In their final season, the St. Pats wore a green sweater with three horizontal white stripes and the team name in white trimmed with green. The St. Pats would play their final game on February 15, 1927, against the Detroit Cougars in Windsor, Ontario. Following the game, the team would be forever referred to as the Toronto Maple Leafs.

> *The Maple Leaf to us was the badge of courage, the badge that meant home. It was the badge that reminded us all of our exploits and the different difficulties we got into and the different accomplishments we made. It was a badge that meant more to us than any other badge we could think of, so we chose it. [We hoped] that the possession of this badge would mean something to the team that wore it and when they skated out on the ice with this badge on their chest they would wear it with honour, pride, and courage, the way it had been worn by the soldiers of the first Great War in the Canadian Army.*
> —Conn Smythe, Maple Leafs governor, 1927–1962

Smythe's memories of fighting for Canada while wearing a maple leaf with great pride directly led to Toronto wearing just a single leaf on their uniform and, by extension, as their primary logo. The very first Toronto Maple Leafs logo and uniforms were put together quickly as a result of the midseason switch in team names. The original 1927 logo was described as mostly resembling what had been worn by Team Canada at the 1924 Winter Olympics which was a maple leaf with "CANADA" arched upwards below it. The uniforms worn in that first game on February 18, 1927, were referred to in newspapers to be "appearing as white as ghosts" with a green leaf on the chest of a plain white sweater; a uniform the team would only wear for two months as they finished up the season.

Once the season concluded, the Leafs got to work on moving away from the St. Pats look. The green and white was dropped in favour of blue and white, colours which were long used across the city of Toronto by the baseball Maple Leafs and the CFL Toronto Argonauts. The new sweaters featured blue with white stripes on the shoulders, sleeves, and around the waist; the large new Maple Leafs emblem on the chest mostly retained the shape used the season prior but was now in white with the full team name scrawled inside in blue lettering.

In January 1929, after a couple of seasons dealing with uniform confusion occurring during games against the New York Rangers and Chicago Black Hawks, the Toronto Maple Leafs became the first NHL team to adopt a second uniform option. Toronto's new white "clash" sweaters with blue pants debuted on January 27, 1929, against Chicago; the *Globe and Mail* saying the team "looked like strangers" as they took to the ice but were also quick to point out it was a much more eye-pleasing uniform matchup.

Over the ensuing decades, the Leafs continued to evolve their logo; the team's primary crest underwent changes of varying degrees in 1938, 1967, 1970, and finally 2016. For the 1967 Stanley Cup Playoffs and through the end of the 1969–70 season, the team replaced their logo with the same maple leaf used on the new Canadian flag, in honour of the nation's centennial celebration. Its replacement, which debuted in 1970, was the most simplified leaf of the group and was also in use for the longest, least successful era in team history, nearly fifty years associated with poor team performance, alienating fans, players, and staff, and constant turmoil stemming directly from the office of controversial owner

Lieutenant Conn Smythe wearing his uniform from World War I.

Harold Ballard. That change, according to a 1970 story in the *Globe and Mail*, was made because the logo wasn't trademarked, causing issues collecting royalties from the unauthorized sales of boys' sweaters.

Nearly a half-century later in 2014, Hall of Famer Brendan Shanahan was announced as the new president and executive vice president of the franchise, and one of the first tasks he undertook was to change the look of the team.

"When I first arrived in Toronto I spent a lot of time just asking questions, things I had wondered before I had the job and one of them was 'Can someone explain to me why [the logo] changed and who changed it?'" Shanahan told the authors during a meeting at Toronto's Air Canada Centre. "I kept hearing this fantastic story of how they became the 'Maple Leafs' but there was no story about how they got away from that logo, there just wasn't a whole lot of answers. So the next question was really just, 'Can we change it back?'"

"We were leading into our hundredth year and we said 'hey, here's an opportunity to do it,' to look towards changing or rebranding the team," said Shannon Hosford, the Maple Leafs senior vice president of marketing and fan engagement. "We worked on it in the summer of 2015, we went to Boston to the Reebok offices and they gave us a whole bunch of ideas and of course we didn't like any of them! We saw a few in many different colours, the push from different angles was to make it so different which we didn't want to do. Brendan's vision was to go back to a time when the maple leaf really meant something to our fans."

The design team at Reebok worked with the Leafs staff on several different ideas—some aimed at continuing the modernization of the logo and updating its lettering style while others toyed with the idea of adding a lighter blue to the colour scheme.

"They wanted to push us and see how far we would be willing to go, some of the colours were light blues, all blues really," Hosford continued. "There were a number of options and different types of leaves but we came back and talked about what we wanted and then we talked to the NHL. Sophisticated and simple. We aren't trying to do something outlandish with it."

Ultimately, Shanahan insisted they focus on returning to something resembling their older 1950s-style logo, which the team had already been wearing off and on over the past fifteen years as an alternate uniform. "I got caught up in this idea of bookending our century but we didn't want to replicate an old sweater. We wanted it to have classic elements of what it was intended to be, not take a specific year or sweater and just copy it," said Shanahan. "We all felt that the crest was a classic. We weren't trying to outsmart ourselves. We were really trying not to copy something from the past but more taking something from the past that shouldn't have been changed and putting it back to the way it was. I thought there was a lot of symbolism with the team as well, some of the things that occurred with the ownership in the late '60s, things that were done with Stanley Cup banners that should never have been done. To me, I grew up loving that crest and I'm much happier now with this one as a Toronto Maple Leafs fan."

It was late in the evening of February 2, 2016, that the Maple Leafs finally unveiled their first logo redesign in over forty-five years on a program titled *The Leaf: Blue-*

THE LEAFS' LEAFS

1927

THE GREEN LEAF.
DEBUTED FEBRUARY 17, 1927.
WORN FOR 13 GAMES.

1927-38

THE BIRTH
OF THE
BLUE AND WHITE.

1938-63

ASSOCIATED WITH
EIGHT STANLEY CUP
CHAMPIONSHIPS.

1963-67

OUTLINE ADDED TO
CREST. A SHORT-LIVED,
TRANSITIONAL LEAF.

1967-70

THE CENTENNIAL LEAF.
SIMILAR TO 11-POINT LEAF ON
CANADA'S NEW FLAG.

1970-82

THE BALLARD LEAF.
MODERNIZED DESIGN,
ZERO STANLEY CUP WINS.

1982-2016

SUBTLE CHANGES
TO LEAF—WIDER STEM,
MORE ANGULAR.

2016-

LEAF HAS 31 POINTS, A NOD
TO MAPLE LEAF GARDENS'
1931 OPENING.

"Red" Kelly in the blue-and-white in the mid-1960s. Toronto wore several versions of this maple leaf from 1938 to 1967, a modernized version returned in 2016.

print, broadcast on their LeafsTV network. The logo was a slightly modernized version of their 1938 to 1967 logo, some of the inconsistencies that came with a logo designed eighty years ago had been cleaned up and the font was updated and centred properly bringing this classic look up to twenty-first century standards. The leaf included 31 points, in reference to 1931—which was both the first year they played at the historic Maple Leaf Gardens and the first time they had won the Stanley Cup using the Maple Leafs name. Within the leaf were 17 veins, a nod to 1917—the first year of the franchise. Thirteen of those veins were placed above the team name, one for each of their thirteen Stanley Cup Championships.

The new uniforms were revealed at the NHL Draft on June 24, 2016: no shoulder logos or decoration, a single stripe at the waist, two on each sleeve, lace-up collars, and the new logo placed on the front much larger than your standard jersey crest. The overall idea behind the simple design and larger crest was to put all the focus on the new leaf. A series of in-arena tests were conducted with various sized logos to see if such a large crest would negatively impact the players. "We didn't want them to feel this big logo every time they had to bend for a faceoff or crouch for a puck battle," Shanahan said. "We had some made up and we cleared the arena and had a couple of players come in and skate, shoot pucks and give us their feedback on whether or not they liked the uniform or whether they felt the crest was so big that it was in the way."

Changing the Leafs' uniform and logo, the mere idea of which likened to a sacrilegious crime in the city, was embraced immediately by "Leafs Nation." The new team logo and jerseys now seen throughout the stands in arenas all across North America, home or away, are ones that transcend generations. A logo that evokes passion for the game in parents, grandparents, and children alike as they fall in love with this glorious game.

For more than 45 years, the Leafs wore the simplified "Ballard Leaf" on the chest of several different uniform styles. The jersey illustrated above was used from this logo's introduction in 1970 until 1992. The "Ballard" logo lasted through the 2015-16 season, before the team took a trip back in time to the older-styled leaf seen in the photo at left.

VANCOUVER CANUCKS
1970-PRESENT

THE TEAM

The city of Vancouver was home to several successful hockey teams long before the National Hockey League came to British Columbia, even a Stanley Cup Championship courtesy of the Pacific Coast Hockey Association's Vancouver Millionaires in 1915. Following the Millionaires, there were the Maroons, Lions, Norvans, and Maple Leafs—all competing in various levels of hockey, before the pro-level Pacific Coast Hockey League (later the Western Hockey League) added the original Vancouver Canucks in 1945.

With the success of the Canucks in the PCHL and WHL—including a championship in their very first season—the Vancouver hockey scene had their hearts set on securing an NHL franchise. They even built a brand-new arena, the Pacific Coliseum, in hopes of attracting interest from the league. A failure to land one of the six expansion spots in 1967 was quickly followed up with an unsuccessful attempt to move the Oakland Seals up north in 1968, and then again in 1969. Vancouver's long wait finally paid off and, on December 2, 1969, the NHL announced they were awarding conditional expansion franchises to Vancouver—as well as Buffalo, New York—for the 1970–71 season. Vancouver's franchise was awarded to Tom Scallen, owner of Minneapolis' Medicor Corporation for a price of $6 million US after local candidates balked at the expansion fee, which was three times what each of the six new teams had paid just three years earlier. Medicor was persuaded to bid by Vancouver businessman Coley Hall, who was the original owner of both the WHL's Canucks and the San Francisco Seals before joining the company.

The Vancouver Canucks, originally placed in the NHL's East Division despite being about as far west as you can be, played their first game on October 9, 1970, a 3–1 loss at home to the Los Angeles Kings. Their first win came just two days later, a 5–3 victory over the Toronto Maple Leafs.

Since joining the NHL in 1970–71, the Vancouver Canucks have made three trips to the Stanley Cup Finals in their nearly fifty seasons in the league. They twice took the Finals all the way to a seventh game but have yet to seal the deal and have thus far been unable to replicate the Cup success tasted by the Vancouver Millionaires more than a century ago.

THE NAME

The Vancouver Canucks name dates back to 1945, when the WHL's Canucks first began play in what was then known as the PCHL. Coley Hall was the owner of the franchise and said he named the team on the advice of a "bootlegger friend" of his named Art Nevison, who had been inspired by the wartime comic book character "Johnny Canuck."

Johnny Canuck first appeared in political editorial cartoons during the late 1800s, often shown as a lumberjack, farmer, or soldier standing up for Canada against "Uncle Sam" of the United States or "John Bull" of Great Britain. Johnny Canuck made a comeback in comic books in the 1940s during World War II, where he was portrayed as Canada's version of Captain America; standing up to Axis leaders and helping the Allies win the war.

The first recorded usage of the term "kanuck" appearing was in the 1830s, as an American slang word used to describe a Canadian of Dutch or French descent. The etymology of the word remains a mystery, but could date back to "Kanata," the Iroquoian word for a "village" and the origin of the naming of Canada. Today the term *Canuck* is usually used to refer to any resident of Canada.

When Vancouver was granted their NHL expansion franchise in 1969, it seemed only natural that the team would retain the moniker of their WHL club, who were still active in their 25th season and were now owned by the same group as the NHL team.

The owners, however, had thoughts of something fresh and new for the city.

"Canucks is an outdated slang expression that I don't particularly like," said Lyman Walters, the VP of Medicor. The

"Johnny Canuck" was a popular editorial cartoon character in Canada, seen above in the Winnipeg Tribune, *December 15, 1906.*

Vancouver's original "hockey stick" uniforms, worn from 1970 to '78.

words stung the hearts of every Vancouver hockey fan reading them in the *Province* newspaper on the morning of December 16, 1969. "I'd prefer a name which identified the team as coming from Vancouver and British Columbia," Walters added.

Walters's comments struck a chord with the local faithful, and over the next three weeks, the *Province* published letters from fans on the front page of their sports section, the letters nearly unanimous in their support of sticking with the Canucks name. For those who fancied a change, suggestions included Coasters, Thunderbirds, and bringing back the Millionaires name.

The letter writing campaign ultimately worked and, on January 14, 1970, the team announced that they would indeed be known as the Vancouver Canucks when they joined the NHL. "The fans spoke out and we heard them," said Scallen, noting the newspaper responses were about 80 percent in favour of keeping the name.

THE LOOK

The WHL's Canucks wore red, white, and blue uniforms with the team name arched across the front over each player's number. So, while the Canucks name was here to stay, the new ownership group still had an opportunity to add their own fresh spin on the expansion club by adopting new team colours, uniforms, and a logo.

On June 6, 1970, the Canucks released their brand-new look: the logo was a stylized "C" in the shape of a hockey rink with a hockey stick inside to complete the letter, the colours were royal blue for the Pacific Ocean, white for the snow-capped mountains of the area, and

Kelly green for the forests of British Columbia. Vancouver native Joe Borovich, a thirty-one-year-old freelance graphic designer and lifetime hockey fan who was born "within shouting distance" of the Pacific Coliseum, submitted the winning entry. The only Canadian to send in a design, Borovich beat out hundreds of other designs from eighty US professional artists to get the gig and take home $500 for his efforts.

"When you do a logo they sort of indicate that you should try and bring in the initial of the company and also what they do," Borovich recalled in the video "*Designing the First Canucks Logo,*" uploaded by the Canucks to YouTube in 2014. "I ended up with the 'C' for 'Canucks,' although a lot of people didn't see it initially, made up of the overall shape of the hockey rink with a hockey stick going through making a 'C' and, of course, the stick is a tool that they use in hockey so I had three components there."

In 1978, the Canucks tabbed Beyl & Boyd, a San Francisco–based agency to create a new, more aggressive look for the team. That meant the end of blue and green as the colour scheme, and the elimination of Borovich's "stick-in-rink" logo. In its place was black, red-orange, and yellow, with uniforms featuring a large "V" on the front and a new logo with a flying skate on the sleeve. The look was so radical for the time that the patterns for these new uniforms had to be made by a flag manufacturing company.

"The Canucks colours were all wrong," designer Bill Boyd said in the *Vancouver Sun* on August 22, 1978. "Blue-green is the coolest colour of all, slows the pulse, reduces aggression, and promotes calmness. With the [new] Canucks uniforms we are going from the coolest of colours—

blue-green—to the hottest—red-orange. The cool colour is passive, the hot one aggressive, plus the black. It's the contrast of colours that creates emotion."

Going against tradition, the club opted against wearing a white uniform at home, instead going with yellow.

"White produces no response at all, so we went for yellow," Boyd explained. "Yellow is warm, pleasant, happy, upbeat. What we are attempting to create is an atmosphere that will help create the happy, upbeat, aggressive player—and, hopefully, the happy, upbeat fan." On the "V" for "Vancouver," Boyd said, "it creates the ideal diagonal stripe. All teams have horizontal or vertical stripes. That's static. Diagonal stripes get your attention. They're like the crooked picture on the wall. You have to fix it or it drives you crazy."

Boyd also said that his firm "analyzed the colours and logo of every team in every major-league sport... [and] gave the Canucks 20 different approaches...." This resulted in a primary logo that featured a "pop art" skate speeding over the word *Canucks*. It was created by illustrator Mike Bull and was chosen for its positive attributes of "movement and style." In the design, the team effectively swapped out one piece of hockey equipment (a stick) for another (a skate), but it was the motion associated with how each was presented that inspired the change. The original logo featured a very static stick, the new one a flying skate shown speeding diagonally across the team name.

"So the Canucks will go from 'cool' to 'hot' just by changing their uniforms?" asked the *Financial Post*. "The rest of the teams could wear sunglasses, that is if they aren't already colourblind."

A trip to the Finals in 1982 in their new duds wasn't enough to save the controversial look. The Canucks cleaned things up a bit in 1985, as the skate logo was shifted to the front of each jersey and the "V" design was moved to the shoulders.

In 1989, during a radio appearance, Canucks director of hockey operations Brian Burke complained about his teams "puke-yellow" jerseys, which inspired twenty-year-old Canucks fan Jeremie White to pitch a new uniform design directly to Burke. White originally pitched a series of black and blue uniforms with a logo featuring a hockey stick flying through a "V," but Burke insisted on keeping both the core colour scheme and the team's skate logo.

With that information in mind, White was paired up with Canucks general manager Pat Quinn to finish the job. "At the time I was just pinching myself," White recalled to the CBC in 2018. "I was only 20-years-old and [Quinn] was listening to my opinion."

Together, they brought back a classic white uniform, eliminated the "V"s from the shoulders and reintroduced more traditional horizontal striping around the waist. The Canucks adopted the uniform that autumn and continued to wear them through the end of the 1996–97 season.

On June 3, 1997, out in the rain on the steps outside the Vancouver Art Gallery, several hun-

"Hot and aggressive", the Canucks wore black, red, and yellow from 1978 to 1997.

dred fans showed up to see Canucks players, including Pavel Bure and Trevor Linden, model their latest new look—a killer whale bursting through the ice in the shape of the letter "C" with a colour scheme now of deep blue, deep red, sky blue, and silver.

Initial reactions were negative, with many fans and those in the media noting the similarity to the logo of Orca Bay Sports and Entertainment, the company that owned the Canucks at the time.

"The killer whale is one of the most intelligent creatures in the world and embodies many of the qualities you value in your hockey team," Quinn said at the unveiling event. "We are a proud Canadian city ... our logo will show the world where we're from."

While the killer whale logo still lives on to this day, the colour scheme of blue, red, and silver does not. Ten years later, on August 29, 2007, the Canucks reverted to their original colour scheme of blue, green, and white. In a tribute to the original WHL Canucks, "VANCOUVER" was added to the jersey, arched above the killer whale, a feature which would remain for eleven seasons until it was removed prior to the 2019–20 season.

Henrik and Daniel Sedin before a game in 2010. The Canucks returned to their original colour scheme starting with the 2007-08 season.

VEGAS GOLDEN KNIGHTS
2017-PRESENT

THE TEAM

For several years, the city of Las Vegas was seen as a future home for a top-level professional sports team, but due to the dominance of the local gambling industry, leagues were reluctant to be the first to step into the Nevada desert. That all changed on June 22, 2016, when the National Hockey League announced that billionaire Bill Foley and his group—including the Maloof Brothers, former owners of the NBA's Sacramento Kings—had won the bid to bring an expansion team to Las Vegas for the 2017–18 season, paying a record $500 million expansion fee in the process.

"In the fall of 2017, when we celebrate the 100th birthday of the National Hockey League, we will do so as a league of 31 teams," NHL commissioner Gary Bettman said at the press conference. "We think this is an exciting opportunity not just for Las Vegas but for the league as well." The decision by the league's Board of Governors was unanimous; the league chose Las Vegas over a competing bid from Québec City. Fears of issues with the gambling industry were brushed aside by the league, with Bettman saying it just wasn't as big of a problem with the sport of hockey.

"Well Las Vegas, we did it! It wasn't easy was it?" asked owner Bill Foley. "The NHL stands for the proposition that hockey's for everyone and our great sports town now has a major league franchise."

It was the first new team added to the league since Columbus and Minnesota joined seventeen years earlier, and a new format for the expansion draft was crafted to give the young team a greater chance to compete almost immediately, rather than the many years of difficult seasons, which an expansion team would typically experience. A series of pre-draft trades and savvy selections gave the club a talented roster with a healthy balance of experience, youth, and good old-fashioned determination.

The Vegas Golden Knights played their first game in team history on October 6, 2017, in Dallas, defeating the Stars, 2–1. This was quickly followed up with a second road win in Arizona just one night later. When they headed back to Las Vegas to again play the Coyotes in the big home opener on October 10, they arrived to a city deep in mourning. Nine days earlier, a lone gunman opened fire from a window in a room at the Mandalay Bay Resort on a crowd of concertgoers below, less than a mile from the team's home arena. More than 500 people were shot and 58 were killed in the attack.

Plans for a grand celebration to welcome the team were quickly discarded, as the franchise looked for a way to help their new community. Led by a parade of drummers and circus performers down Las Vegas Boulevard, fans entered the T-Mobile Arena to see each player introduced, one by one, with a member of the local first responder community. Players from both teams joined the first responders on ice, as the names of all those killed were projected onto the ice for 58 seconds of silence. Golden Knights player and Las Vegas resident Deryk Engelland addressed the crowd, "To the families and friends of the victims, know that we'll do everything we can to help you and our city heal. We are Vegas Strong."

This rallying cry was echoed throughout the arena that night, and all advertisements typically lining the boards surrounding the rink were replaced with the saying and a special decal was worn on the helmets of players from both clubs. The Golden Knights embraced their role of helping with the healing process, scoring the first goal just two minutes in, and then another two minutes later, and then another, and another. After only ten minutes of play following the puck drop, they were up 4–0, and well on their way to a 5–2 win. The team wouldn't stop there—not by a long shot. They continued their success winning the Pacific Division and Western Conference championships before they were finally stopped by the Washington Capitals in the Stanley Cup Finals. They became just the third NHL team to appear in the league's championship final during their inaugural season, duplicating the first-season feats of the 1968 St. Louis Blues fifty years earlier and the 1918 Toronto Hockey Club a century earlier.

THE NAME

Immediately after being awarded the team, owner Bill Foley made it clear what his preference for calling the team was. "I love Black Knights, I'm an Army guy but maybe that's not the right name for the team at this time," he said making reference to the Black Knights name used by Army's sports teams. Foley still seems to have given Black Knights a shot as just a couple of weeks later, as he told *Sports Illustrated* "there were too many objections [from the Army] and then pushback from other people, so we've put the [Black Knights] name aside, but the name is going to have Knights somewhere in some fashion, some way," before teasing "or, there's one particular animal, a bird, that we have available to us that we might use."

In the weeks leading up to the announcement, a series of website domain name and trademark registrations made by Foley's Black Knight company were caught by both SportsLogos.Net and DetroitHockey.Net, including the three bird names mentioned in his interview: the Red Hawks, Desert Hawks, and Nighthawks. These were quickly followed up by the discovery of six variations of three different "Knight"-related names: Silver Knights, Desert Knights, and Golden Knights—all three of which were trademarked with both Las Vegas and Vegas as the first part of the name.

On the evening of November 22, 2016, Foley welcomed hockey fans and NHL commissioner Gary Bettman to a stage set up next to an outdoor ice rink to announce the

The Vegas Golden Knights
inaugural season home uniform
features metallic gold and a
sageflower pattern in the shield.

10.10.2017

The Golden Knights' secondary logo is a stylized representation of the starbursts seen on the famous "Welcome to Las Vegas" sign along two crossed swords. This logo is worn on the shoulders of both the Knights' home and road sweaters.

team's name. After a performance from Cirque du Soleil, the big moment finally arrived... at least it was supposed to. The announcement video crashed, leaving the fans in attendance and those streaming the event online staring at a graphic that read only "PLACEHOLDER. VEGAS HOCKEY" with a timestamp running below. After working out the kinks, the video finally played, showing everyone both the team's new name and logo, the Vegas Golden Knights.

"Our logo and our name is really going to exhibit the highest element of the warrior class—the knight," Foley explained at the time. "The knight protects the unprotected, the knight defends the realm, the knight never gives up, never gives in, always advances, never retreats. And that is what our team is going to be."

Foley told the *Las Vegas Sun* the team opted for the shorter Vegas geographic identifier rather than Las Vegas for two reasons: local residents refer to it as such, and a four-word name was just too long. As for why he chose Golden Knights over the other Knight variations. "Silver Knights was an option because this is the Silver State, but Nevada is the largest gold producer in the country. Gold is a precious metal, the No. 1 metal versus silver. I didn't feel Desert Knights had character to it."

Golden Knights GM George McPhee explained the process of moving away from Black Knights to TSN Radio. "We were going to be the Black Knights but we already had the Blackhawks in the league, so the league was trying to get us to come up with another name," McPhee said. "Another name used at [Army] is the Golden Knights for the parachute team."

That quote would come back to haunt the team, as just over a year later, on January 10, 2018, during their inaugural season, Army officially challenged the team's trademarking of Golden Knights. They claimed there was a likelihood of confusion and a false suggestion of a connection between the NHL's Golden Knights and the Army's Golden Knights parachute team. McPhee's quote was included in the challenge as an example of the team's intent. Vegas quickly shot back, issuing the following snarkment: "The two entities have been coexisting without any issues for over a year and we are not aware of a single complaint from anyone attending our games that they were expecting to see the parachute team and not a professional hockey game."

The dispute would drag on throughout the team's run to the Stanley Cup Finals before it was finally resolved on July 19, 2018. "We are pleased that we have agreed to coexist regarding the use of the 'Golden Knights' mark and name," Foley announced. "Our discussions with the Army were collaborative and productive throughout this entire process. We are appreciative of their efforts and commitment to reaching an amicable resolution."

THE LOOK

The Golden Knights introduced their logo as they announced their name at that outdoor event on November 22, 2016. A knight's helmet in gold placed within a black and grey shield with a letter "V" formed by the shape of the front of the helmet. A secondary logo featuring the starburst from the famous "Welcome to Las Vegas" sign was also revealed with the star reimagined using two crossed swords.

"Mr. Foley was a big fan of the symbol of the knight," Jeff Eagles, design director at Adidas told Sportsnet in a 2017 video titled *Building the Vegas Golden Knights Logo.*

"He told us in that first meeting about the original 'Black Knight,' a Polish knight in the late 1300s early 1400s, [Zawisza] Czarny was his name, the first knight of valor, and service. I think the real challenge at that point was coming up with a name that was compelling, but also resonated and captured something very unique to the city of Las Vegas."

Eagles and his division at Adidas began to focus on the idea of Czarny when it came time to design the logo, taking into consideration what type of armor might have been worn by a fourteenth-century knight. This led to them playing with negative spaces to include the "V" into the shape of the helmet. Up to a dozen different versions were presented back to the team before they "quickly arrived at where that primary mark should be."

Team colors were inspired by the "dark storm" grey of a knight's armor, gold from Las Vegas's glitz and glamor (and the team's name, of course), and red for the local desert landscape, which was added to the color scheme near the end of the process as an "energy color."

"Bill Foley is a West Point [Army] guy, using those colors," Golden Knights general manager George McPhee said to the *Washington Post*. "You know his history at West Point. You know about the classmates he had that he lost serving this country. So, those colors mean a lot to us, and will mean a lot to our players. And we're really proud of the logo. It's clean, it's symmetrical, it's kind of bold, and again it stands for something."

On June 20, 2017, the NHL—along with Adidas—revealed the new uniform designs each team would be using as the league switched to their new Adizero jersey style. Held in Las Vegas on the eve of the NHL Awards, the expansion Golden Knights and the unveiling of their uniforms were clearly the focus of the event.

Following a bit of stand-up comedy from host Russell Peters, the sheet was pulled off a mannequin showing the new dark grey jersey with matching helmet. The jersey was complete with black sleeves and sparkling gold and red striping, their primary shield logo on the chest and the crossed-sword starburst on each shoulder.

The uniforms gave hockey fans some brand-new features not yet seen in the league, including the inclusion of a raised embroidered pattern within the logo. The pattern, only visible on the team's uniform, is made up of a sage flower, Nevada's state flower. That floral look was duplicated within the golden stripes as a "tonal deboss pattern" on both sleeves. While the home grey uniform shown at this event was paired with white gloves, by the time the team started playing games those mitts would be reserved for their road whites with the home duds getting a more appropriate black set.

"It was a brand new franchise which gave us unique opportunities; this wasn't a franchise that was moving from one location to another," Eagles added in the aforementioned Sportsnet video. "I think Mr. Foley was really smart embracing the idea that he didn't want to pretend to be something that they weren't. This is not an 'Original Six' team, it's hockey in the desert. It made sense to bring some colors into the mix that have never been seen on ice before and are unique to Las Vegas. Something forward looking, a team of the future."

"The goal was to create this logo and uniform based on strength and power," Foley told the *Post*. "It represents going forward, never giving up and it represents Las Vegas and Nevada in a positive way. I thought we did a really good job."

WASHINGTON CAPITALS
1974-PRESENT

THE TEAM

The District's National Hockey League history dates back to June 8, 1972, when the league's Board of Governors admitted Washington, DC, and Kansas City as the circuit's seventeenth and eighteenth clubs. Ten applicants vied for the two spots, and the final vote to admit Washington came on the fourth ballot. DC was seen as somewhat of a dark horse to gain a new franchise, but power and politics won the day as forty-six members of the US House of Representatives signed a petition directed to the league, helping to goose the bid. President Richard M. Nixon also publicly expressed his enthusiasm for the proposed team, which officially entered the NHL only a week and a half before the Watergate break-in.

Washington builder Abe Pollin, who was also owner of the NBA's Baltimore Bullets, won the right to bring NHL hockey to the nation's capital for a $6 million expansion fee. The team was to have played home games at a proposed arena in downtown Washington, but plans hit a snag and Pollin took matters into his own hands, privately financing and constructing the $15 million Capital Centre in nearby Landover, Maryland.

The Capitals' first regular season game took place on October 9, 1974, at New York's Madison Square Garden, against the Rangers. Washington's maiden campaign was historically abysmal. The Caps won but 8 of their 80 games, good for a .131 winning percentage. They lost 39 of 40 road games, the sole victory coming in Oakland on March 28, 1975, against the California Golden Seals.

Washington stumbled through their early years, languishing at or near the bottom of the NHL standings season after season. The team was getting clobbered financially as well, with losses pegged at more than $15 million over the course of their first eight years. By the spring of 1982, rumors of a merger with the similarly troubled Colorado Rockies filled the press. That summer, Pollin outlined a set of criteria that would allow the team to remain in the area, and a successful "Save the Caps" campaign ensued. The franchise's fortunes were further buttressed by a stellar 1982–83 season, which included the team's first Stanley Cup Playoff appearance.

This seemingly catapulted the Capitals into a new and prosperous era, as the 1982–83 season represented the first of which would become fourteen consecutive playoff seasons—all of which, however, came up short.

As the twentieth century drew to a close, Abe Pollin financed and built another new arena, this time in downtown Washington, DC. The Capitals christened the new MCI Center on December 5, 1997, with a 3–2 overtime win over the Florida Panthers. The 1997–98 Caps went all the way to the franchise's first Stanley Cup Finals and were embraced by the region's fans with affection and fervor, despite having been swept by the mighty Detroit Red Wings.

The new millennium brought new ownership and, after a few fitful years, the foundation for a true contender was firmly established. Multiple Presidents' Trophies followed and, on June 7, 2018, the Capitals won the franchise's first Stanley Cup Championship, vanquishing the expansion Vegas Golden Knights in a decisive fifth game of the Finals.

THE NAME

The team kicked off a contest to name the new outfit on New Year's Day, 1974. More than 12,000 entries were submitted, and hundreds of different names were considered. Three weeks later, on January 21, 1974, a press conference was convened rinkside of the Capital Centre to announce the winning entry. A suspenseful scene unfolded as Pollin discussed the matter at hand and finally said to an assistant: "The envelope, please."

With anticipation in the air, Pollin opened the envelope and dramatically hoisted a hastily scribbled piece of cardboard aloft that read "WASHINGTON CAPITALS," officially naming the team. Observers were underwhelmed.

"Capitols" was the moniker applied to Red Auerbach's pro basketball team of the late 1940s. Charter members of the NBA, the franchise folded after a few years. An ABA team—also called the "Caps"—played one season in the District in 1969–70, and "Capitals" was the placeholder name of a World Football League franchise that was announced on the very same day the NHL team was christened.

Pollin was undeterred. "In my opinion the 'Washington Capitals' best typifies Washington's new professional hockey team," he declared. "We had thousands of names that were novel, clever, and extremely original." Pollin, along with his wife, Irene, served as the final arbiters, overruling the results of the contest. "It took me eight to ten hours, but I looked at every one," he said. "It wasn't until 11:30 last night that my wife and I came up with the final name."

Domes, Cyclones, Streaks, and Comets were listed as finalists, with Comets suggested by some 250 entrants. At the end of the day, eighty-eight people sent in either "Capitals" or "Caps," and Ruth Stolarick of Alexandria, Virginia, was declared the winner.

Mrs. Stolarick, a native of Canada, told the *Washington Post*, "Washington Caps is what I had in mind. It's better than Capitals. It's easier to put on the jerseys." Pollin thereby overruled both the results of the contest *and* the winning entry by insisting on "Capitals," not "Caps."

"It's '*Capitals*,' not '*Caps*,'" he told the *Post*. "It's appropriate for the area and it ties in with the Capital Centre."

Regardless of local reactions, the name of the team could have been worse. Among the other entries that were considered were Watergate Bugs, Buggers, Pollinites, and Capital Abes. Pink Violins, Ice Caps, Blades, Delegates, Whips, Troopers, Colonials, and Pandas also did not make the cut, along with Eagles and Metros, which were deemed to be too similar to baseball's New York Mets.

THE LOOK

The Capitals' first visual identity was a study in DC-centric red, white, and blue. The new entry's core look was anchored by contemporary lowercase sans serif letterforms that announced the name of the team, rendered in a backward-facing italic, with the "t" in "capitals" cleverly formed into a stylized hockey stick. A series of alternating blue and red stars above the wordmark and down both sleeves framed the whole thing on the white home sweaters, while red was the order of the day on the road, with blue and white stars.

The Caps paired their red jerseys with white pants for the first four road games of the 1974–75 season. The look was met with derision, with the *Detroit Free Press* saying that they "looked like the sissy team of the NHL.

"What else would you make of the Capitals' red sweaters, white pants and red stockings? It appeared they were playing in their shorts."

Good taste prevailed, however, when the team quickly shifted to blue shorts for both home and road usage. This look saw the Caps through the first two decades of their existence.

A sharp pivot was announced on June 22, 1995, when the team unleashed an entirely new visual identity. Red, white, and blue were out, replaced by a muted blue, accompanied by black and metallic bronze. A swooping bald eagle was the centerpiece of the new look, which was created by New York–based Sean Michael Edwards (SME), a sports branding giant of the era.

The *Washington Post* reported an "unofficial count revealed seven members of the Capitals' organization used the phrase 'We hope to soar like an eagle' 17 times" at the introductory press conference.

The Capitals wore these patriotic red, white, and blue star-studded uniforms for their first 21 seasons, 1974–75 through 1994–95.

With hopes to "soar like an eagle", the Capitals switched to this look in 1995, even taking it to the Stanley Cup Finals in 1998.

"We have a new logo, a new uniform, and a new spirit," said owner Abe Pollin. "I think the new spirit is what counts," he added, noting that the previous look was "outdated and staid."

Team communications official Ed Quinlan noted that the Caps were soon moving into a new arena, and another team official added that the team "never had a logo; we always had a 'word.'"

The change took place at a time when many sports teams were adopting more aggressive stylings, characterized by complex logos with multiple outlines and focus-tested colors. The Capitals, however, like so many other clubs, eventually reverted back to familiar and comfortable visual territory.

Exactly twelve years after the team moved to blue, black, and bronze, the Capitals returned to their roots. On June 22, 2007, the team unveiled a new/old look, developed by Reebok, which drew inspiration from their first set of uniforms. This time the lowercase letters that spelled out 'capitals" leaned forward, "representing the team's commitment to innovation and forward thinking." Three stars graced the fronts of the sweaters, a subtle homage to Maryland, Virginia, and Washington, DC—"the three main geographic areas in the Capitals' market," according to the team, "[aligning] with hockey tradition, as each game's top players are named its three stars."

Team owner Ted Leonsis, who purchased the Capitals from Abe Pollin in 1999, explained the backwards turn. Leonsis, a Georgetown grad, said, "I grew to be a Caps fan in college. I loved the red, white, and blue. It feels natural. And I got emails from 900 fans telling me to go back to these colors. It's tradition and history, brought into the future."

Nearly eleven years later, the Capitals concluded their 44th season by finally winning Lord Stanley's Cup. The uniforms that captain Alex Ovechkin and his teammates wore that night bore a very close resemblance to those worn by their distant ancestors—DC-centric star-spangled red, white, and blue outfits—once associated with humble beginnings, ultimately the look of champions.

WINNIPEG JETS I
1979-1996
WINNIPEG JETS II
2011-PRESENT

THE TEAM

Hockey has been a fixture in Canada's Gateway City since the dawn of the organized game. The Winnipeg Victorias were the first team to successfully defeat a reigning Stanley Cup Champion, ultimately taking home the Cup three times: in 1896, 1901, and 1902. The Winnipeg Falcons represented Canada, winning the gold medal at the 1920 Olympics in Belgium, and the Winnipeg Hockey Club duplicated this feat at the 1932 games.

On July 4, 1966, Winnipeg businessman and former CFL player Ben Hatskin was given a franchise for his hometown in a new junior "Super League," consisting of nine teams across the Canadian prairies. This league would morph into the Western Canada Junior Hockey League (now the WHL), which would include the Winnipeg Jets as one of its charter franchises for the 1967–68 season.

After three years in the WCJHL, Hatskin—along with the owners of the Edmonton and Calgary teams—began floating the idea of a new major professional league to be known as the World Hockey Association (WHA) that would draw star players away from the NHL. On November 1, 1971, it was made official, and ten franchise holders—including Hatskin's Winnipeg Jets—were introduced at a New York luncheon as the clubs that would compete in the WHA's inaugural 1972–73 season.

"We're going to have one hell of a league," Hatskin told the *Winnipeg Free Press*. "And mark my words, before long we'll give the National Hockey League plenty to worry about. In fact, they're worried now."

Hatskin wasted no time giving the NHL something to worry about when he teased the idea of having Chicago Black

Hawks star Bobby Hull suit up for his team. "The Winnipeg Jets are going to ice the best hockey club we can. How would you like to see Bobby Hull playing in Winnipeg? Don't laugh. It's not beyond the realm of possibility. I'm prepared to give Bobby Hull one million if he'll sign a five-year contract with the Jets." Good to his word, Hatskin signed Hull in the summer of 1972 to a 10-year, $1.75 million contract, making Hull the first "million-dollar man" in the game of hockey and giving instant credibility to the upstart league.

The Jets played their first home game on October 15, 1972, and nearly 8,000 fans showed up at Winnipeg Arena to see the Jets take on the Alberta Oilers. Hull, who was unable to play due to a legal dispute over his new contract received a minute-long standing ovation. He addressed the crowd before the game, and thanked Hatskin, saying he "owed him a deep debt of gratitude." Winnipeg mayor Stephen Juba won the line of the night, telling the crowd "the NHL turned deaf ears on us for years; I hope they go into receivership." Unfortunately for the home side, the Jets lost to the Oilers, 5–2.

During their seven seasons in the WHA, the Jets would go on to win three Avco Cups—including a cup clincher at home over those same Oilers in the final game ever played in the history of the league, on May 20, 1979. Though the league was ending, the victory wasn't a bittersweet one, as two months earlier on March 30, the Jets—along with the Edmonton Oilers, New England (Hartford) Whalers, and Québec Nordiques—were granted entry into the NHL as expansion clubs for the 1979–80 season.

Winnipeg's home debut in the NHL came against Don Cherry's Colorado Rockies on October 14, 1979, with 12,648

Hall of Famer Serge Savard in the Jets' original NHL uniform, 1982.

in attendance at the freshly expanded and renovated Winnipeg Arena. Hatskin, who had since left the team, was invited back to drop the ceremonial first puck as the Jets topped the Rockies, 4–2.

Stuck behind the Edmonton Oilers and Calgary Flames in the strong Smythe Division, the Jets struggled to advance anywhere in the Stanley Cup Playoffs over the next decade despite performing among the league's best in the regular season. A quickly weakening Canadian dollar and a sudden increase in player salaries left the Jets in a financially difficult situation. An attempt to relocate the franchise to Minnesota following the 1994–95 season was so close to being reality that the team even raised a banner retiring their logo before their final home game that season. An issue securing a lease at the Target Center in Minneapolis gave the Jets renewed life in Winnipeg, but it didn't last long. On January 19, 1996, the NHL approved the Jets' relocation to Phoenix, where they'd continue on as the Phoenix (now Arizona) Coyotes, starting with the 1996–97 season.

Winnipeg immediately received a new pro team, as the International Hockey League's Minnesota Moose moved to town that fall, taking the name Manitoba Moose and would keep the market warm as hopes for the NHL's return to town never faded among the local faithful. Moose owner Mark Chipman and his True North Sports and Entertainment group had a new arena and a hungry market and the NHL seemingly had a different team in danger of relocating every year; the Nashville Predators, Pittsburgh Penguins, and even those Phoenix Coyotes all at one point or another looked to be a prime candidate for relocation, though for various reasons none of the teams left their home market.

For most of 2010 and early into 2011, it looked as if the Coyotes could possibly return to Winnipeg but delays in getting approval from the league and local city council to relocate the franchise effectively ended any hope of a return of the original Jets. Chipman then quickly turned his attention to the struggling Atlanta Thrashers, announcing his purchase of the team on May 31, 2011. Jubilation in Winnipeg led to fans flooding the streets in celebration of the potential return of NHL hockey to their city. Finally, on June 21, 2011, the NHL made it official when the league's Board of Governors approved the sale of the Atlanta Thrashers to Chipman's True North group and its relocation to Winnipeg for the 2011–12 season. "We are delighted that NHL hockey is returning to Winnipeg and to a fan base that already is showing so much support for its team," said commissioner Gary Bettman.

THE NAME

There's no definitive story as to how and why the Winnipeg Jets ended up with their name, but what's clear is that it didn't begin with the original NHL or even the WHA team; the first use of the Winnipeg Jets name was by Ben Hatskin's WCJHL junior team, which began play in 1967. On October 7, 1971, Hatskin announced his new WHA franchise would also use the name Winnipeg Jets. "I like the name," Hatskin told the *Winnipeg Free Press*. "Then we'll have the junior Jets and the Jets, just like the Canadiens and junior Canadiens."

The most popular theory as to how they got the "Jets" name, and one that seems to have been accepted by both local journalists and now the NHL itself, is that Hatskin was a friend of Sonny Werblin who owned the New York Jets of what was then the American Football League. A story about Hatskin's 1990 death in the *Free Press* says he "chose the nickname out of respect for Sonny Werblin and the New York Jets." The book *Yankees to Fighting Irish* repeats this same claim but adds that it was also "because of the city's growing air transport business." A 1988 statement from Jets public relations director Ralph Carter to author Mike Lessiter for his book *The Names of the Games* doesn't help much with any of this, saying "the team name of Jets has no distinct reasoning that ties in with the city of Winnipeg. There is no true document on the subject. The name was just popular with the fans."

After the Jets "retired their logo" in 1995, in anticipation of an expected relocation to Minnesota, the *Free Press* speculated that the team would likely be known as the Manitoba Jets if they were to stay in Winnipeg. Of course, they simply continued using Winnipeg Jets as their name for that final season before they moved to Arizona and became the Phoenix Coyotes in 1996–97.

When it looked as if the Coyotes may return to Winnipeg in 2011, going back to the Jets name "was the logical way to go," Mark Chipman said to Jon Waldman in his book *100 Things Jets Fans Should Know & Do Before They Die*, but "when it turned to the Thrashers our organization had a different feeling." The Thrashers were an entirely different franchise, and Chipman's True North group considered respecting that difference by giving the team its own name, and the leading contender internally was the Manitoba Moose, the name of their American Hockey

League team. Chipman said he had also considered using the name "Bears," with a polar bear as the focus of the brand, saying that "the future of the prosperity of our province, a lot of it was going to come from the north, [the polar bear] is an incredible iconic image that's unique to the province." It was also around this time when reports began to leak out to the media that the team was considering a name other than "Winnipeg Jets," which led to public outcries that they'd even consider using anything else.

On June 24, 2011, the team headed to the podium at the NHL Draft in St. Paul, Minnesota, to announce their first pick, still without a name. Introduced only as "Winnipeg," Chipman had to wait for the loud chants of "GO JETS GO!" from the Winnipeggers who made the drive down. He first thanked the city of Winnipeg, the province of Manitoba, commissioner Bettman, and the NHL's Board of Governors before introducing his general manager.... "It is now my pleasure to introduce our executive vice president and general manager Mr. Kevin Cheveldayoff, who will make our first pick on behalf of the Winnipeg Jets." The Jets fans in attendance took to their feet in celebration, clad in original Jets jerseys, waving flags and roaring at the return of the Jets name, while those thousands watching at the draft party back in Winnipeg did the same.

"To be honest we thought about it long and hard, it wasn't an easy decision to make at first," Chipman told TSN. "We thought about the possibility of doing something new and going in a different direction. In the end, we just kept coming back to it, it was the right decision to make. So much great heritage and history behind the name and we're really honoured to carry it forward now."

THE LOOK

As was the case with their name, the WHA Jets simply took the logo of the junior Jets when they played their inaugural 1972–73 season. The logo showed a blue and white hockey player skating on a red circle, the team name scripted in white to the left and a blue jet soaring above leaving a white contrail below. And while the junior Jets wore New York Rangers jerseys, with *Jets* in place of "Rangers," the WHA Jets went in a slightly different direction. They kept the blue, red, and white colours and the Rangers' striping pattern, but introduced a new logo across the chest featuring a hockey player skating with the puck next to the word *Jets*. Home whites had blue shoulders and, for just the opening season, both their home and road sweaters used a rounded, coloured nameplate on the back.

For their second season, in 1973–74, the Jets introduced a new logo, keeping the rest of the uniform intact. "Jets" was now in white with the "J" doubling as a hockey stick, placed within a blue circle trimmed in red; WINNIPEG was squeezed in below in red and a blue jet inside a red circle was to the left, just above the "J" in JETS. Winnipeg used this logo and these uniforms until the end of the 1978–79 season, with the only change in that time being the addition of white shoulders to their road blues in 1977 and switching from red to blue pants in 1978.

As they made the transition to the NHL in 1979, the Jets kept their logo but updated their uniforms. When general manager John Ferguson arrived from New York, he brought along his controversial and since-scrapped Rangers uniform worn from 1976 to 1978 up to Winnipeg, and simply replaced the Rangers' shield logo with the Jets' circle logo. The uni-

forms were blue on the road, white at home, and featured a thick stripe that went from the collar down the length of each arm and a stripe at the waist. Believe it or not, this quick "Frankensteining" of a uniform design stuck around the Jets for eleven years, worn until the end of the 1989–90 season.

During their first NHL rookie camp in 1979, the Jets had their players wear an experimental new uniform in which stockings were replaced with pants, known as "Cooperalls." The design of the uniform included a continuous white stripe starting at the back of the jersey looping around the neck around the shoulders, travelling down the sides of the jersey, continuing down the player's legs before stopping at the skate. The sleeves were red with white and blue stripes, and a second red stripe went down the side of the jersey, stopping at the waist. The Jets had hoped to get this unconventional new style approved in time for their 1980–81 season, but both the wild jersey design and the Cooperalls would never be worn by the team.

As the 1980s came to a close, the Jets reached out to Rod Palson, creative director at Palmer Jarvis, for his thoughts on a new look for the team. Palson, who had earlier conceived the idea of the "Winnipeg Whiteout," teamed up with Palmer Jarvis art director Darryl Hartle for about a year to develop a new Jets logo and uniform. "It was a long burning process. They knew that they had to update the look but nobody could really come to grips with what they needed," Palson told the authors. He also recalled that his group presented what was ultimately the winning design early on, but the team still wanted to explore other options, turning to a team from Vancouver for ideas. They presented "a radically different look and colour," Palson said. "I remember there

Palmer Jarvis art director Darryl Hartle's 1989 illustration of what would eventually become the new Winnipeg Jets logo and uniforms for the 1990–91 season. While their colours remained the same, the Jets logo was modernized and uniform striping cleaned up.

Some of the many proposed and ultimately rejected logo and uniform concepts Palmer Jarvis pitched to the Jets in 1990. An on-ice test shows the uniform re-design finalists above.

was rage, there were dyed-in-the wool people on that executive [board] who said, 'There's no way that we're ever changing our logo to look like this!'"

"At first we gave them totally new logos but it soon became apparent that fans didn't want such a drastic change," Hartle said at the time. "I really reworked the style of the [previous] uniform, making it much more modern and a lot cleaner. That led me to the cleaner look of the logo."

The team eventually settled on three uniform designs and two logos before inviting about a hundred season ticket holders to Winnipeg Arena to conduct an on-ice focus test. One by one, the three new uniform sets, as well as the existing uniforms, were shown to fans as the models skated around the ice. Two of the three sets removed red altogether, going with a blue-and-silver colour scheme; one included an entirely new logo made up of a interlocked "W" and "J" with the top the of "J" forming a jet flying skyward, while the other two featured the logo of the eventual winner in two different colour schemes and jersey designs.

The new look was finally unveiled the evening of June 5, 1990, at Winnipeg's Grapes Pier 7 restaurant and televised live to viewers at home. The winning choice was a re-coloured red, white, and blue version of one of the blue and silver uniforms modelled at the on-ice focus group. The *Winnipeg Sun* proclaimed it the Jets' new "look of the 90s," it featured a heavily modernized version of the previous logo, "JETS" was still laid out across a circle but now slanted to the right, like before the "J" was a hockey stick and a red jet was placed to the left of the team name but now with a contrail shooting through the team's name. Uniforms removed the large stripes down each arm in favour of a simple large

blue stripe (white on the road blues) trimmed in red at each elbow, and a return back to the red pants of the WHA days.

"In the final evaluation, it was clear: Winnipeg Jets fans were loyal to red, white, and blue," read the press release. "They told us they were not opposed to a re-design of the uniform as long as it maintained a sense of the identity which they have held with the Winnipeg Jets for nearly two decades." The Jets, in turn, would remain loyal to this uniform for six seasons, which made up the remainder of the original franchise's time in Winnipeg as the team left for Phoenix in 1996.

A new Jets franchise came to town in 2011, giving an opportunity to go in an entirely different visual direction. Officially unveiled on July 22, 2011, the new logo incorporated a silver CF-18 Hornet jet flying over a two-toned red maple leaf all within a blue circle trimmed in grey. A small notch on the blue circle points north as a compass would, a subtle nod to the True North group's own corporate logo. Overall a very similar design to that of the Royal Canadian Air Force roundel.

With the new look the club had moved forward while still looking back—not to the original Jets, but instead to the AHL's Manitoba Moose; specifically a commemorative sweater the Moose had worn three years earlier. "In '08 we honoured the 1948 RCAF Flyers and it was from that imagery we drew a lot of inspiration," owner Mark Chipman said at the unveiling. "Our desire was to authenticate the name and make it as meaningful as we possibly could."

Chipman credited the Department of National Defence, the NHL, and Reebok for the design of the logo while also thanking the Toronto Maple Leafs, who gave permission to the club for using a maple leaf on the logo. The Jets had planned on unveiling the new look a few days later, but an

eager Jets fan broke into a merchandise container and shared a photo of one of the team's new T-shirts to the Internet, forcing the team to hastily unveil the logo that evening.

On September 6, 2011, two months after the logo was released, Jets players Eric Fehr, Mark Stuart, Nik Antropov, and Andrew Ladd helped the team unveil their uniforms in front of three large air force jets at the 17 Wing Winnipeg Canadian Forces base. With dark "Polar Night" blue jerseys trimmed in lighter "Aviator" blue for home games, the uniforms featured the roundel logo on the chest and a shoulder logo made up of stylized wings similar to a patch you'd see on an air force uniform and a series of white and "Aviator" blue stripes on each sleeve and around the waist. "We are proud to see the Air Force roundel incorporated into the logo of our home hockey team," Colonel Blaise Frawley, a commander at the 17 Wing Winnipeg base, said at the unveiling. "Today's announcement at our home in Winnipeg certainly lends a boost to our morale." The Jets also announced a series of donations expected to total $1 million over the following ten years to various soldiers, military family, and Air Force heritage related charities.

"It's very, very exciting. Once you see the logo, the sharpness and the colours and how rich and vibrant it is, then if you walk around our dressing room right now, you start to see the different colours unfolding, well, in your mind's eye, you wonder what that jersey is going to look like," GM Ken Cheveldayoff told the *Winnipeg Free Press*. "For those four players who were up there as part of the unveiling that's something they're always going to remember. They get a chance to score goals but they don't get many opportunities to be part of a historic opportunity like this."

CONCLUSION

"The past is never dead. It's not even past." —William Faulkner

*   *   *

Your authors met up in Toronto in October 2017 to research what would become *Fabric of the Game*. In the spirit of conducting said research, we attended a game at the Air Canada Centre between the Toronto Maple Leafs and the Detroit Red Wings. The home team won, 6–3 (this made Chris very happy), but we also witnessed a uniform matchup for the ages . . . one that could have taken place in 1938 or 1950 or 1964.

The Maple Leafs, garbed in blue and white, faced off against the Wings, clad in red and white. In other words, this contest featured two teams who sported a combined total of two colors. (Some readers may be thinking, "What about white?" White is not a spectral color, dear readers, but we will dispense with the physics discussion and get back to the topic at hand.)

This aesthetically pleasing, timeless combination of uniforms stands in very stark contrast to some of the other looks that we have discussed in the preceding pages. We can all debate the merits of the Mighty Ducks of Anaheim's *oh-so-'90s* five-color logo, but it definitely speaks to a moment in time. There are plenty of examples of teams that opted to make a clean visual break from their respective pasts—think of the Stars, Panthers, and Kings. But a remarkable number of clubs have made changes, lived with them for a while, and pivoted back to their roots—the Penguins, Oilers, Islanders, Sabres, and Blues to name a few. Additionally, the annual Winter Classic outdoor game is arguably the most aesthetically pleasing event on the sports calendar, and part of that appeal rests with the throwback-inspired uniforms that are such an integral part of the game. Original Six teams like the Leafs and Wings look perfectly at home in this setting, but relative newcomers such as the Predators, Stars, and Capitals have trotted out uniforms that evoke an NHL of the distant past.

Why is this?

As a society, we tend to have a habit of romanticizing the past. The memories of our youth and older relatives who share with us stories of their own will often gloss over much of their hardship or troubles, focusing instead on the better times. Of course, there were always plenty of problems in years gone by; time heals all wounds, they say, but reflection can allow a momentary escape from what feels like an infinite present in which hardship can seem dominating.

A throwback uniform can present similar feelings.

We see the simpler designs of an old Bruins or Rangers uniform from what we perceive as a simpler time. We watch these familiar patterns from long ago face off and can immediately remember what it was like when we all fell in love with our team, with this game. That first wave of wonder and endless discovery of what would make up such an integral part of us for the rest of our lives. The stars of today wearing the same outfits of those legendary athletes of the past, who are regarded and regaled about in almost mythological fashion, giving us a clear visual bridge across the entire history of our team.

As we watch and enjoy our teams today, wearing their latest "next generation redesign," let's take a moment to realize that someday we will look back upon this time with much fondness. If your team plays or dresses terribly, even if things aren't the greatest, you'll likely gloss over the more unpleasant bits and focus on the good. These are the good old days. Future generations will inevitably call for their teams to throw things back to our present, so they can reminisce about the past and escape their present for a while.

Is time travel possible? We may not know Marty McFly, but we have seen Marty McSorley, and we can say with all certainty that, yes, the Carolina Hurricanes have, in fact, cloaked themselves in the uniforms once worn by the Hartford Whalers.

It's entirely possible that Seattle and Vancouver will soon form an NHL rivalry that echoes the one that Montréal and Québec once shared. There was a time when Hartford and Boston were NHL rivals, and two New York franchises, the Americans and Rangers, shared an arena for seventeen seasons. Likewise, Montréal's legendary Forum played host to both the Maroons and Canadiens. The Habs have won two dozen Stanley Cups; the Maroons folded.

The Fabric of the Game connects generations, and, as we mentioned a couple of hundred pages ago, continues to both bind and separate us—with fervor and passion. The founders of the National Hockey League, who convened at Montréal's Windsor Hotel in December 1917, would surely have understood.

ACKNOWLEDGMENTS

We first discussed working on a book together in the spring of 2017. The opportunity to create the definitive resource exploring the story behind each team's identity, accompanied by a rich and informative array of visuals, was one that neither of us could pass up.

Of course, a project such as this could not be done without the aid of some fantastic people along the way.

That summer, we were fortunate enough to be granted an exclusive meeting with Toronto Maple Leafs president and alternate governor Brendan Shanahan, and chief marketing officer Shannon Hosford for an in-depth discussion on the team's rebranding efforts the year prior. We'd like to thank Brendan and Shannon for their time, and MLSE senior director of communications Dave Haggith for arranging everything.

Later that year, Todd flew up to Toronto from New York to join Chris for an incredible two-day visit to the Hockey Hall of Fame's D. K. (Doc) Seaman Hockey Resource Centre. The treasures of the game are here, curated and secured in a climate-controlled environment—thousands of artifacts that represent the largest collection of hockey resource materials on earth.

We examined vintage sweaters (several of which are featured in the preceding pages) and dug deep into the history of every NHL team, surrounded by ghosts and legends, with the Conn Smythe Trophy close at hand. We are grateful to the chairman of the board himself, Lanny McDonald, for writing our foreword, as well as Craig Campbell, Phil Pritchard, Bill Wellman, and Kelly Masse for all of their assistance and support. Their knowledge and love for the game of hockey is inspiring and we are relieved knowing hockey's most irreplaceable treasures are in the best hands they possibly could be.

We attended a Maple Leafs-Red Wings game at the Air Canada Centre, followed by late night poutine and beers at Wayne Gretzky's Toronto Sports Bar. As we enjoyed our evening, we crossed paths with The Great One's father, Walter—cosmic confirmation that our mission was indeed on the right track.

We are indebted to our editor, Jason Katzman, who helped shepherd this project through with skill and patience. His enthusiasm for this book never wavered, even as we got bogged down in details such as what really was the name of the team in the movie *The Mighty Ducks*, and whether or not the word "color" should include a "u" (Ed. "it absolutely should!" —Chris). Our partnership with Jason and Sports Publishing was forged in Cooperstown, New York, at the kitchen table of the former mayor of the village, Jeff Katz, over a spread of pizza and limited-edition Oreos. Props to Ken Samuelson for his keen eye and savvy, veteran copyediting skills.

Thanks goes to the NHL's Chris Foster, who brought Chris on board the league's centennial project, which inevitably planted the seeds of *Fabric of the Game*. He later invited us to join him for a Rangers-Senators game at the world's most famous arena, Madison Square Garden, in April 2019.

To the friends in our lives who love this wonderful game or those who were just there for us when inspiration was needed, as a good friend does...Stu Gottlieb, Eric Beaton, Brian & Nadine Cook, Paul Conway, Joe De Luca, Jenny Dixon, Marc Agnifilo, Lisa Follows, Dana Hough, Matt Irving, Chris Lancaster, Shawn & Lisa Maynard, Clark Rasmussen, Jamie Sawyer, Will & Erin Stokes, Keith Williams, and anyone else who stopped to ask us "how things were going."

A special shout out to Paul Lukas of *Uni Watch*, who started off as a colleague and very quickly became one of our true friends, and to those who have followed and supported SportsLogos.Net over these twenty-three years.

We are forever grateful to old friend Bill Frederick for his contributions and recollections across several chapters of this book. Stick taps to David Haney for his generosity and insight. David's tenure as the NHL's director of creative services came at a critical time in the history of the league as the circuit expanded and multiple franchises shifted locations. Our many hours of discussion yielded some terrific details and contextual flavor. Our sincere appreciation to Seymour Knox IV and his mother Jean for all their stories regarding the founding of the Buffalo Sabres, as well as the club's 1996 re-design. Joe Bosack's memories of working on the Colorado Avalanche's visual identity were both valuable and comical. Special thanks also goes to Dan Price for his time and thoughtful words on developing the same logo. John Viola of the Florida Panthers, who is truly "one of us" and was integral in the Panthers new 2016 design. *Merci beaucoup* to our friend Marc Gibbons for some bi-lingual support in the Québec Nordiques chapter. To Rod Palson and Darryl Hartle for their invaluable insight on the Winnipeg Jets 1990 rebrand, including some never-before-seen photos of the development process.

To our families...

From Chris: Thank you to my parents, Mike & Cheryl, for encouraging and embracing my passion for sports and computers, which together would form the base of my career. To my grandfather Wilf, the biggest Jets/Blackhawks fan there is. My in-laws, Andy & Karen, for their understanding when I suddenly couldn't make it to a few family gatherings in order to hit a crucial deadline. My children, Ollie & Rosie, who really enjoyed Todd's illustrations—yes, daddy can come out to play again! And finally to my wife, Kristen, who truly went above and beyond during this project—everything from laying out my initial steps when this idea first popped into my brain right up through continuous reading and editing of chapters to just being there to help me through the entire process, I absolutely could not have done this without you.

From Todd: Eternal thanks to Susanne for her sage advice on writing and daily creative inspiration.

Finally, special thanks to those who played the game. The dedication and passion you've shown to the sport of hockey is what truly made these uniforms as legendary as they are. Without the likes of Maurice Richard and Jean Béliveau, the Canadiens sweater is no more than a blue stripe on a red field. It was their fire, and those like them, that took a colourful collection of wool and turned it into the sacred symbols we worship now and forever.

ABOUT THE AUTHORS

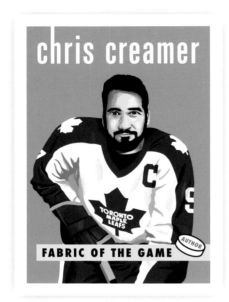
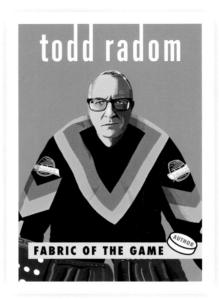

CHRIS CREAMER is a writer, historian, and world-renowned expert on sports logos and uniforms based in the Toronto area. His passion for logos resulted in the creation of SportsLogos.Net, an ongoing 20-plus year project dedicated to the history of team logos and uniforms. He has worked closely with the National Hockey League acting as a historical consultant for their centennial season celebration, written for NHL.com, the *Buffalo News*, and has been featured or quoted in several publications including *The Hockey News, The Athletic, Washington Post, Toronto Star*, and *Sporting News*.

TODD RADOM is a graphic designer, sports branding expert, and writer. His work includes the official logos for Super Bowl XXXVIII, the 2009 NBA All-Star Game, the graphic identities of multiple Major League Baseball teams—including the Washington Nationals and Los Angeles Angels—and league and team identity and branding for the BIG3 basketball league. He has provided commentary about sports logos and branding for ESPN, National Public Radio, and the *New York Times*. In addition, he has been profiled or quoted in numerous publications including the *Washington Post, Philadelphia Inquirer, Chicago Tribune, Sports Illustrated, The Athletic*, and *Sporting News*. Radom is the author of *Winning Ugly: A Visual History of Baseball's Most Unique Uniforms*.